M000315787

The New Symposium

POETS AND WRITERS ON WHAT
WE HOLD IN COMMON

Edited by
Nataša Ďurovičová
and Christopher Merrill

AUTUMN HILL BOOKS
& 91ST MERIDIAN BOOKS
IOWA CITY, IOWA
2012

The New Symposium, editors Nataša Ďurovičová and Christopher Merrill

Copyright © 2012 by the International Writing Program at the University of Iowa and Autumn Hill Books. All rights reserved.

Individual essays copyright © 2012 by their respective authors. All rights reserved.

The cover image, *Abandoned Windmill* by Troy Ziel, is used with permission. All rights reserved.

Design by Shari DeGraw

Library of Congress Control Number
2011912901

ISBN 978-0-9843036-8-7

To contact AHB:
Autumn Hill Books
P. O. Box 22
Iowa City, IA
52244 USA

www.autumnhillbooks.org

91st Meridian Books is an imprint of Autumn Hill Books published in collaboration with the University of Iowa's International Writing Program

To contact 91st Meridian Books:
International Writing Program
100 Shambaugh House
The University of Iowa
Iowa City, IA 52242-2020 USA

iwp.uiowa.edu/index.html

91°ST
M
BOOKS *AB*

CONTENTS

7 Introduction
Christopher Merrill

THE COMMONS

13 What Is a Commons?
Lewis Hyde

35 The Commons: Hardin's Anguish, Midas' Quest
Yvonne Ouwor

45 From Bones to Sky: What We Hold in Common Through Differences
Rustom Bharucha

59 What We Hold in Common in this Uncommon Era
Barry Sanders

79 On the Edge of a Common Space: Geography and Exclusion
Ameena Hussein

89 Defending the Common Wealth
Scott Russell Sanders

101 The Ten Common-ments: Some Experiences From Indonesia
Ayu Utami

121 Under the Watchtower or, First Growths of a "Commons" Capitalism
Gregory Norminton

JUSTICE: ONE OR MANY?

131 Justice: Four Windows
Jane Hirshfield

147 On Justice, Memory, and Compassion
Tony Eprile

159 Poetic Justice: A Shared Irresponsibility?
Mohamed Magani

167 American Labasha
Daniel Alarcón

173 The Writer in Search of Justice
Helon Habila

181 Justice and its Image
Anastassis Vistonitis

191 Justice on the Waiting List for the Burmese
Ma Thida

199 On the Images of Justice
Ksenia Golubovich

HOME/LAND
209 Odysseus Goes Home
Jeffrey Carson

219 Home/lands
Nick Papandreou

229 Liturgy: A Meditation on the Mississippi Gulf Coast
Natasha Trethewey

237 Ain't Got No Home in this World Anymore: Notes on a Son's
Homecoming ⋄ David St. John

247 The Sacredness of Home My Question is: Who Deserves a Home?
Kavery Nambisan

255 Home and Places
Eiléan Ní Chuilleanáin

263 A Small Home
Kei Miller

271 I Land Home in the Waft of Sibyls with their Ruthful Smiles
Stephanos Stephanides

277 Afterword
Nataša Ďurovičová

281 Contributors

Introduction

CHRISTOPHER MERRILL

The discussions took place each spring in the House of Literature, on the Greek island of Paros, an ancient site of cultural exchange. Writers from around the world gathered to explore an idea – the commons, justice, home – in an atmosphere conducive to discovery. The brilliant sunlight of the Cyclades, the cypresses and palms and blossoming oleanders, the church bells ringing in the village of Lefkes – these framed the debates, which ranged across history, literature, politics, and religion, not to mention architecture, film, and music. Inspired by Plato's symposium on love, The New Symposium was an occasion for more than forty writers from twenty different countries to engage in a conversation, punctuated by jokes, philosophical asides, and heartfelt testimonies, that sparked new ways of thinking about what it is that holds us together.

In 2005, Artemis Zenetou, executive director of the Fulbright Foundation in Greece, suggested to me in my role as director of the University of Iowa's International Writing Program (IWP) that we host a literary seminar on Paros to promote cross-cultural dialogue. What better place to meet than the House of Literature? she said – and so began The New Symposium, which in the next three years created a wealth of insights and arguments and camaraderie. With funding from the Bureau of Educational and Cultural Affairs at the U.S. Department of State, and support from the Athens-based

European Translation Center, we enlisted a diverse group of writers, many of them IWP alumni, to embark on a journey to sharpen our thinking, foster connections, and, with any luck, inspire literary works that might add to the intellectual fabric of our time. The spell of those days, we trust, endures in the essays gathered here.

Paros proved to be an ideal setting. Long a crossroads in the Mediterranean, the island bears the marks of many civilizations – Phoenicia, Crete, Macedonia, Rome, Byzantium, Venice, the Franks, the Ottomans, modern Greece – which contributed to the freewheeling nature of our talk. We came to regard Paros as a palimpsest through which to glimpse layers of history, from the era of conquest and empire to the age of commerce and terror. Our charge – to articulate questions about age-old issues – took on added meaning in a place defined by its long tradition of exchanging goods and information. The talks began informally on the ferry ride from Athens, and by the time we made landfall on Paros plans for new collaborative ventures were already in the works. For the opening night of the symposium the women of Lefkes prepared a variety of local dishes, the men served their homemade wine, and the mayor of the island welcomed us to a cross-cultural space, which for the next several days became our home.

We assembled each morning in the sitting room of the House of Literature to discuss the papers the writers had prepared in advance, and there for several hours we debated the merits of various arguments and ideas, following the drift of our thought into new rivers and eddies.

The commons was the theme of the first symposium, in May 2006: our shared heritage, the collective trust that all human beings hold together, which must be passed on undiminished to our heirs – sea and sky, art, culture, science, customs and laws, rites and rituals, the airwaves, the seedbeds of creativity. The commons are the source of our sustenance and knowledge: water and land, air routes over which we travel, the public square, the Internet. How to protect our precious resources? How to build a self-sustaining, self-correcting whole?

For our next symposium we turned to the subject of justice, operating on the assumption that while it seems to be a basic human right it is understood and evaluated in different political and cultural structures. If the Greco-Roman heritage figured justice as a blindfolded woman with a set of scales, a force for egalitarianism and leveling, we wondered if there were other ways of conceiving it. Can there be justice apart from order? we asked. How to summon justice when the law fails? What is the proper scale on which justice should be sought—in each individual life, or in some larger time-span? Is it time to revise the ground rules for justice in a virtual world in which we are but a click or two away from one another?

Home, the topic of the last symposium, generated the most emotional essays, perhaps because it is the subject dearest to a writer's heart. Indeed the idea of home is tested in the terrain of emotion: it is in every sense a visceral construct.

A scattering of lines from the essays about home may give some sense of the drift of the conversation:

> People carry with them the blueprints of memory for a place.
> NATASHA TRETHEWEY

> The meaning is, then, home
> is where we can be ourselves most fully.
> JEFFREY CARSON

> There are layerings, like the fall
> of everything to the bottom of the sea.
> MACDARA WOODS

The right to possess also comes with the right to dispossess.
KAVERY NAMBISAN

Perhaps all this writer can hope to do is to write a literature from within that is so large it begins to push the walls and doors and the roof—slowly, slowly—that it begins to expand the territory of his home.
KEI MILLER

We leave and return home so many times that we take it for granted sometimes. We forget that it is not merely an abode but the storehouse of our experiences and emotions.
AMMA DARKO

Some stories are too complicated to tell.
DEBRA MARQUART

A particularly poignant aspect of this symposium was that our filmmaker, Nigol Bezjian, could not attend, because on the day that he was to fly to Athens Hezbollah closed the airport in Beirut, and so our discussions on Paros, filmed by a cinematographer from Cyprus, acquired an altogether different coloration.

And there were other conflicts. The wars in Iraq and Afghanistan provided a dark backdrop to our reflections, and in the birthplace of Archilochus, who in the seventh century BC wrote what are considered to be the first lyrical poems in Western literature, it was not unusual for writers to weave fragments of his work into the conversation: *I am the servant of the God of War/ and I have received gifts from the Muse...* What we sought to understand, then, was not only the relationship between literature and politics but the larger issue of the writer's role in a world undergoing profound change.

The discussions inevitably spilled over into the meals we shared at local restaurants and into our excursions around the island — a descent into the ancient marble quarry, with the director of the Aegean Center, the American photographer John Pack; a tour of the Byzantine Church of One Hundred Doors with the poet-translator Jeffrey Carson; a hike down the Byzantine Trail, through olive groves, sheepfolds, and stands of gorse, which brought us to a seaside village for a feast of grilled octopus. The conversations continued deep into the night, on the ferry back to Athens, and then via email. What we have assembled in the following pages is a testament to what took place on Paros — twenty-four essays from *The New Symposium*, many of them revised to take into account points raised in our meetings. We hope that this book will bring to life some of the thinking that contributed to the spell of those days in the hills above the sea.

What is a Commons?

LEWIS HYDE

The "commons" means many things to many people. Take John
Locke's *Second Treatise of Government* (1690) in whose chapter "Of
Property" the commons is not to be found in then-contemporary
English villages but in a time and place more reminiscent of the
Book of Genesis. "God...*has given the earth*...to mankind in common,"
writes Locke. Nature is "the common mother of all," albeit a "wild
common," for she lacks the improving hand of man. For Locke,
that original wilderness resembles a thing called "America" whose
"wild woods and uncultivated waste" call to mind the world before
it was first peopled by "the children of Adam, or Noah." "...In the
beginning all the world was America, and more so than that is
now; for no such thing as money was any where known." Call
it America or call it Eden, in this seminal document of modern
liberalism the commons bespeaks a primordial first condition,
one that existed before labor, before cultivation, before money,
and before the constitutional state with all its apparatus for the
protection of property.

Or take Lawrence Lessig's book, *The Future of Ideas* (2001), which
bears the subtitle, "the fate of the commons in a connected world."
The "commons" here is the internet, and the shared technology
that enables it, but it is much more besides. At one point, speaking
of the Linux open-source operating system, Lessig asserts that,

"Like Mother Nature herself, [Linux] is quickly becoming universal and free." Elsewhere, speaking of the possibility of technologies that would open up broadcast spectrum to an unlimited number of users, Lessig writes: "The realist in all of us refuses to believe in Eden. But I'm willing to believe in the potential of essentially infinite bandwidth."

Here again we have the aboriginal commons that preceded the fall of man, and again we have an Adamic New World, a place where nature and technology sweetly jump together. In the nineteenth century this fantasy was embodied by an endless series of patented devices for coring and peeling apples, as if the problem that arose in the Garden of Eden were not about the apple itself but about apple technology. In this century we find Lessig imagining that Adam in the Garden had all the bandwidth he needed and dreaming that now (as figured by the Apple Computer logo: rainbow over bitten apple) we shall have it again, have it just as soon as we get the optical switches perfected and all the patents fall into the public domain.

Among other things, then, the commons is the name of an answered longing. If there is a commons, perhaps we can be quit of the chitinous skin of scarcity. Perhaps life is abundant and capaciously supporting. The commons is the fantasy that more than air can be like air, always there for the inhaling lung. Infinite bandwidth, codfish of such bounty that fishermen walk the sea on their backs, passenger pigeons darkening the air, all of literature instantly available on the computer screen, unfenced prairies stretching to the sea, unmown meadows where the ancient cattle graze. There are psychological, spiritual, and mythic elements to "the commons" and we should mark them at the outset so as to attend to how they refract our thinking about the other, more concrete commons.

As for these concrete commons, I propose to elaborate one image of them using some actual data from the kind of English agricultural villages that Locke ignored, though before entering the history it will help to sketch a few matters of definition. I take a commons to be a kind of property (not "the opposite of property" as some say, following Locke I suppose) and by one old dictionary sense, "property" is "a right of action." Take some simple object in your house, a pencil say, and imagine all the actions that you might take in regard to it. You can use it to write a letter, but you can also give it way, or sell it, or rent it, or bequeath it to your heirs, or use it to stir soup, or break it in half, or burn it, or bury it in the backyard. We don't normally separate out all possible actions in this manner because normally what we mean by "property" is the whole bundle. If the pencil is my property I can do anything I want with it. William Blackstone, the eighteenth-century British jurist, defined ownership as such: "That sole and despotic dominion which one man claims and exercises over the external things of the world, in total exclusion of the right of any other individual in the universe." The word "dominion" here, by the way, was the same word that John Adams chose to describe the political power that some men hold over others. In Adams's politics, the opposite of "dominion" is "liberty." If I own a pencil in Blackstone's sense, I am its despot; it has no liberty.

Enslaved pencils aside, if we return to this atomizing idea of "a right of action," it soon becomes apparent that ownership even today rarely consists of the entire set of possible actions. To move from the pencil to the house where the pencil lies: if I own a house in an American city I have many "rights of action," many "properties," in it, but not all. In the city where I live, for example, I cannot put a herd of cows in my yard; I cannot convert my home into a soap factory; I cannot build a tower ten stories high; I cannot even rent an office to a friend, for I live in a noncommercial zone. And all these are things I cannot do even if I own the house outright, a rare case, for most homeowners have mortgage contracts that further restrict their rights of action.

We have moved from a pencil to a house to the city where the house is found, and this last widening of the focus allows me to suggest a "right of action" that will complicate the picture. Adult citizens in American cities have the right to vote; I suggest we consider this right to be a "property." It is certainly a right of action, and one of the few remaining for which there is no market. The right to vote comes with citizenship and though there are ways in which citizens can lose it, in the normal course of events we consider it inalienable. You cannot sell your vote; you cannot give it away. There is no material property, only an action that expresses the political agency of persons who have it as a right. In fact, by its inalienability it is one of the things that makes such persons who they are. We usually say that citizenship gives me the right to vote but one could as easily say that the right to vote gives me a property called citizenship. Something along these lines is what James Madison was getting at when, in a 1792 essay, he wrote that "As a man is said to have a right to his property, he may be equally said to have a property in his rights." Madison's prime example was freedom of speech: "A man has a property in his opinions and the free communication of them." The right of free speech, like the right to vote, we usually think of as a "civil" rather than a "property" right, but the distinction begs the question of where to draw the line between the material and the social worlds. Defining property in terms of actions keeps that question open so that "property" is never just some physical thing (pencil or house), nor a person's rights of action, nor the social regime recognizing those rights, but some combination of these joined together.

Pencils, houses, or a democracy built of inalienable rights, my point is that the idea of property as a right of action suggests a simple first definition: a commons is a kind of property in which more than one person has such a right. You and your spouse might own a mutual fund as "tenants in common"; your account is a commons with two commoners. In Puritan New England the family was called "the little commonwealth"; family property was the commons of all members.

Couples and families are, however, among the smallest of possible commons, the simplest compounds, the sand and gravel of the set of institutions we are out to understand. To describe the more complicated commons that the term more usually denotes, the rest of this essay will expand on the simple definition through a look at one set of historical conditions that gave rise to the term in the first place.

Traditional English commons were lands held collectively by the residents of a village, the fields, pastures, streams, and woods that a number of people, none of them the owner in Blackstone's sense, had the right to use in ways organized and regulated by custom. Those who held a common right of pasturage could graze their cattle in the fields; those with a common of piscary might fish the streams; those with a common of estovers might cut bushes, gorse or heather; those with a common of turbary might cut turf to burn for heat. Everyone, poor cottagers especially, had the right to glean after the harvest. Those to whom these various rights of action belonged were called commoners.

Systems such as this were the norm in most premodern communities. Alpine grazing fields in Switzerland were village commons for millennia. Early landholding practices among Native Americans offer other parallels, as with this description in regard to California Indians:

> Sometimes people owned plots of land, particular trees, or special fishing places outright; in other situations they owned "rights." One family, for example, might own salmon-fishing rights from a particular place along a river; another family might own the eel-fishing rights there; and a third family might own the rights to cross the river at the same place.

In this case, no one absolutely owns that "place along a river"; it is, rather, the object of a set of use rights, multiply owned and embodying or reflecting the fact that communities have many interrelated members with many interrelated needs. In both this and the traditional English case, the commons is not so much the land in question as the land plus the social relations and traditional institutions that organize its use.

The system of English common land tenure lasted for over a thousand years, a span of time that can roughly be broken into three periods. In the Saxon age, before the Norman conquest, it is assumed that all village lands were held and worked in common, except for a few enclosed gardens and orchards. No one person or family was the ultimate owner; what belonged to people were use rights, the commons being the place those rights were expressed. During the many centuries after the Norman conquest the lands of any village were more likely associated with a local manor, the assumption being that the commons belonged ultimately to the lord of the manor and that rights of common were granted on condition of fealty to him and attendant acts of tribute (military service especially). The third period, the age of enclosure, ran from the early eighteenth century to the end of the nineteenth. During these two hundred years as much as one-seventh of all English common land – about five million acres – was divided up, fenced, and converted into private property in the modern sense.

It should be said that the notion that feudal commons ultimately belonged to the lord of the manor is more likely a legal fiction promulgated during the age of enclosure than an accurate description of how feudal peoples themselves understood their situation. It would be hard to find a case during all those many centuries in which any overlord acted as owners today might act (evicting tenants, say, so as to sell land to speculators). The commons were managed collectively; no overlord alone could set in motion any significant change in how they operated. Significant changes required consensus agreement among the commoners which meant, for one thing, that the commons was a very stable form, unchanged for centuries. It also meant that when landlords finally moved to enclose the land they could not simply do so, they had to go to parliament and persuade the legislators to change the rules of the game. Most enclosure in England was "parliamentary enclosure," a legally sanctioned act of appropriation often justified by the convenient notion that the landlord's ancestors had anciently bestowed use rights upon the commoners, the idea being that if someone granted the rights in the past, his descendants might recover them in the present.

Later in this story we will come to the colonial American idea that the best kind of land to own is "fee simple," and it will be useful to pause here to explain what the phrase means because it arose by contrast to true feudal ownership. In the Middle Ages, an estate in land granted by a lord to a vassal was called either a "feud" or a "fee." A fee was not a sum of money, it was an estate held on condition of the vassal's loyalty and service. A "fee simple," on the other hand, was an estate held subject to no such obligations. A fee simple is a simple estate, an unconditional or unencumbered estate, one held free of the many reciprocal duties that were the mark of medieval hierarchy.

In all of the grain and complexity of the story of land tenure in England before enclosure, several things are worth marking for the present discussion. First, a point already touched on bears stating more fully. The commons are not simply the land but the land plus the rights, customs and institutions that organize and preserve its communal uses. The physical commons – the fields and woods and so forth – are like a theater within which the life of the community is enacted and made evident. A bit more detail about the medieval case will illustrate what I mean. Under the manorial system, an overlord had obligations to the free tenants of the manor; the tenants had rights to meadow land and so-called "wastes" (land not cultivated), and the lord could not alter those rights, nor diminish the amount of land involved. On the other side, these tenants usually owed the lord military service and other kinds of tribute. Below the free tenants were serfs or "villeins" who, again, had rights in the common land, but whose obligations to the lord were fuller and more burdensome.

A serf's holdings obliged him in money, labor, and kind. Of money, for example, he was obliged to give the lord a sum upon the marriage of one of his daughters. Of labor, he was obliged to come with his own plow and oxen to plow the lord's acres, and when the plowing was done there was harrowing, reaping, threshing, and so forth, for an allotted number of days in the year. Of kind, he might be required to provide honey, eggs, chickens, and so forth. Such a commoner had use rights in the land, but certainly no fee simple. He lived under what Daniel Defoe called "the great law of subordination." Manorial commons were the land, yes, but more substantively the land was a place where an aristocratic society staged and displayed its rigorous and inescapable hierarchies.

Feudal commons are only one case, of course; different societies will have different kinds of commons, even when at some level they all involve multiple use rights in land. Pre-conquest English commons were much more egalitarian in practice, for example, at least according to the stories the English tell about their Saxon past.

Such historical cases aside, the idea that attention must be paid as much to social life as to the land means there are some simple questions to ask of any commons, existing or proposed: What social structure does its use rights embody? What political form is being enacted? Given that the commons arose in premodern agrarian villages, to what degree can the form be translated into modern contexts? If there are commons in the United States today, can their form be continuous with our inherited politics and ideas about property? Can there be democratic commons? Can there be capitalist commons?

I said above that, for present purposes, several issues are worth marking in the complex story of the English commons. The first is this suggestion that commons and community will tend to map one another. A second has to do with the longevity of the institution. English commons lasted for centuries, possibly for millennia. To what might we attribute such remarkable stability?

All who are in the least familiar with literature on the commons know that no discussion of that question can proceed without addressing Garrett Hardin's influential 1968 essay, "The Tragedy of the Commons." Hardin was then concerned with the problem of controlling world population growth and, in the course of a thoughtful meditation on that topic, he paused to consider why it so often happens that human beings find themselves destroying their own resources.

Fisheries such as those off the coast of New England are one of the examples Hardin used to illustrate the diagnosis he offered. The fish stocks in question could be treated as a common property for centuries, so long as "the commoners" were limited in number. But there came a time, quite recently, when unlimited fishing with unlimited means threatened the fish populations with utter collapse. Every common has a carrying capacity, a limit on its use beyond which the common itself will begin to suffer. A forest where commoners gather wood will replenish itself so long as the commoners never exceed the forest's carrying capacity. The moment they do, the forest will die out.

As many have since pointed out, Hardin's tragic model may have been well applied to modern fisheries, but it had little to do with how commons were managed historically. Hardin began, for example, by asking us to "picture a pasture open to all," and then to imagine these "all" invading it beyond its carrying capacity. But no commons was ever open to all; access was always limited in some way, a point I'll come back to shortly. Beyond this, Hardin had people using the commons who seem to have no neighbors they know or care about:

The rational herdsman concludes that the only sensible course for him to pursue is to add another animal to his herd. And another.... But this is the conclusion reached by each and every rational herdsman sharing a commons. Therein is the tragedy.

Hardin was prompted to this individualist daydream by his reading of an 1832 essay on population control by an amateur mathematician, William Forster Lloyd. Written during the height of the enclosure period in England, Lloyd's essay included a supposed story that Hardin did not reproduce but which is worth citing here for the parallel strangeness of its assumptions:

> Suppose two persons to have a common purse, to which each may freely resort. The ordinary source of motive for economy is a foresight of the diminution in the means of future enjoyment depending on each act of present expenditure. If a man takes a guinea out of his own purse, the remainder, which he can spend afterwards, is diminished by a guinea.
>
> But not so, if he takes it from a fund, to which he and another have an equal right of access. The loss falling upon both, he spends a guinea with as little consideration as he would use in spending half a guinea, were the fund divided.... Consequently..., the motive for economy entirely vanishes.

Just as Hardin proposes a herdsman whose reason is unable to encompass the common good, so Lloyd supposes persons who have no way to speak with one another or make joint decisions. Both writers inject laissez-faire individualism into an old agrarian village and then gravely announce that the commons is dead. From the point of view of such a village, Lloyd's assumptions are as crazy as asking us to "suppose a man to have a purse to which his left and right hand may freely resort, each unaware of the other." The "Prisoner's Dilemma" is the label that game theorists now give to one of the conundrums that can arise when self-interest and common purpose are set at odds. The name is telling: difficulties are easy to generate if you assume the parties cannot communicate, and it is handy therefore to begin your parable in a prison, almost as handy as assuming a herdsman who acts as if he had despotic dominion over the commons.

Both Hardin and Lloyd posit a kind of freedom that custom never allowed to those who held use rights in the commons. The simple fact is that the commons were a form of property that served their communities for centuries because there were strict limits on the use rights. The commons were not open, they were *stinted*. If, for example, you were a seventeenth-century English common farmer you might have the right to cut rushes on the common, but only between Christmas and Candlemas (the 2nd of February). Or you might have the right to cut the branches of trees, but only up to a certain height and only after the tenth of November. Or you might have the right to cut the thorny ever-green shrubs called furze, but only so much as could be carried on your back, and only to heat your own house.

And these are simple restraints; most stints were more fully elaborated. If you were a farmer who held what were called "rights of common, appendant," you were constrained in the following ways: you must own land within the manor; you must actively cultivate your own land, your rights to the common pasture on "the lord's waste" arising out of your need to pasture your cattle in summer when you are cultivating; you may only pasture beasts needed in agriculture (oxen and horses to plow, sheep and cows to manure); you may only pasture your beasts during the growing season, when your land is under cultivation; you must not put more animals on the lord's land in summer than your own land can feed for the winter. In short, you must own and cultivate land distinct from the commons, and your use of the commons is limited by the size of your holding, limited in the kind of animal you may pasture, and limited to certain times of year.

In sum, use rights in the common were typically stinted, rarely absolute. No common was "open to all" and no "rational herdsman" was ever free to increase his herd at will.

It should be noted, too, that as the commons were stinted, so was the market in goods (especially in grain). Markets could not operate without regard for the provisioning of commoners and the poor. Farmers, for example, were obliged to bring grain to market rather than sell it in the field to wholesalers, and markets themselves were fenced, as it were, so that speculators couldn't outbid the poor. A description of "the orderly regulation of Preston market" dated 1795 reads:

> The weekly markets...are extremely well regulated....
> None but the town's-people are permitted to buy dur-
> ing the first hour, which is from eight to nine in the
> morning: at nine others may purchase: but nothing
> unsold must be withdrawn from the market till one
> o'clock, fish excepted....

In another town "hucksters, higlers, and retailers" were excluded from eight in the morning until noon.

Nowadays it would be hard to find a time or a place where there *wasn't* an available market, and certainly it would be hard to find a market carefully fenced to make sure the poor could provision themselves. But in premodern England a market was a limited thing, a stinted thing. In a seven-day week, only one day was "market day," and on market day only the afternoon hours were a free market where anyone could buy.

As with the constraints on the commons, markets were stinted for social and moral ends. No one was left to follow his or her own ends without regard for the group. In *Customs in Common*, the historian E.P. Thompson cites a pamphlet from 1768 that, he says, "exclaimed indignantly against the supposed liberty of every farmer to do as he likes with his own. This would be a 'natural,' not a 'civil' liberty." The pamphlet itself declares that such liberty

> cannot then be said to be the liberty of a citizen, or of one who lives under the protection of any community; it is rather the liberty of a savage; therefore he who avails himself thereof, deserves not that protection, the power of Society affords.

To these eighteenth-century eyes, a stinted market, one constrained by moral concerns, is a social market while a wholly free market operating without limits is savage.

There is one last point to make about the way that the commons operated in premodern England. The commons were gated institutions—only certain persons could use them, and only for limited uses—but these uses, once established, were not to be cut off. In general no one could erect barriers to customary common rights, not the lord of the manor, not even the king of England. In fact, if encroachments appeared, commoners had a legal right to throw them down. In some locations, villagers would annually walk the boundary of the commons, carrying axes and crow bars to tear down any building or fence which had been raised without permission. In the early seventeenth century, King Charles I enclosed Richmond Park by building an eleven-mile wall around it; regularly thereafter parishioners would pull down those parts of the wall that blocked their perambulations of the parish bounds.

The enclosure of common lands in England began as early as the fourteenth century when plague killed so many people that overlords could simply appropriate common land, the constraining use rights having died with the users. There was another wave of enclosures early in the sixteenth-century, but it was in the years 1750 to 1850, more or less, that the bulk of the commons in England were converted to private land. Many forces lay behind the change. An emerging wool market encouraged fenced, single-use pastures for sheep, for example, while a rising industrial economy introduced rural peoples to wage labor, the freedoms of which many found preferable to the obligations of village life. The claim was also made that enclosure promoted agricultural efficiency. Separated fields could be planted with single crops to improve the soil, or they could be drained to improve the health of livestock, changes which were almost impossible to affect in land held by many different people for many different uses.

The early modern phase of enclosure coincided with many other changes in how persons, their work, and their public lives were imagined, and in an associative sense the meaning of "enclosure" lies in those changes as much as in the overt fencing of fields. Enclosure means a shift away from lives guided by customs preserved in local memory toward those guided by national law preserved in writing. It means a shift in the value of change itself, once suspect and associated with decay, now praised and linked to growth. It means the loss of the right to tear down encroachments, which is also the loss of any protective barrier between the values of the commons and those of the marketplace. It means a change in the measurement and perception of time. In the mid eighteenth-century, factory time–coordinated, precise, and finely divided–arrives to judge agrarian life and find it wanting. Enclosure took the village sundial, hung it on the wall, and added a minute hand. Before too long it would strap the wall clock to the wrist and add a second hand. We who wear those watches, skilled now in what Wordsworth called "the usury of time," are the late inheritors of enclosure.

To my mind, though, the central meaning of enclosure's erasure of the commons lies in the way it carved that thousand-year-old animal, the commoner, into his constituent parts, then reshaped him for the new world of efficiency, law, progress, and time-as-money. A commons depends on a special sort of property that can, in theory, be broken into three parts: there is the use right, there is the commoner who has the right, and there is the land where the right is exercised. "In theory," yes, this division can be made, but not in practice, at least not if the goal is to preserve a viable world of common holdings, for these three things are one thing in that world, and it would cease to exist if they were picked apart.

To illustrate by an analogy to a kind of "property" I suggested some pages back, in the United States, if you have a home in the state of Florida, say, you have the right to vote in that state's elections. All such elections have some sort of residency requirement, so the home helps establish your right. Again, we have three things—a residence, a person, a right of action—and in a viable democracy, these things cannot be separated one from the other. In theory, perhaps, we could design a system where the right to vote belongs to the house and not the householder, but then we would have created a situation in which the rich can multiply their votes by buying up houses. Or we could, perhaps, say that the right to vote is a property that the citizen can transfer at will, though again by doing so we would open the door to the kind of plutocracy where the rich can buy more votes than the poor. Residency, resident, and right are bundled together to produce a "citizen of the state of Florida." No part can be split off as a separable property, at least not if we wish to preserve our kind of democracy.

But exactly this kind of severing attended the enclosure of common lands in England. During the days of Parliamentary enclosure, the understanding was that people holding use rights in a commons should receive something – cash or some equivalent in private land – in exchange for the loss of those rights. In theory this seems fair; it is hard to imagine how enclosure could have proceeded without some such conversion. In practice it amounts to a sea change in how persons and communities are imagined and given their agency.

To flesh this out with but one example, in 1812 the eight-thousand-acre Delamere forest was enclosed, half of the land going to the king. Except in regard to a few moss pits and peat bogs, all rights of common in the forest were extinguished. The chief forester and his assistants, whose uses had included a right to raise rabbits in the woods, were given cash. Local landowners had their use rights exchanged for alienable plots of land. The tenants of these landowners, who had enjoyed a centuries-old right of estovers, got nothing, though the landowners were instructed to offer cash compensation.

Such a conversion severs the land, the users, and the use rights, commodifying the first and last of these and leaving the middle term – the human being who once used the forest – changed from a commoner into a modern individual.

The story of enclosure wakes a resistant pastoralist in many readers, so it may be worth pausing here to say a few words in favor of the modern and against these agrarian commons just to be sure that nostalgia does not fog the edge of thought. I mentioned in passing that along with enclosure we find the rising appeal of wage labor. Remember that feudal vassal who owed his lord the service of his sword, and below him that simple commoner obliged in honey, chickens, eggs, and time at the plow. Such people have no employers, they have lords and masters, and little or no freedom to alter the terms of their work. The great stability of the commons is a great confinement too; those with inherited rights to common land were the fortunate heirs of a world resistant to change, but by the same token they had little way to modify that world should they so desire.

Wage labor unsettled all that. It brought its own kinds of confinement, to be sure, but it also brought a promise of mobility and choice. To illustrate with one of the classic American cases, no one wants to be Benjamin Franklin apprenticed in Boston to his bullying brother the printer; everyone wants to be Franklin the runaway, going to Philadelphia, setting up his own shop, and advertising his do-it-yourself self by wheeling a barrow of printer's paper through the dawn streets.

Early-modern political thought long linked personal mobility with the mobility of property or, more specifically, linked political liberty with the right to hold an estate in "sole and despotic dominion." After the Puritan Revolution, the distinction between the vassal and the freeholder became marked and full of meaning. The vassal's land and sword were not his own, they were his lord's, and therefore so was he. For the freeholder, both land and sword were unencumbered and consequently so was he. A right to own land in fee simple and the "free" individual appeared together, each knit to the other. Wool was not the only crop to be taken from post-feudal fields; God's Englishman grew there as well, a new animal — at least in the rhetoric of the time — bred to become an actor in the public sphere.

It is not hard to feel a sentimental attachment to the premodern commons, but the sentiment should at least be informed. Let us not elide the fact that agrarian commoners lived embedded in a set of obligations most of us would find onerous if not actually oppressive. Enclosure and all its attendant meanings loosened up that "great law of subordination" and brought modern choice and political agency. Even E.P. Thompson, not a pastoral moralist but an apologist for the commons nonetheless, is willing to concede that "the older ... culture was in many ways otiose, intellectually vacant, devoid of quickening, and plain bloody poor."

All this said, I have not offered this short history of one country's actual commons in order to weigh it against the modern; the point has been to gather material that might help in fleshing out an image of the institution. We began with a simple assertion: a commons is a kind of property in which more than one person has a right of action. A useful start, but traditional commons are of course larger than the two-person or family holdings this definition first suggests. Traditionally, the bundled rights of action that constitute a commons embody a community and, in so doing, reflect its shape or structure. A commons comes to life around some matter, tangible or not (pastures, fish, ideas, tricks of the trade), but the commons is not that matter by itself. Because the matter of the commons is the focus of rights of action, it soon becomes a kind of theater within which people enact their set relationships—to one another, to the past and future, and to the natural world. Consequently, an accurate description of any commons should suggest answers to the question, What kind of social life finds its being here? or, more fully, What structures of power, obligation, reciprocity, gratitude, status, honor, learning, dependence, inheritance, intimacy, and so forth are fostered by this thing?

To say this briefly by way of beginning to answer the question posed by this essay's title, a commons is a social regime for managing a collectively owned resource, and the emphasis should be on *social* rather than on resource. In addition, although it is not hard to split a commons into the parts that make it up— the commoners, their use rights, the fields where those rights are enacted—in actual practice these parts cannot easily be separated one from another because (and this is a second part of my definition) it is the parts *bundled* that constitute the commons, that bring it into being. The things (fields, fish, ideas) are where the common use rights meet, and that means that the things are encumbered, not readily available for trade. Likewise, because the use rights are in an important sense what make the commoners who they are, the rights are also not readily available for trade, at least not if the people and the community wish to preserve their identities. The agrarian commons I've been reviewing was not made of alienable rights or alienable things.

Another feature of most durable commons is their stints, the constraints placed on use in the name of longevity. Moreover, the inalienability of rights and resources means that the right to resist encroachments or tear down enclosures should be considered a primary kind of stint. The commons is never the only kind of property at large in the land; there is always some form of despotic dominion and some form of market nearby, and for the commons to endure it must be protected from these. It needs some kind of built-in border patrol, a defense against the undue conversion of use rights into rents or the fencing of open fields into sheep pastures. Almost by definition, the commons needs to stint the market, for if the "free market" is free to convert everything it meets into an exchangeable good, no commons will survive.

As a subset of this point about stinting it should be noted that limits to use will be less important where there is no issue of carrying capacity. Garrett Hardin was wrong to ask that we "picture a pasture open to all," but he was right to make carrying capacity a central question. Especially in a case like an agrarian commons, there will always be the problem of how to make sure that the land remains productive generation after generation, and the solution has always been to set clear limits to use. Where there is no problem of carrying capacity, as with ideas and inventions in the public domain, there may be little need for limits on use except for the all-important limit on encroachment. An invention or discovery beneficial to all is not by its nature a private property, but it can be made into one by the artifice of law. Where we wish the wealth of ideas to be a commons we will need to set a boundary on that artifice. (If the internet is to be a commons, for example, the primary stinting will have less to do with limiting use as with limiting encroachments. When motivated advertisers or propagandists have managed to insert themselves into every link, we will no longer have a common good.) Finally, the management of any commons can be seen not just as responding to the nature of its materials but also as organizing action toward certain ends and purposes. (In the internet case, the goals could be equal access to knowledge rather than maximizing wealth.) Every form of property raises political, ethical, even eschatological questions. The catechism of the old *New England Primer* used to ask, "What is the chief end of man?", the Puritan response being, "to glorify God and to enjoy Him forever." Such declarative faith may not always be available, but that does not mean that questions about ultimate purposes disappear. Toward what ideals have we adopted the ways in which we live? To what end should one or another thing be open to common usage rather than held in private by individuals?

We have already seen some ways in which questions like these might be answered. It is not hard to nominate goals, both positive and negative, in the case of traditional English commons. They were, at various times, organized to ensure the sustainability of arable lands, to give village life stability over time, to lock in the hierarchies of medieval life, and so on. Some time ago I mentioned that poor cottagers were entitled to glean: whatever remained in the fields after the harvest belonged to them by right of common. In addition, the poor always had a right of access to the non-arable commons, to forests and other "waste" lands. Gleaning and access rights were especially important in times of dearth or scarcity and, along with the stinted market that kept "hucksters, higlers, and retailers" at bay, were part of a system of communal tenure that knew one of its ends to be the provisioning of the poor.

The modern ends toward which commons might exist are similar if more various. Issues of sustainability have not left us; if we wish to preserve watersheds, the oceans and their bounty, the atmosphere, aquifers, and so on, some modern form of commons is in order. Issues of social equity and distributive justice are always with us, too – not just in regard to the internet, but in discussions of radio spectrum, for example, or of medicines that can be brought into the public domain. Many argue (myself included) that treating ideas, inventions, and discoveries as a commons fosters creativity and innovation. Finally, the commons is a form of property that gives body to, or brings to life, human sociability. It is one of the places where we can express, demonstrate, and foster the fact that the human self is not a solitary but a collective thing, embedded in family, community, history, and nature. There are plenty of forms of property that express our individuality; the commons expresses our mutuality. One of its ends, that is, is to give presence to the collective portion of our humanity.

May-September 2006
Paros, Greece and Gambier, Ohio

This essay is the earliest iteration of what eventually became the second chapter of *Common as Air*, published in 2010 by Farrar, Straus and Giroux.

The Commons:
Hardin's Anguish, Midas' Quest

YVONNE OUWOR

How should one live?
SOCRATES

There is a fable shared among Kenyans of Luo ancestry of a
distinguished hyena being invited to two different parties on
the same day and time. One party is in the east, the other in the
west. Hyena reaches a crossroad, and he has to decide whether to
go east or west. The aromas emerging from both directions are
equally yet differently sublime. Hyena dashes west, changes his
mind and heads east, stops and hastens back to the crossroads.
He thinks about it and then with an explosion of energy, sprints
in both directions at once. He experiences a devastating split in
his body and cannot move. Time crawls by. He is on the road,
no help in sight, and he is tremendously hungry. Hyena decides
to nibble his claws. Then he takes a bite off his left leg. Not bad.
He takes a chunk off another leg. As the fable demands, he does
end up consuming himself. Only when his teeth remain, does
he giggle and say, "Oh!"

In previous epochs, the prevailing cultural climate allowed the
idea of the commons as a communal space – not necessarily physical – to evolve. The commons were where the experience of existence that transcends time, tradition, environment, culture forms
and perhaps even destiny could be met, shared, discovered, built
upon, and learned. The commons today are still seen as a repository
of energy, heritage, shared experience and resources, imagination,

and meaning. They are accessible and entrusted to "the public." They belong to all. The idealized commons encompass all life and knowledge of life under the trusteeship of responsible human citizens. By common consent, the commons and the things they contain should not be owned, possessed, or sold.

The commons are also constructed to assume that their meaning is common to all cultures. That the San people of Southern Africa express repositories of life and experience – such as the commons represent – in the way immigrant Australians do.

On further reflection, the commons do seem to gesture to a collective human expectation of a destiny that transcends the fragile, ephemeral present, a defiant signal to each creature's last, sighed breath. Legacy, heritage, future. A statement of what it means to be (or have been) human at a certain point of history. The commons could be seen as a manifestation of the personality of existence of a people and life forms in a shared time of history.

One might then see the commons as the inner life of a shared existence out of which a collective, creative energy, vision, and meaning may be drawn upon, learned, shared, taught, grown, and asked to inspire. The cynically inclined, however, might point to the commons as all those things that finite, mortal life does not take with it after death. It is almost inevitable that an exploration of the commons should accommodate the themes of time, place, and space in and of history: Does the twenty-first century conversation about the commons begin as a tragedy – the inherited consequences of the value the previous century has placed on the commons?

If regarded as such, this tragedy is not of the commons as much as it is of profane human action that now arouses an Aristotelian *fear* and *pity*. The commons would therefore not only be an arena, but also – in keeping with twenty-first century sensibilities – the *spectacle* upon which the cosmic tragedy of human choices are acted out. And as the Poetics advises, those who hear this account are filled with horror and pity – far more, however, overflow with indifference.

Given the above – an admittedly polemical peek at the context – the unrolling vista of the twenty-first century merits some consideration, here where the contemporary drama of the commons is playing out.

Beyond memory, in the "presence" of globalization and "market driven" theories of economic sustenance, the contemporary personality of existence seems to be stuck on a treadmill of a special brand of nihilism. This nihilism is characterized by a quasi-religious cult of relativism where anything is "good" as long as it is can be controlled and branded as "rights" or "freedom." Overt socio-political ideologies of the past centuries lie in tatters and from their ruins capital-driven universal lifestyles explode. The epoch's language elevates what pope Benedict XVI terms the "thingification" of life (bling-bling, slasher, regime-change, sustainable use, collateral damage *etc, ad infinitum (ad nauseam?)*). This epoch craves amorphous lines yet the integrity of anything seems to rest in the money it bleeds (or will bleed). Decision-making and technology are intertwined – have superior technology, will reign. Fiber optic cables hook the world up to stars but significant provinces of earth are blanketed in darkness, written off as meaningless.

Creativity has its owners, Atlas Shrugs.

Death as a topic of discourse or enquiry, even for the sake of catharsis, is... dead. Very angry human beings give "the finger" to existence in absurd acts of self-immolation that take others out with them. The provocative acts of life negation, sometimes screamed in the name of a god, are merely reduced into a non-negotiable, no-enquiry-required word – terrorist.[1] Horrified respondents engage the terrorist with shocking and awesome

---

1 from "La *Personnalité humaine, le juste et l'injuste*," as translated in "Human Personality," in *Simone Weil: An Anthology*, edited by Sian Miles (New York: Grove Press, 1986).

"just wars," to annihilate *the Threat*, invoking gods no longer trusted. If there is an education constructed to learn the language and mores of this new world, it has not been diffused. Therefore, in between neon-lit clamor, there lurks a terrible silence of uncertainty.

Alienation has moved from the category of "neuroses to be healed" into quirky acceptability, Eternal Life elixirs are concocted in science laboratories of omniscient PhDs, and there is global glee, renewed faith in Nothing when a sheep is cloned; infinite possibilities and no moralizing God to disrupt the reconstruction of the tower of Babel. DNA is for sale, as are replacement human body parts, biogenetics is the new oil rush, Reality (sic) Television is the opium of an enlightened people, hours of gazing into other human beings acting out life, tantalizing voyeurs with the gift of humiliation (also for sale). The air heats up, and the hole in the ozone layer widens. A judge struggles for words to articulate judgment in a case where one human has traveled to another country to murder another over a deal-gone-wrong. The commodity? A virtual sword won and sold in a virtual game played by a community of humans who do not speak to each other. An epoch fueled by the obsession with possession, transient thoughts, the elevated "I" (and the I extricated from the environment and community), institutionalized distrust where a battle for the collective human imagination is acted out, where knowledge and the basic things that sustain life — like water — are steal-able, patentable items.

Whither the commons, in this climate?

This question and others may be addressed to the commons themselves — How does the idea of the commons correspond to the demands of this epoch? Is there a contemporary, accessible universal method of articulating the *meaning* of the commons? What *is it to be human* in this epoch, what does the human feel, seek, imagine, need and grapple with, and how would the commons articulate this? With regard to the idea of the commons, is it likely that a language of shared interest that draws in most world cultures can develop? What if the commons were a mirror of a condensed ideal of the world, like that of tranquil sheep browsing in pastoral peace in the gorgeous English commons?

There is a curious human habit, a throwback to the previous century – of finding places of the earth and anointing them "UNESCO World Heritage and Culture Sites." This formula is supposed to ensure the preservation and conservation of the place for "future generations." The twenty-first century conflicts, though, negate the blessings and ensure that artifacts from such sites are stolen and sold to collectors and keepers worldwide, such as happened in Iraq.

This anointing could be augmented by in-country legal protection as has happened in Lamu, North Coast, Kenya. Narrow labyrinthine streets, coral houses, *bui-bui* clad women, chilled-out *kanzu*-adorned men, fish galore, blue seas, balmy weather, supremely skilled boat craftsmen, and a flowery language. A treasure trove of mystery, knowledge, and high-art charm. So attractive that the whole island lifestyle, succumbing to the laws of supply and demand, is for sale. Right now, at the waterfront where wooden for sale signs drift in with tides, if the Kanzu-wearing, land- and artefact-owning male population were to be counted, all the nations of the earth, apart from Tuvalu – and that could change – would be represented.

This begs yet another question: How do the commons in this epoch translate for an African country such as Kenya, uneasily straining towards an unknown economic nirvana? What are the commons for a "developing country" that must make choices for its own future but in a world in which the rules of engagements are determined elsewhere?

In the Rift Valley, between Mt. Longonot and the 15-kilometre diametre of Lake Naivasha, lies Hell's Gate Gorge. All creatures great and small gather there. Hell's Gate has seasonal watering holes that dry in seasons of drought. However, trails stored in the memory of creatures great and small lead to the riparian commons abutting the lake. Hell's Gate's creatures have never felt the impact of a drought season before.

Until early this year.

Drought came. As is their wont, creatures great and small headed to Lake Naivasha.

But agro-industrialists, commercial flower farms, multinational companies have not only lain pipes to drain water from the lake and other pipes to pour effluent back into the lake, they have also built around and blocked all access paths to the lake.

True, Kenya is a global leader in flower exports. Yes, the farms employ over 50,000 people, provide a solid livelihood for many, and generate significant cash for the exchequer. This year, though, carcasses and skeletons of creatures great and small dotted sealed lake entry points. Many creatures died along fences and electrocuted themselves on gates looking for water from a lake they had imagined was also theirs.

What happens to the human being when the common room is closed for sapient and sentient species to play out their special role in existence?

A somewhat mischievous look at King Midas, who essentially wondered what it was to be a *human fully alive*: Midas as is known, acquired the power to touch people and things and turn these into gold for his pleasure. It was exciting until he found himself existing in splendid golden isolation. Midas found himself the prisoner of an idea that had originally sounded so good but had turned out to be a map to Profound Idiocy. In his golden self-constructed cage he encountered despair, loss of intimacy, the death of surprise, and the defeat of validation and value. Here he found time to crave raw, messy lived experience and the desire to tangle with life on life's terms. Midas' terror in his golden jail was compounded when he discovered he had inadvertently locked out the possibility of creating a grander paradigm that encompassed his deepest longings to transcend his now despicable gilded Eden, because almost immediately, his thoughts and desires all turned into gold.

Imagine a hypothetical play: this epoch's drama about the commons. Act One seems to suggest a theme of humanity's disenchantment with the course its collective life has taken. King Midas is legally permitted to touch everything, anything, even the things humans love and are most proud of. His touch grazes the human mind and imagination, the heart and collective soul. Now the reservoir of life's imagination is threatened by a chronic golden drought, and to find a way back to a transcending philosophy of humankind and the hint of a glorious destiny is Sisyphus' toil.

(The only grace in this performance is that it is just a play, and therefore the offspring of imagination and creativity. Even in an epoch nodding to the beat of Hobbesian misanthropy, there is a commensurate consciousness that creative covenants, laws and other contracts, can be re-examined and re-envisioned for a recognized, imagined, good.)

Act Two in the hypothetical play opens to a desert inhabited by a people called Turkana. They are a nomadic people who have managed through the centuries to draw sustenance from the desert for their cattle that in turn sustain their lives, contribute to their meaning in life. Their lives are governed by dry weather quests for pasture and water for their livestock, wet weather cattle restocking ventures not necessarily recognized as "legal" in the statutes. Their philosophy of life submits to an idea that Mystery-Being/God/Akuj presides over existence. Begotten from Akuj, all life, therefore, particularly human life, remains a mystery to itself. The sense of the sacred imbues even the most banal circumstance and the concept of ownership is confined to a loose structure of trusteeship and communal agreement.

The dialogue is between the audience and Turkana representatives – an elder or two. The Turkana opinion of biotechnology and ownership of DNA is required because unknown to them – and this is true – an Australian animal breeding company trawling for genetic advantages now holds the DNA patent on their generations-nurtured, desert-bred cattle – the Borana/Zebu, hardy, resilient, and prolific.

In this dramatic journey mirroring real life, amidst dust storms and a yellow weaver's song reminiscent of the northern Kenyan desert, it is probable a friendship might emerge between the elders and the audience – that sometimes happens when humans share a deep laugh. The audience would have perceived that this play can also be read as the memory of a season of ridiculousness in human beingness.

Today, the Australian-patented African Zebu/Borana cattle are tended by a people who sing to them because they simply are – the moral recognition of shared existence, a tribute to that which sustains a human's life, a living repository of life. These are a people who do not give a marabou stork's squawk about patents or gene data ownership. To the Turkana, enforcement of copyright, intellectual property is not a problem. Should Australian enforcers arrive to impose the Zebu cattle gene ownership rule among them, the enforcers will discover what it means to be among humans who have a low tolerance threshold for fools. (Fools: special category of humans who imagine they own/possess/ are entitled to/should be paid for yoga postures, turmeric powder, "polo," and mathematical algorithms.) Persistent enforcers would discover the concept of "War Commons" where the accumulated martial imagination is invoked and deployed in the art of threat-elimination, and laws are created as circumstance demands.

Act Three of the hypothetical play is a blank slate, empty stage and human imagination... Deus ex machina permitted.

What if the commons evolved into a multi-level space in the heart of life where humanity goes in order to remember what it means to be human? A garden where Man does not try to live by bread alone? A place of listening to and learning from life's dialogue with life? Hubris may cause deafness to the conversation of life with life. This conversation, like some rivers, may also flow beneath the radar of human sensibility, but it flows nevertheless, unimpeded by legal abracadabra.

Life is its own knowledge.

The untamed pulse of truth, meaning-seeking; the irrepressible, immortal personality of existence morphs at its own will. All human beings, even if they wear the pseudo-sacred robes of IP lawyers, are vulnerable to this personality. And as part of life (not above it), the human being leaves a narrative of existence, a footprint of choices made, the story of relationship with the cosmos. Arguably, perhaps only the extremely alienated twenty-first century soul would be pleased with a tragic end to the play.

"Oh!" said the Hyena.

There is an ineffable redemptive grace in the fable; the wry laughter of lessons learned. In this giggle there is hope. Hope is another possible beginning for the story of the commons in the twenty-first century.

> If man as a being (person) is something greater than the world, then as one who exists (living dynamism), he is part of the cosmos. Therefore, while in the final analysis the aim of his actions is his own completeness or happiness, in the immediate terms it is to serve the whole of which he is a part. Even though the objective of the entire universe is to help man attain happiness more fully, man, as part of the world must also serve it.
>
> LUIGI GIUSSANI
> At the Origin of the Christian Claim

BIBLIOGRAPHY

Giussani, Luigi. *At the Origin of the Christian Claim*. Montreal: McGill-Queen's University Press, 1998.

Miruka, Okumba. *Oral Literature of the Luo*. Nairobi: East African Educational Publishers, 2001.

Rand, Ayn. *Atlas Shrugged*. New York: Signet, 1957.

Rosenstand, Nina. *The Moral of the Story; An Introduction to Ethics*. California: Mayfield Publishing Company, 1999.

WEBSITES (SELECTED)

http://www.bollier.org

http://www.bollier.org/pdf/PA Report-pdf

http://www.creative commons.org

http://www.dieoff.org/page95.htm

http://www.gci.org.uk/

From Bones to Sky:
What We Hold in Common
Through Differences

RUSTOM BHARUCHA

The invitation to reflect on the weighty environmental category of "the commons," lightened by the simpler gloss of "what we hold in common," brought us to the magical island of Paros. Here, in the midst of the Cyclades, the clarity of light and water and the incessant chirping of birds contributed to the sparkle of conversation between strangers from different parts of the world. Undeniably, the invitation was seductive, but it also came with a sense of obligation, an expectation that "we" would have something in common, when, in actuality, we discovered our affinities through deep differences in our relationships to the world and its pressing problems. Like all invitations, which have the aura of a gift that cannot be refused, it was necessary in the course of the symposium to respond to its generosity, as well as to question its premises in a more reflexive mode. Inevitably, we were compelled to travel back to the roots of the word "common," which has been derived in one of its etymological avatars from *com*, "together," and *munis*, "under obligation."

In the elegant formulation of the invitation, there was a turn to universals, to the "shared interests of humanity," which compelled us to re-visit—and circumvent—the somewhat moribund premises underlying the discourse of humanism and the utopian rhetoric of One World. Not unsurprisingly, we were guided towards the reassurance of an apparently common "inheritance": not financial or economic, but elemental. This inheritance of "sky, water, public lands, and the airwaves" was somewhat too expansively linked to "culture, science, customs and laws, rituals and rites," and later extended to encompass the "the public square" and "the Internet." Even as these diverse phenomena were subsumed within the continuum of the commons, it was more problematically assumed that they could be passed on "undiminished to our heirs."

Nothing, I would propose, passes on undiminished. All tradition is flux, forever on the point of disappearing even as it persists. Within the rigor of rules informing any inheritance, the laws of mutation—and possible extinction—prevail. Or else, there would be stasis, dogma, and frozen truths. In the desperate onus to "protect" the commons, we run the risk of forgetting the death-in-life of creation itself. Moreover, at every step of the way in this web of connections constituting the commons, there is an elision at work. What is being passed off as elemental, universal, and therefore shared, is, in actuality, subject to more individuated, class-ridden, nationally and racially determined norms and laws of ownership. What is being presented as normative is not representative of the real.

From my location in India, for example, I know that water is not something that "we" (the people of India) share in common. Not only are vast sections of the population denied the right to water through the sheer lack of its availability on a regular basis—and not just in emergency states of drought and famine—the more cruel fact is that low-caste communities, the so-called untouchables, continue to be denied access to water. This includes children in rural schools who may be prevented from drinking water from a common tap out of fear of pollution. The problem, therefore, does not merely concern the transformation of "nature" into "natural resources" through different processes of commodification, by which water is now sold in vast quantities through the sale of bottled mineral water. In addition to the exclusionary power of commodification, whereby vast sections of the population can't afford to buy water, there are other more locally determined taboos on the free access to water enforced by religious sanctions and fundamentalist pressures.

Contextual differences, I would emphasize, have to inflect any reading of "what we hold in common" before we can arrive at a respect for differences. For what would be the point of upholding the commons if this respect did not exist? Wouldn't the commons then be another form of coercive submission to what is incontrovertibly right? At times the differences being elided in the name of the commons appear to be merely sociological: the public square, for instance, drawing on European concepts of civil society and the public sphere, cannot be readily translated into notions of community that continue to prevail in many cultures of the South. In these cultures, pre-modern/anti-modern religious and cultural practices may still be dominant, defying the civic norms determined by the democratic uniformity of citizenship and the dictates of the State.

Yet another difference underlying the ostensibly shared benefits of global modernity can be linked to the indeterminacies of access. The much-hyped ubiquity of the Internet, for instance, is a hoax, even in technologically savvy countries like India, where barely 1 to 2 percent of the entire population has access to the Net. Underlying these global "commonalities" is the stark reality of inequalities, inequities, and imbalances *within* the borders of specific regions and nations: those who have access to education and technology, and those who don't; those who are surfing the Net, and those who have to yet to obtain electricity in their homes.

Perhaps, these differences would become more evident if we chose to speak about the commons in more than one language, namely English. Even within English, which is the language we shared in our symposium, I would point out the inadvertent dissonances underlying our discourse, as, for example, when "the tradition of robust communal dialogue" in Greece is invoked as a common point of reference. To my ears, unavoidably tainted by the discourse of Partition and religious violence in the Indian subcontinent, the word "communal" cannot be separated from "sectarian." There's blood in this word, and, therefore, I cannot readily associate it with dialogue, but rather with the breakdown of dialogue into irreconcilable differences.

In what language, therefore, can a discourse of the commons be envisioned that does not camouflage these differences? Even as one accepts that no one language is superior to another, and that we are compelled to use English as the language of global convenience, we need to be more alert as to how we *think* within its shifting contours and usages. In this regard, it would be useful to remind ourselves that universals do not just drop out of heaven: they are grounded and emerge out of specific cultural and historical particularities. Indeed, what is interesting is not so much the fact that universals exist, but that one arrives at them through significantly different routes and modes of signification.

So, for example, when one thinks of elements like water or the sky, one is not expected to ask: What is water? What is sky? These elements are taken for granted; they are the givens out of which an exchange of thoughts can materialize. But what happens when a man from the Bavari tribe in the Rajasthan desert, for instance, is asked this very question, "Akash kya hain?" (What is sky?) He points to an earthen pot and traces his finger on the inner rim of the pot's periphery: For him, this interstice of space between the circle made by his finger and the rim of the pot is *akash* (sky). In this gesture, we are compelled to *see* the sky differently. It is no longer that canopy on top of our heads, which is, in actuality, controlled by the surveillance of national governments.

The sky evoked by the Bavari man from the desert is a symbol, I would suggest, of something that is not readily designated, marked, or prescribed. Indeed, its signification is left somewhat open, and in this regard, his sky is not just a compilation of politically correct attributes, which is how the sky normally gets legitimized in the economistic and developmental languages of the commons. In these languages, the sky's benefits are calculated in terms of its maintenance of the earth's temperature, its production of oxygen, its absorption (within limits) of exhaust fumes, and its seemingly infinitesimal capacity to transfer radio signals. As Peter Barnes puts it so succinctly, "It's not oil we're running out of, it's sky."

However, the sky that he identifies becomes not just a diminishing resource, but also something that needs to be owned, claimed, bought, and sold, rather like any other commodity in the business world over which one can set limits, claim rights, and thereby protect what is in the process of being destroyed. Working unabashedly within the logic of capital, Barnes is clear that unless the sky can be owned on the basis of a *trust* with all the requisite payments, penalties, and dividends, it will no longer be the nourishing force of our lives. This argument, indeed, is grounded in the pragmatics of survival and scarcity, and would seem to be antithetical to the more open-ended gestural envisioning of the sky by the Bavari man from the desert.

And yet, I wonder whether these positions need to be quite so diametrically opposed. Perhaps, Barnes does not sufficiently work through the discriminations of his multiple understandings of the sky—for instance, between the "sacred trust" of the sky, and its more material manifestation in a "nationwide trust" (more specifically, a U.S. Sky Trust). These "trusts," I would submit, are not easily reconciled. Likewise, while acknowledging that there is "intrinsic value" to the sky, he is unable to work out in the language of economics and business what form this value could assume. By the time the Sky Trust is mapped out, it is an eminently "extrinsic," pragmatic business proposal that hinges on the premise that the "use" of the sky implies "ownership."

Invoking Wittgenstein, I would counter this premise and suggest that "use" is unavoidably linked to "meaning," but not necessarily to ownership. If I partake of the benefits of the sky or, for that matter, any aspect of nature, I cannot claim to own it. Ownership needs to be further differentiated from the modalities of belongingness. If I belong to something, or more specifically, to someone, as in the state of love, that doesn't mean that I own that someone or something. Belonging is about sharing, about losing one's self in a state of imagined affinities, where, in the best of possible worlds, as envisioned by John Donne in "The Good Morrow," "each hath one, and is one."

In short, I see no reason to uphold the commons on the grounds of ownership if only to "save capitalism from itself," which is Barnes's specific plea. I hold no such brief for capitalism. My interest would be in seeking other ways of envisioning the commons outside the logic of capital. Indeed, the agencies of capitalism, whether in the forms of real estate, genetic engineering, or the mechanization of agriculture, could be the greatest sources of destroying the commons, both at ideational and practical levels. To turn to capital for its rejuvenating possibilities and to disarm it of its negative potentiality through some kind of mimicry of its operative functions is to play into a dubious logic. Indeed, this logic is not dissimilar from the rationale of deterrence fuelling the race for nuclear power, in which the accumulation of nuclear missiles is viewed as one way of ensuring world peace.

To offer a different understanding of the commons, not anchored in the logic of capital, let me take you to vast stretches of grasslands in Rajasthan called the *oran*. Here, in these empty stretches of the desert, marked by clumps of grass and stubbly plants, studded with wells and small shrines of folk deities, with lizards and insects glistening in the desert sun, one is alerted to a very specific *ethos* of the commons going back many centuries, but which continues to resonate in contemporary India. This is not a history that has its roots in the enclosure movement of medieval England, destroyed by the capitalist greed of feudal landowners and the incursion of new agricultural technologies. Nor is the *oran* a repository of customary laws or common sense affirming a pristine rationality. More emphatically, it is not the surviving remnants of what some bigoted critics of the commons have viewed as primordial competitiveness, which has divided individuals over centuries, driven by their dog-eat-dog vested interests in property and wealth.

I do not wish to romanticize the social and political context surrounding the continued existence of the *oran* in contemporary Rajasthan, where there is no dearth of greedy and venal land-owners, steeped in upper-caste notions of entitlement. Clashes between agriculturists and pastoralists over the grazing rights of animals, for instance, continue to be virulent, provoking bloody feuds that defy the laws of the State. How then does the *oran* continue to exist, seemingly oblivious to all these problems and tensions? I would suggest that it has a spiritual sanction which withstands the very real attempts to appropriate the land within its territory. Even as so-called religious trusts and State agencies like *panchayats* (courts) have attempted to claim the *oran* in many dubious ways, its ethos remains resilient. At a psycho-logical level, one could claim that the guardian deities protecting the *oran* are feared, so much so that no one would presume to exploit its resources for profit without facing dire consequences. Such is the weight of belief invested in this taboo that it begins to function like an irrevocable law.

At a less mythic level, the *oran* is at once similar to and yet differ-ent from western environmental models of the commons. For a start, it is not so much a free space as it is a fertile wasteland. The fact that it is not functioning to its maximum capacity does not mean that it ceases to be significant. In its refusal to be other than what it is, it rejects the imperatives of productive utilitarianism.

Instead, it teaches us a profound humility that goes beyond the logic of John Locke advocating "enough, and as good left in common for others." The *oran* does not valorize "enough" or even what is "sufficient." It does not legitimize either scarcity or abundance, existing in its own right as much for nature and animals as for human beings, reminding us of the interconnectedness of life itself.

One should qualify at this point that the commonality of the *oran* is something understood within the boundaries of a specific region or locality. It does not have any larger national significance as such. Most people living outside of its precincts may not be aware of its existence. However, this does not stop the State from using the land of the *oran* for the most violent purposes, notably nuclear tests. India is not alone in this regard. It is said that the vast majority of nuclear tests in the world have taken place on the commons, at times in the breathtakingly beautiful islands and atolls of the Pacific Ocean. Just imagine: If Paros had to be subjected to nuclear tests, what would we feel?

Some years ago I remember witnessing the trauma inflicted on local people living in the vicinity of Moruroa following the nuclear tests of the French government on this island. I encountered this disturbing evidence in a video documentary screened in the ethnographic museum of Dahlem in Berlin, more precisely within its panoramic collection of Oceania. Here, surrounded by a vista of fishing nets, hooks, boats, and large National Geographic portraits of islanders fading into sepia tones and staring out into the wilderness, I confronted the "commons" of the museum: a collection made available to the public at large, but which, like other such collections, is not easily separated from the legitimization of colonial loot. Against this eminently civilized commons mediated by the institution of the museum, I was alerted to the harsher destruction of the natural commons in Moruroa.

Is it less violent if nuclear tests take place not in beautiful sites like Moruroa but in the barren interior of the Sahara Desert, which is where the French government had first conducted its tests before infiltrating the sanctity of the Pacific Ocean? In Rajasthan, the nuclear tests were conducted in a bleak part of the desert in a place called Pokharan, where life is harsh and poverty omnipresent. When these tests were shown on Indian television, the villagers in this area were interviewed, and, for some of them, it was a matter of pride that Pokharan had finally been recognized in the world map. The irony is savage, compelling "us" (the global interlocutors of the commons) to think harder about our assumed sensitivities. Of what use, one could add, is all this talk about the commons, if it fails to recognize those marginalized sectors of the world's population that appear on our television screens only in times of disaster? Indeed, does it even matter that one should feel a rush of moral indignation in response to the insidious words, "The Buddha is Smiling," which is the official Indian mantra announcing the "success" of nuclear tests?

With this perverse reminder, one is compelled to return to the logic of deterrence that I had mentioned earlier to recognize its lucrative benefits. Today, after the nuclear tests in Pokharan and all the appropriate noises made by the "big boys" in the nuclear club not wanting to accept a Third World encroacher, India is more widely accepted as a "global partner" precisely because it has proved its credentials as a principled nuclear power. Finally, we have joined the club, another kind of "commons," but arguably at the expense of respecting wastelands like Pokharan and the people living there. In the larger considerations of geopolitical security, they simply do not exist.

Shifting the emphasis of the commons from universals (and the destruction of universals) through experiments in nuclear power and other such atrocities, we might be better off calling attention to a more productive reading of the commons in relation to what is ordinary. If the ordinary doesn't always get named or recognized, it could be that it is too common to matter. Relegated to the margins and the vanishing points of everyday life, it does not appear to warrant attention. And yet, perhaps it is in these very undistinguished areas of ordinariness that one can begin to arrive at a new understanding of the commons, incorporating what we can potentially hold together through an embrace of differences.

The ordinary is not to be equated with the homely, with what is comfortable and capable of warming the cockles of our hearts. At times the ordinary is harsh, even terrifying in its capacity to survive and struggle for existence. Keeping this truism in mind, I would like to share a story with you now that has some elements of harshness and terror, but which can illuminate the vital differences encompassing the commons.

I am standing in a wasteland on the edge of the desert in the border region of Jodhpur, Rajasthan. This is not an *oran* stretching in front of me. What I see for miles and miles is a field of bones. Animal bones: bones of buffalo, cow, camel, goat, sheep, and other unrecognizable creatures. Bleached under the sun, these bones have acquired the colour of dust. Surveying these bones, it is hard not to imagine a battlefield signifying the end of life itself, from the ancient sites of Armageddon and Kurukshetra to the contemporary killing fields in Iraq, Afghanistan, and elsewhere.

Bones: what we hold in common. The common denominator of what remains after death, in different states of disintegration.

Suddenly I notice colour: pinpoints of bright blue and shocking pink, surreal dots and patches punctuating the monochromatic dust of the bones. I realize that these colours are pieces of plastic wedged within the skeletal remains of the animals. A daunting thought: In the absence of food, these animals have eaten plastic in their lifetimes, and some of them have died with the plastic intact within the cavities of their stomachs. Even in death, plastic remains non biodegradable.

Plastic: what we hold in common. This anachronistic but still lingering menace of modern technology accumulates in noxious piles in different parts of the world, contributing to disease and pollution. No amount of grassroots resistance, official bans by environmentally sensitive governments, or biodegradable alternatives has been able to banish plastic from the surface of the earth. We seem destined to live with it.

Back to the bones, I am alerted to yet another dimension of what we have in common, but in a singularly uncommon context. My travelling companion and guide is a seer of the desert, who has spent many years in close contact with tribal and nomadic communities, whose knowledge systems he has closely investigated. He is not content to stop with the observation of mere bones and plastic. He urges me to look more carefully. "See," he instructs. "Are the horns and the hooves of the animals intact?"

I am unable to see the difference. Why is he asking me to see something that is so obviously macabre, if not grotesque? Better not to see such meaningless minutiae in the remains of the dead: aren't the bones enough? Then I realize that he is asking me to make a connection between the bones and the larger world of trade and commerce. The buying and selling of animals doesn't end with their deaths. Their bones can be used in the local glue and pharmaceutical industries, where they earn a lot of money for shrewd speculators in the bone industry.

Trade and commerce: what we hold in common. If not in animal remains, then in the body parts of human beings–kidneys, hearts, livers, and skeletons: these too are part of a roaring global trade, with the detritus of the Third World contributing to the health of First World consumers.

Returning to the bones, my seer-companion is in no mood to stop his reflections on material culture. I am duly reminded that there are skills involved in severing bone from bone, horns and hooves from the joints of skull and feet. These unrecognized surgical skills belong to the most downtrodden of scavengers. In India we have many words for them: untouchables, *harijan* ("children of God"). This patronizing category popularized by Gandhi has now been replaced by *dalit*, the more dignified and proud designation of the low-caste oppressed.

Untouchability: what we hold in common. At first glance, this seems like an exaggerated reflex, if not an insult to the laws of democracy and civility, guaranteeing equality of citizenship, hygienic disposals of the dead, and sanitized garbage clearance, which are the *sine qua non* of developed countries. No bones of animals are to be found in their public spaces or urban hinterlands. Indeed, more often than not, there are no animals in sight in their social landscapes, everything squeaky-clean and neat, in place. But a closer look at the interstices and undergrounds of global cities would reveal the scavengers at work: those untouchable non-citizens, the toilers and laborers, who keep the city clean. More minutely, in the cosmopolitan sectors of the global metropolis, untouchability is reaffirmed as the citizens avoid staring into the eyes of strangers, walking past them as if they do not exist. The Other, in its proliferating avatars of suspicious Muslims and grubby immigrant workers, pollutes the gaze of the citizenry, even in the most disciplinary regimes prohibiting eye-contact.

In the midst of these dark thoughts, I turn to my seer for guidance. But he is silent, munching betel nut with equanimity. Then I remember what he has told me many times: these scavengers are not just bone-collectors. They are also singers of the most prodigious and metaphorically rich songs. One could call these songs the epics of the downtrodden, far less recognized than those of Homer and Vyasa. These epics incorporating ancestral genealogies encompass the sky, earth, water, fire, and ether: the *panchabhuta*, or the five elements constituting life itself. Rich in cosmic allusion, these songs are also inseparable from the actual struggle and survival that go into the degraded practice of bone-collecting.

Songs: what we hold in common. But who is listening to the songs of the downtrodden? How can they be heard? Would it not be better if there were no such songs so long as they continue to be linked to debased actions like scavenging and garbage collecting? Our readiness to answer these questions with an emphatic denial is jeopardized by our absence of exposure to the realities of the downtrodden. These realities seem to annihilate the possibilities of "commonality," even while sustaining the livelihood of entire communities.

From bones to sky, the antinomies and injustices of the universe are interwoven into the contradictory songs of the downtrodden that cry out to be sung and shared. Perhaps, this too we have in common: the need to share stories and narratives, and to listen to forgotten or marginalized histories, just as we attempted, in a spectrum of registers and cultural contexts, in our meeting in Paros. Back in Calcutta, speculating and thinking aloud on what we could still have in common through our articulation of differences, I face the New Year with the growing realization that we need a commons, more urgently than ever before, for our survival, sanity, and peace of mind. The lessons of Paros linger with continuing doubt, inner dissent, and an openness to positive failure.

NOTE:

All references to Rajasthan in this essay are drawn from my book *Rajasthan: An Oral History* (Penguin India, 2004), which is a compilation of conversations with the late Komal Kothari, the "seer" addressed in the latter part of the essay.

What We Hold in Common in this Uncommon Era

BARRY SANDERS

> Great spirits now on earth are sojourning. These, these
> will give the world another heart/And other pulses:
> hear ye not the hum/Of mighty workings?
> KEATS, to a friend, 1816

Last Sunday, we celebrated something in America called Mother's Day. Restaurants serve more meals on that occasion than on New Year's Eve; florists sell more roses than on Valentine's Day. Sweet shops typically run out of chocolates. Though many people think of that holiday as ridiculously commercial, it came about in quite the opposite way, through the agitation of a single person of heroic persistence, a woman named Julia Ward Howe. She has fairly well faded from history, but at one time the mere mention of her name would make Howe's toughest opponents stammer and spit. She fought passionately her whole life for the freedom of slaves, for the recognition of the poor, and for the rights of women. She saw the bloody Civil War up close, and it shocked her to realize that the newest republic in the world could wind up short-lived – in continuous turmoil if not utter and absolute destruction.

She shaped her entire life in the pursuit of peace. After an evening spent comforting a cadre of dying soldiers in a Civil War camp, in 1861, she returned to her own tent and, as she reports, in one sitting wrote the anti-war anthem, "The Battle Hymn of the Republic." In the song, God extends his mighty hand and crushes hate until it's gone for good. While few people know anything about Julia Ward Howe, almost every American can hum "The Battle Hymn" and, even if they can't quite catch its meaning, know by heart the song's powerful, almost intoxicating, opening image: "Mine eyes have seen the glory of the coming of the Lord;/He is trampling out the vintage where the grapes of wrath are stored." We face a reckoning, Howe insists, for this transgressive act of brother killing brother on and off the field of battle: We face a reckoning with the Maker. There must be an end. There will be an end.

In spite of 700,000 or more men killed in the war, and another three hundred thousand wounded, Howe believed that all human beings hold in common a desire for peace. Her own experience told her that such a peace, however, would never come from men. For her, the radical transformation of the world could only be generated by mothers. The question, Howe wrote, "forced itself on me, 'Why do not the mothers of mankind interfere in these matters to prevent the waste of human life, which they alone bear and know the cost?' I had never thought of this before. The august dignity of motherhood and its terrible responsibility now appeared to me in a new aspect."

Perhaps influenced by ancient Greek celebrations for Cybele, a great mother of the gods, and Rhea, the wife of Cronus, Howe conceived of an international day for the celebration of motherhood. To set the idea in motion, she wrote a proclamation, in 1870, in her favorite literary form, the poem: "Arise then, women of this day! /Arise, all women who have hearts, whether your baptism be of water or of tears! / Say firmly: 'We will not have questions decided by irrelevant agencies./Our husbands shall not come to us reeking of carnage for caresses and applause./Our sons shall not be taken from us to unlearn all that we have been able to teach them of charity, mercy, and patience./We women of one country will be too tender to those of another country to allow our sons to be trained to injure theirs./From the bosom of a devastated Earth a voice goes up with/Our own. It says: 'Disarm!

Disarm!/The sword of murder is not the balance of justice./Blood does not wipe out dishonor, nor violence indicate possession.'" She had her statement translated into French, Spanish, Italian, German, and Swedish and then distributed thousands of copies around the world.

In 1872, she traveled to London to organize what she hoped would be the first of many conferences for peace. Group after group, however, shut her out because none of them wanted to work with a female leader. So she returned to America to begin promoting her yearly festival and held her first one, significantly, on the Commons, in Boston, on June 2nd, 1872. She proclaimed it Mother's Day for Disarmament and Peace. For many years after, thousands upon thousands of women, along with an increasing number of men, gathered in Boston, New York, Philadelphia, Edinburgh, London, Geneva, and even Istanbul to celebrate Howe's founding vision of Mother's Day.

Howe thought big. She wanted nothing less than an international congress of women that would make the issue of world peace its only priority – an international witness for that radical political commons called peace. Women across America carried with them copies of Julia Ward Howe's impassioned plea to rid the world of war. Declaiming it wherever they could find an audience, they gave voice to Howe's political ambitions. In the deepest meaning of conspiracy, they shared one breath. They breathed together:

> As men have forsaken the plow and the anvil at the summons of war, let women now leave all that may be left of home for a great and earnest day of counsel.
>
> Let them meet first as women, to bewail and commemorate the dead.
>
> Let them solemnly take counsel with each other as to the means whereby the great human family can live in peace, each bearing after his time the sacred impress not of Caesar, but of God.

In the name of womanhood and humanity, I earn-
estly ask that a general congress of women without
limit of nationality be appointed and held at some
place deemed most convenient and at the earliest
period consistent with its objects, to promote the
alliance of the different nationalities, the amicable
settlement of international questions, the great and
general interests of peace.

Howe's festival of peace morphed over the years into a more
placid, more general holiday, a sunny day that salutes mothers
for making it through yet another year. Howe would have seen
the change, I am convinced, as just another act of aggression. In
1914, President Woodrow Wilson declared the second Sunday in
May as the holiday Americans now know. Although he made his
announcement just several months before the start of World War I,
he mentioned nothing at all of the holiday's roots buried deep
in a movement dedicated to ridding the world of wars of any kind.

While I have always had my doubts about Wilson, I believe in
Howe. Like her, I believe that we all desperately crave peace, even
though it seems strangely naive these days to utter such a sentiment. Still, what we hold in common does not, I firmly believe,
change. At times, because of a rapid-fire life of getting and spending, our priorities shift, and what's common – including common
sense itself – gets occluded or distorted or, worse yet, deferred and
slowly forgotten.

I focus on one such moment. I am indebted here to Raymond
Williams and his bracing little book, *Keywords: A Vocabulary of
Culture and Society*. He points out that the root word for *common*,
the Latin *communis*, derives from two separate sources: *com-*,
"together" and *munis-*, "under obligation"; and *com-*, "together and
unis-, "one." In practice, the word refers sometimes to a concept or
idea common to humankind in general or to a specific group. The

idea of the common can thus create community, but it can also cause serious divisions within the larger community. Because of its dual nature, the word has always carried a political charge.

This is true from its earliest use, where *common* celebrated a serious political division between the noble, knightly, or gentle ranks, as opposed to the lower orders. So, for instance, while the sixteenth-century phrase, *the commons*, reveals what's blessedly undistinguished and ordinary – what's shared – it does so by granting power to those lower ranks or orders. The upper crust, as we know, does not cede power without a struggle. And so, by the early nineteenth century, *common* took on a derogatory meaning, as something "low or vulgar."

I spend some few minutes with etymology and definitions here because it sets into focus my own particular framing of this conference. For as I think about our gathering, I find this same potential for division in the rubric, "What We Hold In Common," with an emphasis, for me, on hold: *to clutch*, keep safe, maintain near at hand. Every one of us, I suspect, is desperately trying to hold on to some one idea or concept that we would like to see integrated, some time soon, into the society at large. In my own case, I move onto the commons by suggesting that we all hold an indebtedness to, and a dependency on, mothers and motherhood. I further argue that this quality that we all once recognized as so defiantly universal has been knocked aside by that negative meaning of common.

I ask you to keep Julia Ward Howe in mind and her nineteenth-century singing and trumpeting and trampling for her beloved commonweal. I wish to use her century as my decisive break, when community started turning common, that is, cheap and vulgar. In the early decades of the nineteenth century, through the intrusion of technology, in the West at least, the idea of the common began to fracture in that most fundamental area to which Howe calls our attention – the spirit of mother. The relationship between mother and child got demeaned, brushed aside, replaced, and we have paid a high price for that loss.

Mother is the ultimate host. All other forms of graciousness, of unconditional reception, derive their model from the idea of motherhood. Witness this week. Our own hosts have wrapped us generously in a most powerful Greek innovation – what Homer refers to as *philoxenia* – or simply, *hospitality*. In Homer, alone, I count eighteen instances of hospitality. In that spirit, I start my story with a figure from the ancient world, a prominent second-century Greek physician named Galenus, who practiced in Rome. I focus on only one of Galen's many medical interests, the human *pulse*, a word that does not appear in English before the early twelfth century and then as *pous*, Middle French for "push." If we hope to understand the historic idea of the pulse, we must abandon our modern notions of it. For example, in the Middle Ages people were not limited just to feeling their own *pous*, but, quite extraordinarily, to tasting and smelling it, as well. I quote from the French poet Wace, from his *Chronicles of Britain*, where the word first occurs: "He tasted his pous, he saw his uryn, He said he knew his medicine." Wace provides a description of an aesthetic self-diagnosis, one that involves a fairly sophisticated play of the senses.

Galen counted some twenty-seven different pulses in the body, each one beating out its own particular tune, each one varying in qualities like size, quickness, frequency, regularity, and rhythm. Galen delighted in discovering pulses that, in their quirky behavior, resembled, as he delights in pointing out, worms, ants, waves, and gazelles. He can also describe a particular pulse, he says, as saw-edged, hectic, undulating, twisted, chord-like, beat-decreasing, beat-increasing, and on and on.

For close to 1500 years, the body's seemingly anarchic rhythm continued unabated. In the eighteenth century, however, as the Enlightenment demanded order and uniformity from the disorder known as culture, the pulse, like so much else, came under the unifying principle of mathematics. Here, we enter dangerous ground. For to regulate the pulse is also to regulate the pulse-giver, herself, mother.

Galen described the pulse's many variations as a way of understanding it, perhaps even of containing it. For he knew the basic nature of the pulse as inherently wild and manic, an unruliness which revealed itself even in its etymology. At its base we find the vigorous Latin *pellere*, "to push," hence "to chase," or "to chase away." That action increases in the Greek *pallo*, "I shake" and *polemizo*, "I agitate violently," and in its close kin *polemos*, "polemics" and, by extension, "to make war." Such an unpredictable, irascible creature just begs to be conquered and tamed.

An early eighteenth-century English physician named Sir John Floyer led the charge. In a treatise entitled *The Physician's Pulse Watch*, Floyer introduced, as a key indicator of health, the idea of a quantifiable, regular pulse. That small, unassuming work, published in 1707, helped to transform the entire medical profession. Floyer exerted great authority. When he spoke, people listened. They obeyed. It was Floyer, for instance, who advised the mother of the great Samuel Johnson that, if she ever hoped to cure her son of his severe case of the King's Evil, she must take him, without delay, to be touched by Queen Anne. The King's Evil was a quite serious disease—nothing to fool around with—what physicians would later call scrofula. Johnson's mother heeded the advice and took her young charge, on March 30, 1714, to the Queen. Johnson was the last person, it turned out, that the Queen cured, as she died later that same year, bringing to a close the practice of healing through the royal touch. But if royal intimacy had ended, so had other, more mundane forms of touching. For this, we can hold Floyer greatly responsible.

Floyer had absolutely no truck with Galen's riot of pitches and punctuations. Where Galen heard a richness of rhythms all over the body, Floyer heard only common meter, a continuous string of iambic feet emanating from one point only, the wrist. (The phrase "common meter" first appears in English poetry in 1718.) Where Galen heard tap dancing, Floyer found the steady regularity of the waltz. Floyer established a universal measure, a mean for the human heart, at rest, of 70 to 75 beats per minute. A lower number, even of one or two beats, indicated lassitude, a higher number gave evidence of a state of hyperactivity. Either was cause for alarm. The heart was headed for machine status, as regular and stable as a locomotive.

But Floyer represented only the beginning of the new medical regime. In 1816, a French physician named Rene Laennec forever changed the practice—the *practique*—of medicine. Unable to hear the heartbeat of a particularly heavy patient, Laennec fashioned a crude listening device out of a paper tube to amplify the patient's beat. For the first time, an instrument—perfected three years later, in 1819, and marketed as a stethoscope, a "chest looker"—came between the physician and the patient. For the first time, an instrument "tells" the physician that his patient is pulsing "normally"—within that fairly narrow range that Floyer had decreed, between 70 to 75 beats per minute.

At one time, the physician would press his ear deep into the patient's back or chest, for the doctor needed to know what the patient "sounded" like; indeed, he needed to sense whether the patient was *sound* or not. Mothers easily performed that same simple and intimate task. Doctors listened for congestion, for light airy echoes of the heart called wisps. Galen, of course, heard a cacophony of rhythms. A Galenic doctor does not aim for numeric accuracy, but rather, using his nose and eyes and ears, slowly constructs a story, a narrative, that makes sense of the patient's interiority. Only then might he think about prescribing some remedy. We generally think of that kind of procedure as fuzzy and impressionistic thinking at best—certainly not as science. But that's how medicine proceeded.

If you want to return to health, you better participate. To paraphrase Walt Whitman, good doctors required good patients. While the doctor needed to prod and probe and listen up, the patient needed to talk up, to tell the story of what brought him or her there—where he was when he got struck down, what the weather was like, who was with him, what time of day, and so on. Even as late as the early nineteenth century, we have records of physicians, in small German villages, say, examining female patients by listening to their stories, reflecting, and asking the wildest of questions—like "Do you hear the wolf still howling in your womb?"—listening again, and asking a new round of questions, like "What have you been dreaming?" In this way, patient and doctor slowly developed a story together. The procedure took time. The word *patient*, we must remember, carries two meanings: suffering and composure. Laennec's tube altered the relationship. It not only amplified the heart, but narrowed it as well. Bio-logy (*bio-logos*, or "life-story") gave way to science (*scientia*, or "knowledge"). Patients gradually surrendered their voices.

Up to the nineteenth century, physicians worked in consort with that wise person, who traditionally knew the patient best—the mother. The mother drew out the early details of her child's story. Where does it hurt? She might ask, as she laid a hand on the forehead, or threw her arms around the child in a tight embrace, or planted a kiss to make it all better. It was the mother who first delivered the news to the doctor. After the nineteenth century, the physician took over the job, assumed the role of mother. The child's answer to the mother's question, "Tell me how you feel?" went from a sometimes fairly lengthy, time-consuming, and rambling story before the advent of instruments, to a simple, I feel sick, or I don't feel well, or it hurts here. What did the story ultimately matter after Laennec? The instrument would tell the doctor whatever information he needed to have. The instrument would, so to speak, deliver the facts. It would help in quantifying illness. The stethoscope did not merely interrupt the narrative between doctor and patient, it helped break the intimate and decisive storytelling connection between mother and child. This in service of the modern doctor who got what he wanted, an efficient and instrumental relationship with the patient.

Today, a doctor – a specialist – definitely does not want a story. Rather, the doctor – and I think the verb here tells it all – the doctor *takes* a history of the patient. The stories those patients once told migrated out of the physician's office, in roughly that same period, to become a fixture in the office of a new doctor, the psychiatrist. Doctor Freud used those pent-up stories for a new treatment that came to be known as the Talking Cure. (To work in any efficacious way, naturally, the good talker had to search out its partner, the acute listener.) These stories were a luxury, told by adult patients who had the spare time and money to rattle on, for forty-nine minutes, in the sanctum of the psychiatrist's office. Indeed, Freud's clients turned out to be wealthy, and mostly women.

The modern, regulated systole and diastole pulse, that tiny beacon of life flashing on and off 72 times a minute, gets rigidified in Western medicine, as we have seen, on a particular afternoon in Doctor Laennec's office in the autumn of 1816. (An English inventor produced the first metronome that same year, in 1816.) Only some thirty short years later, in 1847, the word impulsive enters the vocabulary as a new and negative word. The *impulsive* person acts, not out of cautious or deliberate reflection, but on the immediacy of the emotions – from the wrist and not the head. The impulsive person's heart is just too "amped"; it pumps over-time. But the idea of impulsiveness may reveal something more, a vestige, really, of Galen's uncontrollable, manic, even war-like little beast within each of us, just struggling to assert itself.

Support for such a theory may come from popular culture.

Anthony Storr, in his book *Music and the Mind*, makes the point that "the demand for accessible musical entertainment grew during the latter half of the nineteenth century...." I find buried in that sentence a statement about pulse in the following way. When our own internal music narrowed and even died out, people filled that void in other ways. They forged a new musical connection, this time with an externalized, man-made pulse. In other words, when the medical profession broke the nexus between child and mother—a musical break; a pneumatic break—people, young people especially, needed more than ever to recapture that full range of rocking, pulsating rhythms they recognized as their mother's. Mother is, of course, the creature who bestows on us our own pulse. We can have no more basic connection with another human being.

The entry for *mother* takes up three full pages in the *Oxford English Dictionary* (*father* occupies one). The Indo-European root for *mother* is *mat*, an extension of *ma*, "breast" (as in *mama*)—or "breast feeder." And from that tiny root *mater*, an encapsulated history of life emerges. We get Demeter (literally, Mother of the gods), metro-polis (Athens), matriculate, and matrimony. All that is missing is death. But, then, mother is the life-giver. We must find death elsewhere.

Along with the common definition of *mother*, the word takes on scores of connotative meanings, as is said of a city, one's university, of nature, the earth, of the head of a female religious community, of church (*Mater Ecclesia*), of the womb, of wit, of water ("mother liquor"), of the names of certain parts of the brain, of certain aspects of astrology and geomancy. Recall Saddam Hussein's prescient phrase, warning George W. Bush that, by invading Iraq, the U.S. would experience "the mother of all wars." In the most basic matter of civilization—language itself—one speaks "a mother tongue." And in that other world of binary language, what enables me to pound this essay out, my geek friends tell me, is a complex of processors located in the inner sanctum of my computer known affectionately as the mother board.

To turn to the more sublime, we come across the hardness of mother of pearl, the softness of mother of thyme, the absolute truth of mother naked, and the absolute nurture of mother womb. Think of the difference in calling a country a fatherland as opposed to a motherland. Since the seventeenth-century, the British have celebrated, in the middle of Lent, a holiday called Mothering Sunday. On that day, the spirit of motherhood seeps into the entire community. Children traditionally visit their parents, and everyone exchanges presents. Julia Ward Howe mentions the holiday in her diaries.

We share our first moments with mother, at the breast, in the pulse and rhythm of sucking, and in the ingesting of liquidity. We might also call breast-time the rocking, talking, singing and nonsense-making time with mother—what I once called orality and have since expanded into *baccality*, that is, "mouthing time." We all carry a deep-seated, ancient—and Greek, I may add—longing for a reunion with the mother of all mothers, the mythological mother, the in-spiriting mother. To sing the stories of their people, the ancient Greeks invoked the mother of the muses, Mnemosyne. Greeks imagined her as a babbling, murmuring brook, who gives the community its breath, its voice—its music. I think of her as the pulse of the tribe. "Sing to me of the man, Muse," the *Odyssey* begins, "launch out his story, Muse, daughter of Zeus, start from where you will, sing for our time too." The lesson is an easy one: Mother enables us to breathe. She provides our rhythm. Poetry keeps us breathing with its varied but steady meters. No etymological connection exists between *mater* and *meter*, but of course people forged one for themselves.

Here is what we hold in common—mater, mother, mothering, matrix, matter, meter. When we become disconnected not just from the person but from the concept, the *idea* of motherhood, we have removed ourselves from something terrifyingly basic. We come up against our first unsettling bout of arrhythmia, of de-cadence. What we seem to hold in common these days startles and depresses: common talk turns on hunger, poverty, disease, torture, collateral damage, destruction, and death. We have to remind ourselves who we are, what century we live in.

In a most profound way, I think we all miss what mother represents, what she offers. In the States, our time now is a time, most people would agree, of testosterone, of power and competition, of an imperious determination to dominate peoples around the world. During the presidential campaign of 1999, the press crowed about George W. Bush's manly, macho appeal—something about his saunter or swagger—a characterization that helped in some part to carry him into office.

The stories we began to hear after September 11 were fueled by wrath and revenge and a great deal of fear. When fear is the driver, only the courageous few manage to tell stories of community and love. Out of fear comes huddling up, closing off, shutting down, protecting against some enemy, whom we imagine plotting against us every hour and every minute and every second of every day. Such stories know no joy, no respite, no leisure, and certainly no communitarian spirit. We hear instead tales of dominance and not nurture, hate and not love, revenge and not forgiveness, enclosure and not expansiveness. But we may be hopefully coming to the end of that yarn. There are signs, from various parts of the globe, that people are coming back to their senses, to the compelling power of the heart and the imagination. The weavers have returned. They have strung their looms. They come prepared to use new yarns, to spin new patterns. Let me mention a few commonalties, for they press on our opening motif, the spirit that only motherhood can provide.

As I said, mother allows us to breathe. *Infantum* in Latin means "without sound." *Per-sona*, "person," means to "sound through."

We are defined by our voice. We are made human with our breath. Again, I congratulate the Greeks for yet another invention, this time the creation of vowels, around the eighth century BC, which they introduced into what they received from Phoenician traders as a consonantal writing system. That invention made it possible for people to read silently—that is, to read *in* the rhythm of the sentences, *against* their own rhythm of breathing.

We discover in meditation that it takes very little air to actually breathe. How much breath does it take to blow something as simple as a whistle? I ask this, not as a question about early music making, but one about the power of voice. For the first time in its history, *Time Magazine*, in 2002, chose three people for its annual Person of the Year issue—three women. All three of them blew the whistle, as they say, on acts of corruption and deceit where they worked: Sherron Watkins, an Enron vice president, wrote to chairman Kenneth Lay warning him of bogus accounting practices; Coleen Rowly, an FBI staff attorney, wrote director Robert Mueller complaining that FBI officials totally thwarted her pleas to have Zacarias Moussaoui investigated; and Cynthia Cooper, an accountant at WorldCom, informed her board that she had found a cover up of 3.8 billion dollars in losses through phony bookkeeping practices.

Some recent university studies conclude that women are much more likely than men to call a halt to wrongdoing when they find it. The reasons why women leap on the truth may be endless, but Americans, itching for a radical change, know the truth in their gut. In my own country, a mother, Cindy Sheehan, helped to coalesce a diffuse, inchoate anti-war sentiment, after her son was killed in Iraq, into something resembling a national movement, or at least a coalition. She joined with a women's political and spiritual conglomerate, Code Pink. In the 1960s, the Women's Strike for Peace accomplished the same thing and, according to some historians, delivered the deathblow to the

House Un-American Activities Committee. For me, three women in particular helped define the key issues in the sixties. Their books appeared one year after the other: Jane Jacobs's *The Death and Life of Great American Cities*, in 1961; Rachel Carson's *Silent Spring*, in 1962; and Betty Friedan's *The Feminine Mystique*, in 1963. (I add here that Robert Moses, New York city's planning czar in the sixties, dismissed Jane Jacobs and those like her in the worst way he could imagine, as "nobody but a bunch of mothers.")

Women are making themselves heard and felt in politics everywhere. In America, those bold enough have even begun to whisper about something wholly subversive. It's still a whisper and not a whistle, but if one remains very still, one can hear the words, *what about a woman for president*. It is radical but at least not revolutionary that a major network launched a new series, *Commander in Chief*, featuring a woman as President of the United States. The billboards advertising the program startled a few, and pleased many.

On September 5, 2000, for the very first time, women heads of state and government met at the United Nations. At that moment, nine countries had a woman leader: Bangladesh, Finland, Ireland, Latvia, New Zealand, Panama, Saint Lucia, San Marino, and Sri Lanka. The head of the Human Rights Commission for the United Nations is a woman; she is the former president of Ireland. The current president of Ireland is also a woman. The president of Chile is a woman, Michelle Bachelet Jeria, as is the head of Jordan, Queen Noor. In a recent election, Angela Markel became the Federal Chancellor of Germany, and in Liberia, the new Executive President is now Ellen Johnson Sirleaf. (President Sirleaf has recently asked a New Jersey school teacher, who was born in Liberia, to become the first police chief of that country.) Taya Kaarina Holover serves as the president of Finland; Gloria Macapagal-Arroyo the president of the Philippines; Mame Madior Boye the Prime Minister of Senegal; and Valeria Ciavattia the Co-Captain Regent of San Marino. Beyond politics, in my own country's most sacred pastime, baseball, the National Baseball Hall of Fame, in February 2006, inducted not only its first woman but an African-American woman at that, Miss Effa Manley, who pitched for the Negro Leagues.

We all have a stethoscope pointed at our hearts. Of one kind or another, some instrument is pointed at our vital parts. Some instrument has interrupted, or worse yet, stolen our stories from us. How can we sing a different story line from the tired tall tales that come from this particular administration or that particular corporation? I say that what we hold in common is some version of the inspiriting, pulsating Mnemosyne, the mother of the muses, and that now, more than ever, we need to invoke her power, for we need to sing into existence a brand new community.

I want to underscore the critical importance of this reinvigoration of the spirit of motherhood, which I can do best, I believe, by quoting from one of the most insightful child psychiatrists I have ever encountered, D.W. Winnicott. He apologizes, right off, for writing as a man about the subject of mothers. He admits, he says, that he can "never really know what it is like to see wrapped up over there in the cot a bit of my own self." Nonetheless, he has a central theme, a smart and crucial central theme. Of course, every human being alive is in infinite debt to a woman, a mother. Few men, he insists, are willing to recognize that profound debt. Ignoring that fact leads to the kind of devastation that Julia Ward Howe witnessed on the battlefield. In Winnicott's scheme, civilization can enjoy no end to war until men recognize their indebtedness to their mothers. I must quote Winnicott himself:

> At a time in earliest infancy we were absolutely dependent... The result of such recognition of the maternal role when it comes will not be gratitude

or even praise. The result will be a lessening in ourselves of fear... If there is no true recognition of the mother's part, then there must remain a vague fear of dependence. This fear will sometimes take the form of a fear of woman in general or fear of a particular woman, and at other times will take on less easily recognized forms, always including the fear of domination.

Unfortunately the fear of domination does not lead groups of people to avoid being dominated; on the contrary it draws them towards a specific or chosen domination. Indeed, were the psychology of the dictator studied one would expect to find that, among other things, in his own personal struggle he is trying to control the woman whose domination he unconsciously still fears, trying to control her by accommodating her, acting for her, and in turn demanding total subjection and "love."

Dictators speak. They begin in the Middle Ages, and continue shooting off their mouths for the next four hundred years. That's what *dictare* means. Chaucer is my own delightful dictator of choice, composing his poetry out loud in front of scribes, who write it all down. By the late nineteenth century, Julia Ward Howe's time, however, the definition of dictator changes. Dictators begin to speak with a new tone, with the authority of the absolute. They deny conversation, robbing the average citizen of his or her own voice. While they try to make conspiracy impossible, they make it inevitable. Julia Ward Howe knew this truth. That's why she wanted to preempt the second Sunday in May, not just for her own country, but for the world. She knew how to make the pulse quicken. But, quite obviously, her scheme has not worked well. At least, not yet.

If *mother* has an antonym, *dictator* may come close – the giver of breath versus the robber of voice. Dictators depend for their livelihood on dependency. Poor dears, don't they know that mothers know best, that dependency must come naturally? We might not expect it, but the two female justices on the Supreme Court, Sandra Day O'Connor and Ruth Bader Ginsburg – both of them mothers – have been speaking out on this particular issue, very nearly crossing the line and taking a political stand in public. Justice Ginsburg said recently in South Africa that only the courts stand as a safeguard "against oppressive government and stirred-up majorities." She reminded her audience how crucial it was for a judiciary to act judiciously. The following day, at a gathering at Georgetown University, America's first female justice, Sandra Day O'Connor, raised up on her toes and spoke with shocking clarity about contemporary America. She declared that a judiciary afraid to stand up to elected officials can lead in one direction only, to dictatorship. She had retired from the court several months before; she was speaking to the hard-edged men who replaced her. She was speaking to us. She was speaking. Some people stopped to listen.

We might do well, in May 2006, to honor, once again, the original intent of Mother's Day, reclaiming it as an international day of disarmament and peace. Let us, above all else, acknowledge our common dependency on, and our indebtedness to, mother. Recognition of mother will not suddenly make things all right. I know that. But it might help. It became clear to me in reading a recent homage to the folksinger Pete Seeger in *The New Yorker*. (Seeger's practice of the politics of bravery his entire 88 years reminds me of Julia Ward Howe.) Pete Seeger says about his father, also a musician, a composer, that "he thought the great symphonies would save the human race." Every person has something he or she thinks will save humanity. Maybe the world will hold together as long as people hold on to that belief.

I offer my own suggestion for saving the world, a small start, a try for something new – an infusion of a radically different spirit by returning to what we all hold in common. Can the commons pull off the uncommon? Who knows? It's certainly thrilling to imagine that *only* the common can pull off something so extraordinary.

As Julia Ward Howe told the world over one hundred years ago, so *much* depends on mother. As D.W. Winnicott recently reminds us, so much *depends* on mother.

The rest, I guess, depends on us.

On the Edge
of a Common Space:
Geography and Exclusion

Ameena Hussein

I begin this essay with an anecdote that has almost nothing to do with my subject but one that will, I hope, put my whole essay and mood in context.

One evening a few weeks ago a man fell down at my feet and died. I was one of three judges at the Gratiaen Prize, which is Sri Lanka's equivalent of the Booker Prize. The gentleman, Mr. Shanmugalingam, was one of five finalists. As his name was called out, he wobbled his way through the aisle onto the stage. I remember thinking that I did not expect an old man to have written the book, and as he began to read I noticed that he had an air of great joy that radiated from him. He had written an extremely brave novel, criticizing the Liberation Tigers of Tamil Eelam and hostile towards all parties that perpetuate the state of war. It was a bold and courageous book that told its story from the perspective of a minority people who have endured brutal terror at the hands of almost everyone who was involved in the ethnic conflict that has torn our island nation apart. As he was reading excerpts from the novel, trembling from a combination of what I would like to think as age and happiness, he collapsed and died.

His death shattered me. Later that night, as I wept in bed for a man I barely knew except through his novel, I did not quite understand what I was mourning for. The next day I switched off my mobile phone, I visited friends and did not speak of the tragic event. I bought a pair of red linen trousers and sat quietly with my mother-in-law, who had had a mild stroke a week ago. I called my parents in New Zealand and lent my suv to someone who wanted to transport a large bathroom sink. I arranged my cupboard and kept aside a pile of hardly worn clothes to be given away. I bought Sinhala and Tamil New Year gifts for my household staff. I looked out of my bedroom window and watched the sunset over the tops of palm trees and mango trees. The red roofs turned a rose pink and seemed to glow with pleasure. And then I realized that what I was mourning was what I had in common with that man—and that I too one day would die. That each and everyone in this world would experience that event we call death. And then? What?

Given the frame of mind that I am in right now, I feel that I would not be able to write about anything else but death. For suddenly, death for me has become the very purpose of life. It has taken on a new importance; it forced itself into my mundane existence and reminded me that I am not here for very long. It took Mr. Shanmugalingam, who I have learnt has no immediate family and who had been living with a niece by marriage far from his home town of Jaffna, to bring the immediacy of my transitory existence home to me. I wonder if it is the thought of death that makes us live our life the way we do.

It is the custom of modern times to avoid the topic of death. It is perhaps seen as a failure of life. But luckily here in Sri Lanka, death is still an event. Funerals are crammed with so much ritual and tradition that even if you are a Muslim and you are buried with immediate simplicity you can circumvent it by having forty continuous days of prayer, food, and togetherness, or if you are a Buddhist who is accompanied to the cremation ground with drummers and flutists, or perhaps a Hindu who is set ablaze in an open pyre by his first born son, your death ironically can still reflect a certain *joie de vivre*!

As the world begins to be peopled by a majority who have perfected consumerism to a fine art, I see a kind of death all around
me. It could be a realization of our own mortality as a people, in
that we have lived with a policy of instant gratification. If we look
down through the ages, never before has there lived a people
who has been as selfish as we are. We live as if there is nothing
to leave behind, we live as if there is no-one to leave it for.

I reside in a country that is considered poor by most of the
world. Sometimes, we do not have the basic necessities of life.
Our GDP is 842 dollars per person per year. Our children at times
live on the streets, we do not always have electricity, and if the
monsoons fail we are scared witless. And yet, my philosophy of
life – which is shared by my countrymen – is that of continuity,
a sense of having been before and a sense of being again. It is
the philosophy of rebirth and karma and a sense of justice and
order. But sometimes it is tested.

A long time ago I came to this island in the genes of an Arab
sailor who traded in spices and gem stones. I was then blended
and liquidized first through indigenous, Sinhala and Tamil, and
then later Dutch and Portuguese strains and educated as a brown
Englishwoman. My mother tongue is English, I have tea at four
o'clock in the evening and drive on the left side of the road. I have
lived on three continents over seventeen years, traveled in lands
spanning five continents, and three years ago I returned to my
motherland, hopefully never to leave for long periods again. It
appears that all First World countries have the same concept as I
do – it is the *stay where you are – remain in the land of your birth – don't
trespass if you are brown or black – don't visit us, we will visit you* attitude. A concept that is reinforced over and over again whenever a
Sri Lankan attempts to apply for a visa to visit a country in the
First World. Sri Lankans can only visit Singapore and the Maldive
Islands without a stamped visa. For any other country on earth, a
Sri Lankan citizen must apply for a visa. It is not an easy process.

As I stood for three consecutive days on the street in front of the Italian Embassy with no shelter from rain or sun for a total of 6 hours at a time, with no conveniences, and I mean *no* conveniences, at hand, I had plenty of time to mull on the commons, especially common space and geography. I discussed this with my fellow visa applicants. Some of them had been there for the third or fourth time. They brought little stools and straw mats to sit on. They picnicked and shared personal stories. They littered the area around them with biscuit wrappings and other remnants of sustenance. And they assured me that if they didn't get the visa it would not be a problem. They shrugged with seeming indifference, and yet I knew that like me they were anxious and nervous. They likened the experience to that of taking an examination. Pass or fail. Good or bad. Visa or no visa. Now, with no Schengen visa as yet stamped in my passport, as I write this paper I am still unsure if I can come to Greece, be with my fellow colleagues, and discuss what we have in common. Right now, I think we have very little.

When I read the briefing note that was sent to us where Peter Barnes had glowingly written of our common assets – the sky, water, public lands, culture, science, customs and laws, rituals and rites, the airwaves, seedbeds of creativity, etc – I realized that while we share these common assets, the greatest asset that is common to all of us is denied to most of us. It is that of the world. Earth. The Globe. Our Planet. Call it what you will. With the emergence of nation states and travel documents like the passport, with travel restrictions, visas, and borders, the world ceased to be common property to be accessed by all its inhabitants on an equal footing.

Prior to the Second World War, people travelled the world to trade, to explore, to proselytize, and to conquer. Many of them carried letters of introduction and guarantees of safe passage. The earliest known mention of a passport is found in 450 BC, when an official of ancient Persia, Nehemiah, received a letter from King Artaxerxes addressed to the "governors of the province beyond the river," requesting him safe passage as he travelled through their lands on his way to Judah.

Yet the modern concept of a multi-destination, multi-journey document issued only from the holder's country of nationality arose only from the middle of the twentieth century. Before this, passports were issued by any country to any individual and were valid for a short period of time, acting much the way visas do today. It was only after the First World War that the wide-spread legal requirement to use a passport to travel between countries arose. I grew up on stories of a grand-uncle who piled his Land Rover jeep with gifts, bundled in his wife and two-year-old child and drove pell-mell to England through Afghanistan and Iran. I hero-worshipped my uncle who hitch-hiked from Oxford to Ceylon (as Sri Lanka was then known). He slept on park benches and worked in the kitchens of roadside boutiques. These are experiences I can only dream about, that I know I can never have, for now I am from the wrong side of the world.

Today, there is a new kind of apartheid, especially for citizens of Third World countries. It is the apartheid of the passport. The passport has become an obsession. It is the difference between good and evil. My parents gave up their Sri Lankan passports when they were both in their seventies in order to travel the world with ease. These days they live seven months in warm Sri Lanka, applying for a resident permit in the land of their birth, and two months in New Zealand, their country of citizenship during the summer, and travel for a total of three months of the year to other countries. In Sri Lanka, a foreign passport is unimaginable wealth; it is a dowry or bargaining tool in marriage, so valuable that marriage advertisements carry them like assets. A passport with a valid U.S. or Australian, U.K. or Schengen visa is priceless. You can even be killed for it. Sri Lankan expatriates holding passports from Australia, the U.S., and England or Canada flood the country twice a year, during the summer holidays and during Christmas. They buy luxury high rise apartments, have forgotten to speak their mother tongue, and make it a point to be identified as being from somewhere else. It gives them status.

Some years ago I made a conscious decision to remain a Sri Lankan citizen and to thus be party to all the trials and tribulations that are incurred by being one. In Rome, five minutes after I landed, I was asked by security police at the airport if I had enough spending money and how could they be sure that I was a genuine tourist. In Amsterdam, while still in the air passage that connects the airport to the plane, heavy-booted policemen check the passports of Asians to verify they possess a legitimate visa. In Hong Kong, brown- and black-skinned passengers were asked to surrender their passports to the Cathay Pacific crew, to be returned upon arrival in the United States. Occasionally I get tired of my citizenship. Sometimes I just want to be able to travel and enjoy my planet as if I have the right to it.

Today, Third World citizens will travel illegally in fragile and overloaded boats in order to reach the shores of any country in the First World, be they Mexicans on their way to the U.S., Sri Lankans to Italy, or Vietnamese to Australia. Economically, they become the backbone of their host country. They do the work that birth citizens do not want to do, they live underground lives, their existence barely acknowledged, and for all this they are grateful. There have been times I have mulled on this phenomenon. Why do people voluntarily fall into a state of debt to travel with risk and fear, to leave all that they know and love, to enter countries that are most often cold and inhospitable, to live alongside human beings who regard them with contempt, to make a life that they will eventually consider successful?

When the tsunami of December 2004 occurred in South and South East Asia, the magnitude of aid and personnel that arrived to assist its victims was overwhelming. It was colloquially and humorously termed a tsunami of aid workers. We were touched by the kindness and generosity of the world. And yet, a rebellious corner of my mind wonders if any Sri Lankan doctors or other aid workers had volunteered their services when Hurricane Katrina arrived with all its fury upon New Orleans, they would have been given American visas? I doubt it. It is yet another perpetuation of the way traffic of power or aid should flow.

Thus while it is laudable to think of all these other definitions of what we have in common, I want us to think of the right for all human beings to be treated as human. The right to have access to justice, and a reasonable degree of power and control over our lives. Why is it that the majority of the world's resources are used by the First World even if they are to be found in the Third? Why is it always the First World who will speak about what we have in common, never the Third? And finally, when I asked a few Sri Lankans what we have in common with the world, their replies reflected a morbid and mordant view of the world that worried me – *death, nothing,* and *conflict* were some of the replies.

Taken in perspective, it is only for a short time in the earth's history that we have held this attitude of difference. If we take ancient tales of how the earth was birthed or the ancient edicts on how we are to live, we will find a multitude of beliefs held in common. Even religions as diverse as Judaism, Hinduism, and Zoroastrianism combined elements of earlier religious and philosophical traditions to emerge as organized religions, with priesthoods, texts, practices, and followers. Take for instance the ancient Maori tale of creation and compare it with the Apache story of creation. They both begin with nothingness or darkness and move into light, and they both talk about the separation of the earth and the sky. The Scandinavian, Welsh, and Lithuanian stories of a flood, which includes the survival of living creatures in a boat, talk about a great calamity that befell the world, which after it passed saw an opportunity to start afresh. During these times the different peoples held all the resources precious, and most precious of all was life. It may be interpreted that because it was so valuable, the sacrifice of human life came to mean the ultimate sacrifice or gift one could give a higher being, from the Incas to Abraham to Jesus Christ.

However, from the time where the individual has become supreme we have taken to polluting our commons, wasting or throwing them away, or being greedy for them and inconsiderate about them. When I was young I was told a story of the American government throwing an excess of wheat into the Atlantic ocean rather than exporting it as charity to Asia or Africa because it would bring the global price of wheat down. I do not know if it was a true story, but it has stayed with me even though I could not have been older than nine years, and even then I was horrified. How could they? I raged, living as I was in a 1970s Sri Lanka when consumer protectionism was ubiquitous and we recycled almost everything–clothes, bottles, iron, paper and cans. Green gram or other snacks were wrapped in cones of newspaper, old exam papers lined shelves, and wrapping paper continued to wrap gifts as if in a perpetual life cycle without any hope of nirvana. Bottles were evaluated and retained to house other goods: jam bottles became spice bottles, arrack bottles became kitul treacle bottles, marmite bottles became ayurvedic oil bottles. Clothes were identified and lusted after while still draped on their first owners. They were coveted and treasured and eventually passed down through generations. Iron that held up houses travelled throughout the island, and cans were used as units of measurement or ashtrays or flattened to hold a fan of coir for a broom.

But today I see that even in my Third World island nation where we still live simple and uncomplicated lives, what we hold in common has changed. We have become like anywhere else. We are beginning to think like the others. It is a common frame of mind that is disastrous.

Still, all is not lost; with my Schengen visa almost 80 percent approved (thanks to influence, of course) I would like to end this paper on a slightly more positive note. A month ago my American friend had her baby in Sri Lanka. A single mother, she discovered she could not afford to have her child in America. Surrounded by her adopted family of friends she gave birth to a beautiful baby girl. The child was named Medin after the full moon day she was born on. Though this example still holds to the true-to-form flow of First World visitors being able to travel to the Third World easily, I would like to think that this is the new common – a half-American, half-Indian child born in Sri Lanka, who has the possibility of living anywhere and being a true child of the world.

Defending the Common Wealth

Scott Russell Sanders

What's being sold around the clock and around the world as the "American way of life" is mostly a cheat and a lie. It's an infantile dream of endless consumption, endless novelty, and endless play. It's a pacifier for the ego to suck on. It's bad for us and bad for the earth.

We need a dream worthy of grown-ups, one that values simplicity over novelty, conservation over consumption, harmony over competition, community over ego. We need a story that recognizes our well-being derives not from the private wealth we hold as individuals or as corporations, but from the common wealth we share as members of the human family. We need a new vision of the good life. Or, rather, we need to recover an old vision, one well known to our ancestors but now largely forgotten.

In England, "the commons" originally referred to lands and waters that were used by the community as a whole – the pastures, woodlots, tillable fields, springs, lakes, and rivers on which everyone depended for sustenance. Even if the land was owned by a feudal lord, a church, or a monarch, it was partly or entirely open to use by those who lived nearby, and the terms of that use were defined primarily by the community rather than by the owner.

If one goes far enough back in time, of course, the whole earth was a commons – as the Americas were at the time Europeans first encountered the indigenous people they called "Indians." One must be wary of making generalizations about the hundreds of cultures that evolved in the Western Hemisphere before 1500, but everything I have read suggests that, while indigenous peoples recognized territories for hunting and gathering, they did not recognize private ownership of portions of the earth.

The Europeans who colonized the Americas began carving up this commons and turning it into private property, as the wealthy classes were busily doing back in England and on the Continent. Between the 1500s and the mid-1800s, nearly all of the English commons was privatized, initially through the actions of land-lords and later through acts of Parliament. In the process, centuries-old relationships between people and place were torn apart; a view of land as the source of livelihood for the whole community was replaced by a view of land as a commodity to be bought and sold for the benefit of the propertied class. Those who did not own land became, if they were lucky, the tenants or wage servants of those who did; and if they were unlucky, they starved.

Where there had once been free passage for people and animals, now hedges, fences, wardens, and legal barriers blocked the way. The legal barriers were imposed by Parliament in bills called "acts of enclosure," and "enclosure" thus became the short-hand term for privatizing the commons. The first great surge of enclosures occurred in the late Middle Ages, propelled by the lucrative wool trade. By 1516, the leading character in Sir Thomas More's *Utopia* could lament that mild-mannered sheep, grazing on what had once been common land, were devouring men and villages as well as grass.

By the middle of the eighteenth century, Jean-Jacques Rousseau could trace the origins of social inequality to the privatizing of the commons:

The first man who, having enclosed a piece of land, thought of saying, "This is mine" and found people simple enough to believe him, was the true founder of civil society. How many crimes, wars, murders; how much misery and horror the human race would have been spared if someone had pulled up the stakes and filled in the ditch and cried out to his fellow men: "Beware of listening to this impostor. You are lost if you forget that the fruits of the earth belong to everyone and that the earth itself belongs to no one!"[1]

In a gloss on this passage, Voltaire remarked, "Behold the philosophy of a beggar who would like the rich to be robbed by the poor!"[2]

The following centuries have shown that Voltaire needn't have worried. By the end of the nineteenth century, 99 percent of England's agricultural land was owned by just over half a percent of the population.[3] Except for occasional setbacks, as during the French Terror and the Bolshevik Revolution, the rich in Europe and the United States have easily held their own, and they have done so, in large part, by enclosing more and more of the commons. Today, the fences encircle far more than land. In America, individuals and corporations are patenting life forms and genetic information; they are profiting from scientific research conducted at public expense; they are selling water drawn from aquifers and springs, and they are exploiting public waterworks for farming and real estate development in arid regions; they are building in flood-prone areas thanks to insurance underwritten by taxpayers; they are hijacking the public airwaves and the Internet; they are

1 Jean-Jacques Rousseau, A Discourse on Inequality (1755), translated by Maurice Cranston (Harmondsworth: Penguin, 1984), p. 109.

2 Ibid., p. 180.

3 David Bollier, Silent Theft: The Private Plunder of Our Common Wealth (New York: Routledge, 2002), p. 46.

drilling for oil, mining for minerals, felling timber, and grazing livestock on public lands, paying fees far below market values or paying nothing at all; they are polluting the air, water, and soils and passing on the cost of that pollution to all of us. These private grabs of public goods are widening the gulf not only between rich and poor individuals but also between rich and poor nations, even as they are degrading the commons.

Enclosures are by no means the only threat to the health of the biosphere. Anyone who takes an honest look at the evidence realizes that natural systems are breaking down under the pressure of a swelling human population, which consumes more resources, releases more toxins, disrupts more habitat, and drives more species to extinction year by year. The consequent human suffering—from war, drought, famine, and disease—is incalculable and unconscionable. As a result of these disasters, we now realize that we depend on far more than the lands and waters originally belonging to the commons, although of course lands and waters are crucial. We now recognize that we depend for our well-being on countless shared goods, from a stable climate and a prolific ocean to honest government and effective schools.

We could speak about the whole realm of shared goods as "the commons," as Vandana Shiva does in talking about the indigenous knowledge bound up in strains of rice and wheat developed by generations of Indian farmers; as Jeremy Rifkin does in arguing against the privatizing of the human genome; as Peter Barnes does in proposing how to defend the atmosphere from pollution; as David Bollier does in protesting the giveaway of knowledge derived from publicly-funded research; or as Elinor Ostrom does in writing about the protection of ocean fisheries.[4]

---

4 Vandana Shiva, *Earth Democracy: Justice, Sustainability, and Peace* (Cambridge, Massachusetts: South End Press, 2005); Jeremy Rifkin, *The Biotech Century* (New York: Tarcher/Putnam, 1998); Peter Barnes, *Who Owns the Sky? Our Common Assets and the Future of Capitalism* (Washington, D.C.: Island Press, 2003); David Bollier, *Silent Theft: The Private Plunder of Our*

The Internet, itself a valuable addition to our shared wealth, has become an arena for vigorous efforts to define, defend, and enhance the commons. A sampling of those efforts might include the Global Commons Institute from Great Britain; the "On the Commons" project from the Tomales Bay Institute; "The Leadership for a New Commons" initiative from the Whidbey Institute; the public-domain licensing venture called the "Creative Commons"; and the Digital Library of the Commons hosted at Indiana University.[5]

While "the commons" is a serviceable term with a noble history, the one I prefer to use is "common wealth," which originally meant "the general welfare." I believe we need to recover ways of speaking about "the general welfare," especially in the United States, where public discourse has been taken over almost entirely by the rhetoric of individualism and free enterprise. I separate the compound word into its two parts, "common" and "wealth," to distinguish my usage from that of Thomas Hobbes, John Locke, and other political philosophers, who equated the "commonwealth"—one word—with the body politic.

As I understand it, the common wealth embraces much more than the body politic; it embraces all those natural and cultural goods that we share by virtue of our membership in the human family. A short list of these goods would include the air, waters, soils, and oceans; outer space; the electromagnetic spectrum; the human gene pool and the diversity of species; language in all its forms, including mathematics and music; knowledge in all its

---

Common Wealth (New York: Routledge, 2002); Elinor Ostrom, *Governing the Commons: The Evolution of Institutions for Collective Action* (Cambridge, England: Cambridge U.P., 1990).

5 For the Global Commons Institute, see www.gci.org.uk/.
   For the Tomales Bay Institute project, see www.onthecommons.org/.
   For the Whidbey Institute initiative, see www.whidbeyinstitute.org.
   For the Creative Commons, see www.creativecommons.org.
   For the Digital Library of the Commons, see dlc.dlib.indiana.edu/.

forms, from art to zoology; all manner of artifacts and machines, from knives to supercomputers; the practical arts such as cooking, building, herding, and farming; the practice of medicine; the body of law, the structures of democratic government, and the traditions of civil liberty; parks, community gardens, state and national forests, wildlife refuges, and protected wilderness areas; museums, libraries, schools, plazas, and other public spaces.

None of us, as individuals or even as nations, could create these goods from scratch or replace them if they were lost. For example, no amount of ingenuity or toil on our part could mend the tattered ozone layer, restore balance to a destabilized climate, or revive an ocean fishery that has been depleted below the threshold required for biological recovery. And none of us creates wealth purely through our own endeavors, but only by drawing on this vast inheritance. At most, we may add some mite of value – an idea, an invention, a song – but whatever we contribute is minuscule compared to the riches we inherit. We are born into the legacy of the common wealth, and we pass it on, either enhanced or diminished, to future generations. As recipients of this gift, we should feel obliged to protect and preserve it, and to assure that it remains accessible to all.

For the past quarter century, U.S. politics has been dominated by attempts to ransack the common wealth, benefiting the few at the expense of the many. This plundering takes many forms: below-cost timber sales in national forests, over-grazing of public lands by privately-owned livestock, oil drilling in wildlife refuges, subsidies for the nuclear industry and agribusiness, pork barrel highway projects, sweetheart deals for military contractors, off-shore tax havens for corporations, on and on. The looting of the commons has been carried out through the privatizing of prisons, the transfer of tax dollars to religious schools, the commercial rip-off of the Internet, the scouring of the oceans by factory ships, the opening of national parks to snowmobiles, and the patenting of organisms. The result of all this plundering is to diminish the wealth we hold in common.

Our politicians and merchants seem not to notice that we hold any wealth in common. The story they tell is almost entirely about private wealth and private solutions. If the streets are unsafe, instead of reducing the poverty that causes crime, buy an alarm system, move into a gated community, pack a gun. If the public schools are failing, instead of fixing them, put your kids in private schools. If the water is tainted, don't work to clean it up; buy your own supply in bottles. If the roads are clogged, don't push for public transportation; buy a bigger car. If cancer is epidemic, instead of addressing the causes, try the latest therapies. If Social Security looks insecure, instead of overhauling the system, funnel the dollars into private accounts, so those who guess right on the stock market will win and those who guess wrong will lose. If more than forty million Americans lack any form of health insurance and tens of millions more lack adequate coverage, instead of expanding Medicare to cover everyone fairly, establish private health accounts so the rich can buy superior care and the middle class can take their chances and the poor can live in fear of accident or illness. Even churches, which might challenge this epidemic of selfishness, enlarge their congregations by preaching the gospel of prosperity rather than material simplicity, and personal salvation rather than service to one's neighbor.

✧ ✧ ✧

In the raw young American democracy, Alexis de Tocqueville observed an uneasy balance between the pursuit of personal advantage and a concern for the common good. Since he made those observations in the 1830s, the balance, if it ever existed, has certainly been lost.[6] The spirit of cooperation and philanthropy that so bedazzled the visiting Frenchman is still alive in America, but it has been overshadowed by rampant privatism. The myth of the social compact, which emphasizes our dependence on one another, has been largely displaced by the myth of self-reliance. This trend coincides with the triumph of television, which purveys the solipsistic, hedonistic, ahistorical mindset we blithely call consumerism.

The political assault on the common wealth and the commercial appeal to "consumers" go hand-in-hand. Both urge us to grab whatever we can, to indulge our appetites without gratitude to the people whose labor supports us, without concern for future generations, without acknowledging that we share the earth with millions of other species and that we draw every drop of our sustenance from nature. While the world decays around us, we are urged to buy our way to security, as if we could withdraw inside a bubble of money. This story, the dominant one in America today, is a self-centered fantasy that leads to loneliness for the individual and disaster for the world.

We need an alternative story, one that appeals to our generosity and compassion rather than our selfishness. We need a story that measures wealth not by the amount of money held in private

---

6 In an earlier essay, I noted that "Although Tocqueville found much to fear and quite a bit to despise in this raw democracy, he praised Americans for having 'carried to the highest perfection the art of pursuing in common the object of their common desires.' Writing of what he had seen in the 1830s, Tocqueville judged Americans to be avaricious, self-serving, and aggressive; but he was also amazed by our eagerness to form clubs, to raise barns or town halls, to join together in one cause or another: 'In no country in the world, do the citizens make such exertions for the common weal. I know of no people who have established schools so numerous and efficacious, places of public worship better suited to the wants of the inhabitants, or roads kept in better repair.'" I quote Tocqueville from Richard D. Heffner's edition of Democracy in America (New York: Mentor, 1956), pp. 199, 67-68.

hands or by the Gross Domestic Product but by the condition of the commons. We need a story that links the health of individuals to the health of communities, a story that reminds us we inhabit not merely a house or a city or a nation but a planet. Rather than defining us as consumers, this new story would define us as conservers; rather than cultivating narcissism, it would inspire neighborliness; rather than exhorting us to chase after fashions, it would invite us to find joy in everyday blessings – in the voice of a child or a bird, in music and books, in gardening and strolling, in sharing food and talk. To live by such a story, we need not be sages or saints; we need simply be awake to the real sources of the good life.

In crafting such a story, we might begin by reimagining where we live. Most of us, when asked for our address, will give a street number, a postal code, or other markers of place, but we are unlikely to name the nearest river. As one step toward reviving a concern for the common wealth, we could inscribe on the covers of our phonebooks a map of the local watershed. Grownups would be puzzled at first by this way of describing their true address, but I expect that children would readily grasp what it means. In a number of elementary schools across the country, with help from teachers and parents, students are mapping their local watersheds and monitoring the quality of rivers and lakes. In some communities, after identifying sources of pollution, children have offered testimony to city councils and environmental protection boards. Youngsters readily understand that rivers and lakes gather whatever falls or is dumped on the land, and that streams reveal the state of health for the whole watershed. They understand that each of us lives in the embrace of a river.[7]

7 For a sampling of watershed-based educational initiatives, see Hamline University's Center for Global Environmental Education: www.cgee. hamline.edu/watershed/action/resources/curricula/planting.htm.

My own home in southern Indiana is embraced by the East and West Forks of the White River. With a watershed of 11,350 square miles, wholly contained within Indiana, the White drains roughly a third of the state. So the quality of its water is a fair measure of how well government, municipalities, businesses, farmers, and ordinary citizens of Indiana are caring for this precious common resource. The verdict is: not very well. The White ranks high on lists of the nation's threatened rivers—not because of depletion, as in rivers of the arid Southwest, or because of dams, as in rivers of the mountainous Northwest, but because of pollution. In the upper and lower reaches, it collects runoff from glacial plains, where the deep topsoil is devoted mainly to soybeans and corn and is liberally sprayed with pesticides and herbicides; throughout the watershed, including the unglaciated southern hills where I live, it gathers runoff from lawns, parking lots, highways, factory outlet pipes, municipal dumps, and overburdened sewer systems. The resulting stew of toxins has made it dangerous to drink straight from the river, swim in the river, or eat fish drawn from the river. In 1999, five million fish were killed by a single factory discharge. The Indiana Department of Environmental Management duly issues warnings. But the word "management" is a misnomer here; no one is managing the White River. At best, our state and federal agencies are monitoring its decline.

I spoke recently with a man whose job is to travel around the watershed explaining to farmers new regulations that limit, for the first time ever, the amounts and kinds of poisons they can spray on their land. His standard reception is to be called a communist. The Indiana Farm Bureau as well as the agrichemical companies declare that it is un-American to restrict what a man can do on his own land or what a corporation can sell. Likewise, many developers, industrialists, loggers, and homeowners resist any constraints that might cost them money or sweat. In doing what is easiest and most profitable for themselves, they are obeying the rational self-interest so famously celebrated by Adam Smith and so assiduously defended by apostles of the free market. Added together, however, these selfish choices do not magically serve the "public good," as if guided by an "invisible hand," but instead they defile a portion of the public good called the White River.

Under the twin banners of property rights and free enterprise, rivers are being degraded all across America. Elsewhere, the abuse may come from mine tailings, power plants, livestock feedlots, or paper mills; from barge traffic or jet skis; from the pumping of vast quantities of water for resorts in the desert; or from mountain-top removal for coal mining. The pace of such abuse has increased along with growth in population, in the power of technology, and in the sway of corporations. Regulation alone will not be enough to reverse the trend. In spite of treaties, there are constant battles over allocation of water from the Colorado, for example, and the river is so overdrawn that scarcely any flow reaches the sea. The Clean Water Act has led to improvement in some rivers, but in many cases, it is cheaper for a company to pay the fines for ruining a river than to clean up its effluents. No matter what rules are on the books, any administration in Washington can choose to reinterpret the law, weaken it, or ignore it entirely. Much as we need wise laws and socially-responsible courts, they alone will not protect our rivers or the rest of our shared wealth. The only sure protection is a citizenry that clearly recognizes and fiercely defends the common wealth as the prime source of our well-being, and as our legacy to future generations.

Fortunately, many people sense this need. Around the world, people are shaping a new story about the sources of peace and plenty. You can see the story come alive in farmers' markets, housing co-ops, land trusts, neighborhood councils, and town theaters. You can see it in free medical clinics and Habitat for Humanity building sites. You can see it in the Green Belt Movement, launched by Wangari Maathai in Kenya, which is spreading trees and democracy across Africa. You can witness the story unfolding in citizen forums and simple living collectives, in shelters for abused women and children, in efforts to restore eagles or wolves.

Those who embrace this new story are recovering wisdom known to our ancestors but largely forgotten in our narcissistic age. In spite of what the media tell us, we know that the good life is not for sale. We understand that the good life is something we make together, in partnership with other people and in harmony with nature. Because we realize that happiness, health, security, and meaning come to us largely as gifts, we feel called to preserve those gifts, enhance them if we can, and pass them on.

Love of our common wealth is a root impulse behind countless acts of gratitude and kindness that ordinary people perform every day. We all feel it, but we don't always know how to speak of it, or we speak of it so quietly that our story is drowned out by the blare of consumerism. We need to speak up, to say boldly why we fight for a just economy, inspiring schools, decent housing, and universal health care; why we protect open space, why we clean up rivers and replant forests, why we look after the ailing and the elderly, why we insist that government be a force for public good. In a society obsessed with competition, we need to say why we practice cooperation. In a culture addicted to instant gratification, we need to champion long-term-healing.

The glorification of private wealth will go on around the clock, in every medium, without any help from us. We need to counter that chorus by lifting our voices in praise of the wealth we share, recalling how our lives depend on one another, on generations past and future, on the bountiful earth and all its creatures, on the spirit that lifts us into being and sustains us through every moment and reclaims us in the end.

The Ten Common-ments:
Some Experiences
From Indonesia

AYU UTAMI

Thou shalt have no other gods before me.

So Indonesia became a republic that upholds monotheism. It sounds odd, especially when we imagine that these green and lush tropical islands, settled three thousand and some years before Moses, decided to embrace the concept of a single god in the middle of the twentieth century. Right after the proclamation of independence at the end of World War II, our founding fathers were faced with a decision concerning a crucial issue: the foundation of the new state. While the Islamist groups advocated the *sharia* law, at least for the country's Moslems, the nationalist faction was of the opinion that it was enough to mention a "belief in God," in addition to humanism and social justice, as the state's foundation. The Christian minority from the eastern islands gave notice of their secession if the *sharia* was to be mentioned in the principles. As a compromise they decided to add a cluster of adjectives to "God." So, the first principle of the state foundation *Pancasila* was formulated roughly like this: The Belief in One and Only God. Thus Indonesia was born, a state which is neither theocratic nor secular. And, please be advised, the new state does not acknowledge Judaism. A prominent writer, Linus Suryadi, was once accused of blasphemy against Islam when he said that circumcision was originally a Jewish practice that was embraced by Islam.

Children born in the independence era learn from their beginning years that monotheism (minus Judaism) is one of our common values. This was also what Saddam Hussein learned.

This Saddam Hussein was born in Pekalongan, Central Java. The Javanese do not have family names. His name was Saddam Hussein, full stop, even though he was not the son of Mr. Hussein (in Indonesia, one can find Muammar Ghadafi, Kissinger, Polpot, Mussolini, or Hitler; I believe soon there will be Usamah or Osama, though not Bush). People would call him Saddam, not Hussein. Pak Saddam, not Pak Hussein.

Like other children, Saddam learned state ideology and the history of his nation at school, as well as religion and some other things. He learned that the Republic of Indonesia was established on 17 August 1945, after 350 years of the Dutch colonization and 3.5 years of Japanese occupation. Unlike India and Malaysia, whose independence was granted by the British, we Indonesians fought for ours with blood and tears. We are proud of it. We are taught to be. And what was it that united the 13,000 plus islands? It was, as mentioned in the textbooks, a common history shared between people of different cultures and ethnicities living on those scattered pieces of land. It's that we had a lingua franca. But what does unite us is a common history. In a not-too-impressive expression: the people living on those islands at the end of World War II were coincidently colonized by the Dutch rather than by the British or some others. For the Indonesians this common history is both heroic and romantic. It refers to a glorious past of the Majapahit kingdom and projects a glorious future under the Republic of Indonesia. For a scholar like Benedict Anderson this nation is just a construction. In his formulation, it is not the romantic "great nation on the tropic of emerald, united by a common history" but, more plainly, an "imagined community." An imagined community has no celestial basis.

One of the imaginations of this imagined community is the state foundation on which it aims to grow itself: *Pancasila*, meaning "five principles." The first of its five principles is, again: The Belief in the One and Only God.

And this expression is the very proof of the monotheists' failure to coexist with different values. Before the fifteenth century, the time when Java's interior kingdoms weakened and Islamic power coming in from the island's northern coast surged, Java and parts of the archipelago had been under Hindu-Buddhist kingdoms. The adherents of Hinduism, Buddhism, and local beliefs still live there. Each of these groups has a concept of divinity completely different from the monotheistic concept of god. Monotheistic religions tend to fail, not only in understanding the others' concepts, but more fundamentally in appreciating that such beliefs and practices have their own spiritual and divine dimension. And this certainly is not a trait limited to the Moslems. Travelogues of the first Catholic missionaries to India show the same failure—failure to see Hinduism as a religion, and, worse, failure to see that these "not-religions" could possibly assume the same divine status.

Our common values were thus set up on the failure to coexist fully. I am here talking about Indonesia. Every child learning history knows tacitly that the common platform was arranged after a set of negotiations. In the case of the state's foundation on *Pancasila*, the Islamist group gave in (note that this group does not necessarily represent the majority of Moslems—close to 90 percent of Indonesian population—has never been supportive of an Islamic State of Indonesia). The Christians got what they wanted, as their objection was granted. The Hindus and the Buddhists, having been the most underrepresented during the formation of the republic, gave in the most. In schools, teachers tried to explain non-Abrahamic religions in monotheistic terms. The Hindus have three gods, the Trimurti—Vishnu, Brahma, and Shiva—but beyond them is one absolute entity, the Sang Hyang Widhi. In an effort to put the difficult fact of plurality in accordance with the state's principle of monotheism, school-teachers invariably use simple talk when it comes to Balinese Hinduism. Please don't expect them to talk about the Upanishads, or about any Hindi texts opening the possibility of God's non-existence.

Half of the globe is, or at one time was, influenced by mono-theism. The area covered by the missionary religions has spread to the five continents. Moses, depicted as bringing the tablets of the Ten Commandments, may be the most ancient icon we share in common. Monotheism is the first rule of the Commandments. It is also the rule that creates the most problems when it comes to co-existence and identity. The political dimension of the three branches of monotheism influenced the drawing up of the world map since the time of the Crusades, and, by way of colonization, the two world wars, and the War on Terror today.

What can be said about Indonesia's experience? Monotheism may be the prototype of the problem stemming from the effort to find some common value—particularly when it comes to values related to identity. Common values are a project, a construct, and Saddam Hussein from Pekalongan knew this first rule: common values have always been constructed with the help of hegemony and through the exclusion of the other. This is the first thing to remember: when we list a set of things that we hold in common, something and someone is always excluded.

Thou shalt not take the name of the Lord thy God in vain.

The history of colonization is the common history of the world. Modern nation-states all relate to colonization in one way or another, directly or not; most of them, however, relate to it directly. Indonesia thus used to be the Dutch Indies.

Among Indonesia's Dutch legacies is its legal system. There is a group of notorious articles in the criminal code known by its Dutch expression *haatzaai artikelen*, the "defamation articles." One cannot find these clauses in the Dutch criminal code in the Netherlands. They were initially used to suppress critical voices in the colonies. These articles are preserved as the independent Republic of Indonesia retained the law books in their entirety. We call them the "rubber articles" for they can basically designate any critical opinion as slander. As the government got more authoritarian, the more it used the *haatzaai artikelen* to send activists and opponents to jail.

In addition to a set of modern tools of suppression introduced by the colonial power, we certainly also have to mention, as a matter of historical fact, the transmission of ideas through colonization. In the case of the Dutch Indies, the natives – that's us, Indonesians – were exposed to modern-western education, particularly after the political reforms in the Netherlands at the end of the 19th century. The liberals defeated the conservatives in Holland, and decided to introduce what they called the "ethical policy" to "enlighten" the natives in the colonies. Modern schools opened. Native boys were sent to study in Holland's universities. This initiative introduced modern ideas and ideologies such as liberty, republic, democracy, human rights, socialism, as well as communism, to the Indonesians. Postcolonial studies mention endlessly that it is through the language of the colonizers that the colonized comprehend themselves in the new world.

Saddam Hussein spent his childhood in the thick of the Islamic tradition, as most of Pekalongan children did. The northern coastal town was one of the first Arab settlements in Java; the Islamic tradition, usually referred to as the *santri* culture, is dominant there. As Saddam grew up, he began to read leftist works as well. Socialism and communism were forbidden at that time. The Suharto military regime was a Southeast Asian "dear colleague" of the U.S. during the Cold War. Before the systematic demolition of Indonesia's Communist Party between 1965-1968, there had been some efforts to reconcile Islamic teachings with communism. In that spirit, Indonesia's first president Sukarno, a fiery anti-U.S. politician, had formulated a slogan: Nasakom=Nasionalisme-Agama-Komunisme (Nationalism Religion-Communism). Even though his successor General Suharto, a cool anti-communist, subsequently black-painted communism-cum-socialism as mere atheism, efforts to syncretise Islam and the leftist ideas lingered on among many students-activists. Despite his strong Islamic background, Saddam Hussein joined the anti-government movement through a nationalist-leftist group. He was close to the nationalist Indonesian Democratic Party, a suppressed opponent to the ruling party, as well as to the underground Democratic People's Party. Later, many proponents of this movement were sent to jail under the haatzaai artikelen.

In 1998 the military regime collapsed. Ironically the new government, installed through a democratic election, forgot to invalidate the undemocratic articles of the law book. Or rather, they did not forget. They benefited from it. Already in the era reformasi, Saddam was arrested following a demonstration in his hometown. He was tried with that very same defamation article, and sentenced to some three years' imprisonment. The government he was critical of used to be the opposition party he had earlier supported.

So Saddam entered jail. A formal state prison, the Pekalongan jail is not as notorious a house as Guantanamo or any of the secret detention houses in Indonesia. Yet it was not a comfortable place. During the military regime, when I worked as a journalist, I had friends in jail. We thought we fought for the freedom of the press, but unfortunately the court had a different opinion. Using the defamation articles, the judges sent my colleagues to three to four years in jail. We used to visit them in the men's prison in Jakarta, bringing with us the special foods they were craving.

As long as we kept friendly with the guards and did not forget to offer the necessary lubricant, we could even throw birthday parties, with wine and beer, cakes and jokes. The prisons for women and children are usually harsher, as they contain fewer political prisoners. In the men's prisons, the guards were usually on familiar terms with the visitors–who, in many cases, had themselves once been prisoners, or were prospective prisoners-to-be. One day a guard asked a visitor who it was he was visiting this time. Laughing, the activist answered that this time it was he himself who had been sentenced. Whenever the guards turned strict and unfriendly, we knew an inspection was taking place.

Personal relationships developed between the prisoners, the guards, and the visitors. The visitors, comprised of family and friends, became the main source of strength, a backbone for the prisoners during their term. But this time Saddam was unlucky. The closeness among activists that could be relied on in the past was now waning away as the political situation was changing. It's not a good excuse, I know. For reasons that could not easily be forgiven later, he was neglected by friends and family. Fewer and fewer people visited, or cared about his condition. Neglected by those who were supposed to be closest to him, and victim of the unhealthy condition in the prison, he died of malnutrition and other complications. After his death, his colleagues again organized a protest, demanding that the prison take responsibility.

Saddam Hussein's tragic story is only one of the millions of stories in the wake of colonization. His name was inspired by a global hero. Whether we like it or not, in his time the real Saddam Hussein was a hero for some Indonesian Moslems, for he rose up, roaring against the West, offering the prospect of Pan-Arabism and thereby giving many people, certainly the family in Pekalongan, a hope for a great Arabic center of world power, one that would compete with the West.

But the young Saddam knew that any authority, including the god of the Ten Commandments, dislikes when people make jokes in its name.

Remember the sabbath day, keep it holy.

Soon after the military rule collapsed in 1998, here comes a new old problem. Fundamentalism. The state ideology teachers used to warn schoolchildren of the latent danger of communism. I remember that this was how I was introduced to the word *laten,* meaning "latent," in Bahasa Indonesia. But it now appears that we are facing the resurrection of the latent danger of fundamentalism instead.

Maybe it was a coincidence that the regime crumbled toward the end of the era when the socialist-communist rules were falling everywhere in the world. But it was no accident that it toppled after having been hit by the winds of capital flight and the Asian monetary crisis. During his reign General Suharto was supported by the U.S.; in the Cold War, he was its dear ally. When it came to the accumulation of personal wealth, the U.S. was Suharto's dear ally. In 1998, worth around 15 billion U.S. dollars, Suharto was number 74 on the Forbes richest list (note: his property could not really be distinguished from that of his family – nor, probably, from that of his nation). When he stepped down, his enemies, namely socialism and communism, had already fallen apart. And after the general and the communists have withered away, here come the religious zealots.

But wait. Don't say that we see only the emergence of Islamism. On the other side of the story, outspoken liberal groups within Islam are also emerging. During the military rule they weren't so obvious either. One of them is the Network of Liberal Islam, a circle of Moslem intellectuals who broadcast their ideas through radio programs, the web, traditional print media, and a series of traveling discussions. They believe that, as with any other religion, the Islam that can be discussed is only Islam within the human experience. In this world, Islam always comes with an adjective. The liberal Islam groups call the fundamentalists "the textual Islam" team. The so-called textual groups do not believe that revelation comes with any context; they want to reenact in this present world what they perceive as Islamic reign in the time of the Prophet. One of their priorities is to draw up ordinances based on *sharia* law. Unfortunately this approach touches only upon issues of morality and lifestyle in public places—never on poverty, or the eradication of corruption.

The public space is the place of the battle. Sometimes the battle is really silly.

Let's assume this is a story about the public space. In his last term, the governor of the capital city Jakarta—a general, as has always been the custom—took a decision that should have been taken a decade earlier: to develop a humane public transport system, the TransJakarta Busway. Until then, the public bus system had no schedule, often no shelters, and if the bus did stop—briefly—in the middle of the street, there was at least one pickpocket on board. Or a whole group. The unfortunate passenger was showered by the tropical rain while waiting for the bus, then had his pockets cleaned by pickpockets on the bus, arriving late for his meeting with no money or credit cards; at his destination it was sunny and unbearably hot. If he was lucky, everybody else was also late—which was rather common. It was always like that; because public problems were never settled at a public level, individuals tried to fix them at the level of the individual. The car became a personal priority. The growth of streets could never match the growth of vehicles. Jams were everywhere. Governor Sutiyoso decided to provide a busway.

He was a bit different from most of his predecessors. He announced he gave up smoking, and proved he protects old trees. A hundred-year-old banyan stood where a junction was supposed to be built. The tree was on the government protection list. The general agreed that the bus lane should give way to the tree. This would never have happened earlier.

But now a group of textual youth read the decision with one-eyed glasses. Having been trained to read all texts literally, according to their interpretation, they concluded that the Jakarta government's decision to keep the tree was a superstitious act and, worse, equal to belief in gods other than The One God. The contractor must have believed in the gods of the banyan tree. This is against the State's foundation. Remember, the first principle: Belief in the One and Only God. True, some people do practice older local beliefs by giving offerings to certain trees on days considered holy and in places considered sacred. Old trees are like your great-great-grandmother: surely you'd pay a visit and give an offering if she still were growing.

The gang of one-dimensional textualists cut down nearly all of the tree, leaving only the roots and a meter of the trunk. The only reason they didn't dig out the banyan down to its root was that they didn't have tools strong enough to accomplish the dirty job. Their view of the public space is that they alone are the public.

Other cases were more serious: attacks on properties and members of Ahmadiah, a group considered by the mainstream *ulemas* as an unforgivable deviation from Islam. Or, the effort to attack the office of the Liberal Islam Network. One of the worst cases, as this involved the local government, is the introduction of a regulation banning women from going out after seven pm unaccompanied by a male family member.

What is happening here is an effort to monopolize interpretation. Who owns the copyright of the Holy Book? Revelation, as well as ideas, is supposed to be shared, owned, developed in common.

Honour thy father and thy mother.

With a high rate of infant mortality and a life expectancy of around 65 years, Indonesia's population has reached 220 million. It is the fourth most populated country in the world. The third, the U.S., has reached 300 million. But in the U.S. this is related to the fact that people live longer; it is not because more babies are born but because fewer grannies die. In Indonesia, grandpas and grandmas pass away at the same pace as before. The production of babies is high.

I was the youngest of five siblings. My parents decided I was the conclusion, as it also was the year the government stopped giving subsidies to the civil servants for more than three babies. This new rule didn't apply to me since I was manufactured during the old regulation: until I turned seventeen, I still qualified for subsidized rice. The year I was born was the year General Suharto introduced a Family Planning Program. When it was first launched, it encouraged no more than three children. The policy was a success. At least in my family. My mother, a devout Catholic, decided to take on contraception without much hesitation. In 1970 the population was 112 million.

Only once in my life time did I experience the limit of natural resources – during a drought which forced my family to line up for water at a small and not all too clear spring. During that time, I also liked to have little adventures at the back of our house. There were small canals and patches of trees. I could see what each household pumped out from a pipe into the canal. If the water ran, the formless stuff would be sent to the river. But most of the time the canals were blocked by garbage. Children develop their sense of disgust later. Only when I was older did I think of how filthy the area must have been. At that time people were not familiar with septic tanks – not the middle nor the upper class either. And even now, cities still don't have integrated sewers to process human waste. Again, when public problems are not settled on a public level, people try to settle them on the level of the individual. The middle and upper classes build their own septic tanks. In fact, this private resolve scared an Eastern European diplomat's wife, whom I happened to meet at a dinner party. She was distraught to imagine that beneath every garden of every household there is a bunker filled with human waste. And in her garden is her own waste. Meanwhile, the poor still rely on the common drainage and river.

There are a lot of other, more sophisticated reasons, but it was the memory of the household waste that made me not too keen on seeing so many people in the world. Global warming is the latest warning for humankind, the flock responsible for having caused it. I have decided not to split my cells, the ultimate form of family planning.

Family planning is the one achievement of the military regime I truly appreciate. The authority had a centralized body and a budget to carry out the programs. Starting with a "three children" campaign, the government planned to reduce that number, step by step. In the end of '70s, the slogan was already "Two is enough, girl or boy is the same." There were, however, reports of coerced contraception, which made human rights advocates as well as women's rights activist opposed to the program. Many women do not have autonomous control over their bodies – they are forced, either by the state or by their husband. I think that to be forced to have two kids by the state is still better than to be forced to have ten kids by any husband.

Now, with the regime gone, family planning is no longer popular. The state no longer has either a central body or a budget. The program probably lost its popularity for two reasons. First, it might remind people of the military era. Second, the mainstream view is slanting to the right these days. Coerced contraception is against human rights. Coerced pregnancy too. However, it is easier to put one's finger on the first, as contraception is usually administered in public clinics, while coerced pregnancy happens in private rooms.

Indonesia might well expect a population explosion in the near future. The Justice and Prosperity Party, one of the most modern parties – meaning a political party basing its existence on its networks and programs, not on a charismatic leadership – is in favor of polygamous marriages and encourages big families. This is a party led by highly educated people, and most of its leaders got their PhDs from western universities. A not-so-impressively – educated group is, for example, the Front of Islam Defenders. This is a paramilitary organization that has often been involved in attacks against cafes and pubs, as well as against groups whose view of Islam is different from their view. In an interview one of them, Fauzan by name, said happily that he has four wives from whom he has twenty children still surviving. He'd had thirteen others who did not survive. They did not resign; they died. (The word "resign" was used by a polygamous man who said that one of his wives resigned from the marriage(s), as she was not strong enough to handle the job). At twenty, Fauzan is still not old enough to fight against the U.S. So he fights the U.S. by, umm, making not love but children. As for the children's education and healthcare, he is not worried at all: God will provide.

Even though we don't know each other personally, Fauzan and I share the same world, the same country, the same city (when he is visiting his Jakartan wives). But, to be frank, I don't know if I am able to put him and me in the same box called "us" when we are trying to find answers to questions about what it is we do hold in common. This may sound politically incorrect, but perhaps the problems lie not in what the common is but rather in who we are. Because the commons is defined by who we are, but who we are is also defined by what we hold in common.

Thou shalt not kill; thou shalt not commit adultery;
Thou shalt not bear false witness against thy neighbour.

Now it's time to look at the brighter picture rather than just ponder the problems arising when we try to imagine what the common could actually be.

There is, for instance, at least one thing that I have in common with Imam Samudra, the mastermind of the Bali bombings who so far hasn't expressed regret for his deeds. The bombings killed more than three hundred people. In Samudra's laptop the police found out that he had, apparently, been familiar with adult sites. When the press conference made this public, many people thought it was not relevant to the case. They thought it was the police's smear campaign. Later the police explained that those porn sites could actually be manipulated to cover up correspondence between the terrorist groups. I really don't how it worked technically. However, at least Imam Samudra and I do open porn sites sometimes, albeit for different reasons. I can assure you that I open those sites for, umm, my cultural studies, or pop culture studies, or because I need to gather as much information as possible about pornography in order to be able to contribute to the public debate, as the parliament is now drafting an anti-pornography-pornoaction bill intending to send people who French-kiss in public to five years in jail.

The cyber-world and virtual sites have become the newest media we share in common. I remember hearing about the Internet for the first time in 1995. It was still during the military era, and we didn't know its power would last only a few more years. Some colleagues had been arrested. Many journalists were fired from their offices and blacklisted from the business. I was one of those who lost their jobs. Our underground group, established by mostly young journalists, focused our efforts on breaking government censorship and exchanging information as widely as possible. That was when we started to learn about the Internet and about digital cameras. Both were very tempting. Digital cameras need no film. Soldiers and the low-ranking policemen whom we often had to face in the fields did not know about the new technology. They usually confiscated celluloid rolls inside our cameras if they thought we had taken forbidden pictures. Now for risky situations we would bring two cameras. One digital. One analog, for a decoy. Meanwhile, we could send the stories and the pictures quickly, through the Internet.

At that time the process was still a bit too complicated for ordinary people. We had never heard about browsers or websites. The commercial browser Mosaic started to operate only in 1993, and there were only around fifty websites on the globe. It was still such a new development that we didn't think to create our own website that people could have access to. At that time, for security reasons, our emails had to use an encoding and decoding program.

To our surprise, three years later the regime collapsed. The euphoria of reformation happened simultaneously with the euphoria of www, which was a consequence of the global dot-com boom in the end of the '90s. The government was a lame tiger now. Some years later we know that it is not only the freedom-lovers, the democracy-believers, or the porn-junkies who are connected to the web. Imam Samudra and his terrorist club did the same thing. As long as one can read abc, theoretically one can read the texts on the net. This virtual world is for all.

Today we understand that as far as its substance goes, the www does not have an ideology. But it was not like that during its creation. The concept of a world-wide-web was developed by a British computer scientist, Tim Berners-Lee, who struggled to maintain it as an open system, free and without ownership. He constructed a network in a virtual world accessible to everybody. The www was born out of ideas aiming to democratize knowledge. The virtual infrastructure was later welcomed by communities and groups with the same ideology. They developed computer programs that are free and open to modification. This is one of the latest developments that now make our world flat, according to Thomas Friedman in his new *The World is Flat*.

One of the most phenomenal www inventions is Wikipedia, initiated by Jimmy Wales, head of a new Internet company Bomis.com. To imagine an encyclopedia which is accessible for everybody to read and to edit would sound like a crazy idea — but only until the effort started to bring fruit. Wikipedia was activated in 2001 with articles from a collection that Wales kept from previous free encyclopedia projects. In Wikipedia he invited every visitor to edit and to add to the collection. In the first year the collection added up to 20,000. In 2005, it reached more than 800,000 articles; some of them have been translated to different languages, including Bahasa Indonesia. The collection is growing even as we are reading this sentence. This free encyclopedia now is one of the most visited websites and one of the most used references. Even though Wikipedia has an editorial team, it is not free of false facts or even defamation. However, the idea to create a common encyclopedia where everybody is allowed to participate freely, as a reader or as a writer, is one of the brilliant ideas of this century.

From one vantage point this system might remind us of practices in traditional societies, in which contributions toward "common work" stay anonymous. But then, here is a modern subject and a modern context. Where traditional societies work with myth, Wikipedia claims to work with information, if not facts. While a traditional society has one "site" everyone fully trusts, modern society has unlimited sites that no one can trust fully.

Thou shalt not steal.

The world of the web seems very sophisticated. But where is it located? It is a virtual world, the world of ideas. I nearly forgot about its location until an earthquake shook Taiwan and wrecked the underwater cables that connected internet providers in Asia. Aha, the virtual world is in fact to be found on earth.

The cyber world is a world of intertwining cables. Physical cables. I remember a friend who worked for a financial daily. Secretly he supported our underground movement for press freedom. He had to do it in secret so he would not lose his job. This guy had many ideas, and he was a bit mysterious in some ways. Though we needed to make contact with international organizations such as the International Federation of Journalists, Amnesty International, Human Rights Watch, and the like, our group didn't have any financial support. Phone tariffs were very high as the service was monopolized. But this peculiar friend told us of a way to make a free international call. He invited us to make the telephone contacts from his house on the outskirts of Jakarta. So we filed reports or sent faxes via his house phone, all for free. We were curious, but he said he had a special deal. Anyway, the situation was good for us, so we didn't ask too much. Later we found out that he managed to pull the public phone's cable from a booth near his house. A couple of months later, the telephone company closed that public phone. A couple of years later, I read in the newspaper that a boy, the son of this very friend, was kidnapped by his former business partner.

I realized how mixed-up the concepts of common, public, and state ownership are. Who owns the public phones? The State's monopoly of the telephone network produced bad service, high tariffs, and public disappointment. In turn, people perceived public phones as state facilities and targeted their dissatisfaction at them.

I had a journalist friend who once had a side job selling telephone cards. A hilarious young man. One day he offered an unlimited-time calling card to another friend, a British man who contributed reports to Amnesty International. Keep in mind that this phone card can only be used to make a call, not to receive one. Never to receive a call. She forgot the prohibition and took someone's call. After that, she could not use the card anymore. She could not contact the guy either. He reappeared again one day, when it was too late to complain. Sad story. Years later, he was shot dead by a police squad in front of his house. The police said that he tried to escape when they were arresting him for his alleged participation in fencing stolen cars.

Freedom of the press is fought not only by saints, but by thieves too. The two stories show how a telephone connection is not something you can take for granted here. I have yet to get my cable phone fixed, and I live in the center of Jakarta. Six months ago I submitted the registration, and still no news. A mobile phone is very easy to get these days, but they are much more expensive, and their connection is not satisfying. With a dial-up modem, internet connection is not too cheap, and with a mobile modem it is neither cheap nor as smooth as we hope. Once again, the world of ideas needs the infrastructure. The virtual world needs the cables. The commons is about access.

Thou shalt not covet thy neighbour's house, thou shalt not covet thy neighbour's wife, nor his manservant, nor his maidservant, nor his ox, nor his ass, nor any thing that is thy neighbour's.

A group of students from a prestigious art school in Bandung held an exhibition. They showed some pieces of work made up from collections of pop culture merchandise. The key message was not in the form, but in the process. They obtained the merchandise from the internet. Not through a proper transaction, but in a fraud transaction using fake credit cards. They called this e-buying without real paying "carding." They had manipulated the broker's trust, or his lust to sell. The exhibition was their response to a global culture.

In another student town, Yogyakarta, there are groups of young people who spend time in Internet cafes doing the carding. They like to buy things that they cannot personally use – humidifiers for factories, for example – just to see how far they can go.

How will these things affect not only the brokers but also me? Soon, more and more dot-coms, including Amazon and Barnes & Noble, punished every Indonesian. As a result, I cannot order books from the Internet with my Indonesian credit card and an Indonesian address.

There is a limit. In the end, the inability of the net to connect with and recognize each individual brings about communal sanction.

In the end, our identity is defined by a group, a territory. This situation is best shown by a document we call a "passport." It is true that not everybody needs a passport. My mother, for example, doesn't need to cross the border. That is the only condition in which there is no need to own a passport. For now, only smoke from forest fires doesn't need papers to cross the border. As for the rest, thousands of people see the discrepancy between their hopes and whatever their passports grant them. Like the Internet, passports give people equal status, but in reality there is a hundred and eighty degree difference between individuals or groups. Passports fold us into certain groups and, at the same time, exclude our group from another. It is in this situation that we are groping for what it is we can hold in common.

"The commons" seems like a concept based on an internal contradiction. It includes as well as excludes. But there is optimism in it, as there was optimism when some scattered islands in Southeast Asia decided to become Indonesia. I would like to paraphrase Benedict Anderson here, that the thing we are looking for is nothing but "the imagined commons."

Under the Watchtower or, First Growths of a "Commons" Capitalism

Gregory Norminton

What at first you take for woodchip turns out to be gravel, heaped like slag across a desolate plain. You press on, gnawed by a cold wind coming straight off the North Sea by way of Siberia, until you hear the bright, vertiginous song of a skylark marking its territory. Closer to the ground, a pair of woodlark takes off in alarm, and small flocks of goldfinch twitter among the scrub. After a hundred or so yards the going levels out to reveal close-cropped grass with clots of furze and veins of heather browsed by cattle. If you ignore the sough of traffic in the valley and the vacuous farting of a biplane overhead, you could imagine yourself in Hardy country. Then you notice, in the hazy distance, the control towers and abandoned missile silos.

This is Greenham Common, in the southern English county of Berkshire, half way through the first decade of the twenty-first century: an intermediate place, windswept, devoid of birch or pine or thicket, a land of gorse and overgrazed heather with just the occasional hawthorn needling its way up where fifteen years ago Cold War jets flew.

The landscape has changed more than once in living memory. Victor Bonham Carter, who spent part of his childhood at Greenham, described it after the First World War as "a mighty wilderness... threaded by a single dust road." For centuries this "wilderness" (as it would have seemed to the eyes of a small boy) had constituted a shared public resource where members of the population without agricultural land of their own had the right to graze livestock and collect fuel.

Like many commons across England, including London's now leafy Hampstead Heath, Greenham would have been dominated by heather, with areas of grass and gorse, or furze. The North European heaths constitute a unique biome, evolved over centuries from slash-and-burn agriculture on poor sandy soils. The naturalist and historian Oliver Rackham, writing in the early 1980s, succinctly described the cultural and biological significance of what many continue to regard as wastes.

> Heathland is an ancient and beautiful part of our heritage. It is a symbol of liberty: most heaths are *de facto* open to the public, and their destruction has curtailed the Englishman's already meagre right to explore his own country… It is the habitat of the nightjar, stone-curlew, Dartford warbler, smooth snake, and many other celebrated plants and animals; it is full of antiquities and of complex and fascinating soil and vegetation patterns. It is a special responsibility of England: the Dutch, Danes, and Swedes have been even more single-minded in destroying their heaths, and most of what is left in Europe is ours.

Rackham's anxiety is understandable, for ninety percent of England's heaths have been lost to development and agriculture since 1800.

Until the nineteenth century, the land at Greenham survived as commonly grazed heath, and occasional manoeuvres by the army left only temporary marks. The situation changed radically in 1941 when the Common was requisitioned as an airfield.

Local hopes that the land would be restored after the war were dashed when, in 1951, the United States requested permission to base heavy bombers on the site. Popular protests went unheeded even as work began on the longest military runway in Europe. It is difficult to quantify the ecological damage that followed, and there has never been a satisfactory explanation for the threefold increase in the number of leukaemia cases diagnosed in the Newbury area. What is certain is that a heath that had stood for centuries – a place of biological as well as cultural significance – had ceased to exist.

Although the appropriation by landed interests of commonly-held fields and heaths dates back well before modern times (Shakespeare devoted much of his last years to the assertion of private property rights over common land near Stratford), it was only when innovations in farming practice made it possible to cultivate, for profit rather than subsistence, all but the most difficult soils that the process really transformed rural life. Parliament in the late eighteenth and early nineteenth centuries passed nearly four thousand Acts legalising the appropriation of more than six million acres of land: about a quarter of all cultivated acreage. Those dispossessed, sometimes even of their homes, were invariably poor and deprived of influence, while the needs of a growing population created an understandable desire among the ruling elites to see "Dark frowning heaths grow bright with Ceres' store" (James Thomson, Castle of Indolence).

The dark satanic mills of industry depended on increased yields, but these were amassed at the expense of the rural labourers who produced them. One of these was the Northamptonshire poet, John Clare. When he was sixteen Clare's native parish of Helpstone, where for generations the population had farmed strips in a circular field-system, was the subject of a parliamentary act for enclosure. While it may have been true that "the said Commons and Waste Grounds yield but little Profit," the fact that they offered a subsistence living to many was not deemed worthy of consideration. Freeholders, no matter how poor they had been, were reduced to the status of labourer, set to the hard work of "improving" land they had once shared.

In his poem "The Mores" (moors), Clare marks the passing of familiar native ground, where after enclosure

> Each little tyrant with his little sign
> Shows where man claims earth glows no more divine...

Prior to these "improvements" there had been—according to Clare's biographer, Jonathan Bate—"an intimate relationship between society and environment. The open-field system fostered a sense of community: you could talk to the man working the next strip." In Clare's elegy for this ancient system, where neighbours once met, "Fence now meets fence" and "men and flocks" are "imprisoned ill at ease." The imagery of confinement is significant, for as a boy the poet was able to roam freely about the fields and heaths of Helpstone. By the time he was working as a labourer, the psychological perception of such unenclosed spaces as belonging to everyone had been shattered, and Clare, a true rural conservative, drew a startling analogy for the destruction of an ancient birthright:

> Inclosure like a Bonaparte let not a thing remain,
> It levelled every bush and tree and levelled every hill
> And hung the mole for traitors—though the brook
>   is running still
> It runs a naked brook, cold and chill.
>   LANGLEY BUSH

While it would be disingenuous to pretend that the hard, subsistence life that preceded enclosure was idyllic, there is little doubt that the appropriation, without compensation, of commonly held assets was ruinous for thousands. The nineteenth-century advocate of land improvement, Arthur Young, relented when he saw the social consequences of the changes he had fought for: "I had rather that all the commons of England were sunk in the sea, than that the poor should in future be treated on enclosing as they have been hitherto." William Cobbett, by the 1820s, was speaking of the "madness of enclosures" and pointing out that the increased investment in the land had "worked detriment to the labourer. It was out of his bones that the means came."

This is not old news. Globalisation is unhappily replete with instances in which an economic process seemingly justifiable in its own limited terms has social and ecological results which contradict it. The profits of the soy bean magnates of Brazil are at the expense of the forest itself as well as indigenous people, small farmers and rubber-tappers who depend upon it. Similarly, Japanese and Chinese corporations as they strip their Asian neighbours of their forests dispossess present and future generations of their birthright without offering meaningful compensation. Globally, whether through unsustainable exploitation of limited natural resources or bequeathing a degraded planet to future generations, the enclosure and appropriation of common assets continues at an unprecedented rate. If the process seems to have slowed in Britain, it is merely because we exhausted it generations ago.

But the situation, in my country at least, is not without hope. Membership of conservation groups has grown substantially; government is attempting – in its usual schizophrenic manner – to reverse some of the damage done by intensive agriculture, and it is perhaps indicative of changing attitudes that Greenham Common in 2006 is not yet another civilian airport for London but a place in transition, slowly being restored to nature.

Returning to our wintry ramble, it is not difficult to see – and even feel underfoot – the outlines of the vast runways. Work to remove the hardstanding began in April 1995, with over one million tonnes of material broken up, recycled and sold and the revenue ploughed back into restoration work. Bioremediation to clean up fuel contamination has only recently been completed; on the far north-eastern edge of the plain the stumps of a partly dismantled POL, or Petroleum Oil Lubricant Station, still stand like the remains of some industrial gallows. Exploring the common, one has only a sense of what it once was and may become again. There is little of the biodiversity one would find on long-standing heaths, yet some of the bird and invertebrate species endemic to the ecosystem are beginning to return, and the martial symmetry of the runways is receding.

If the enclosures – a visible manifestation of industrial capitalism – represented the triumph of the straight line, might the restoration of Greenham Common herald a return to non-linear and more sustainable models of behaviour? With the Countryside Rights of Way Act passed by Parliament in 2000, an attempt has been made to reopen landscapes that were enclosed, fenced in, and degraded by private capital. With a renewed freedom to roam come new conceptions of open and natural landscapes, where biological processes may be resumed free of human intervention. Models for such wide-scale "rewilding" come chiefly from the United States where there is more room, but I sense in Britain a growing appetite for wild spaces of our own, be they restored fens in East Anglia or the regenerating forests of the Scottish Highlands. Demographic pressure will necessarily limit such ambitions, but the remarkable success, in the equally crowded Netherlands, of Oostvaardersplassen, proves that with sufficient will (and capital: these ought to be affairs of state), even the most populous regions of Europe can find space for wildness.

Arguments against restoration projects invariably cite the costs involved. This is to persist in outmoded thinking. William Cobbett, at the height of the nineteenth century enclosures, argued in solid terms that the value of bees on a particular Hampshire common was greater than the value of the same common enclosed. This, however, would have cut no ice with the landed interests, whose focus, then as now, was on specialisation and scale. To date, the success of organic farmers to return to the more ecologically sustainable mixed farming methods has been limited in relation to the power of industrial agriculture. And this is indicative of a global failure to recognise the value of nature's services. These – the water we drink, the air we breathe, the very weather upon which we depend – are estimated to be worth trillions of dollars each year. When damaged or degraded, the cost is measured in human lives. Areas with mangrove swamps were less badly hit by 2004's tsunami than those without. Flooding in towns is often caused by the loss of floodplains further upstream. The recent, fatal landslide in the Philippines would probably not have occurred without the deforestation of the hills. Examples of the price paid, in human lives and misery, when the environment is degraded, are sadly legion; and of course we have yet to see the full, catastrophic impacts of global warming. Given our unprecedented levels of scientific understanding, it is maddening that most of the world refuses to place the environment at the centre of everything we do.

Economic value is one thing. Less readily quantifiable is a profound psychological need for access to the green world: what the American biologist Edward O. Wilson calls "biophilia." In Britain this is reflected in a network of "community forests" to soften the impact of population growth: places where woodland and green spaces are being created, with an emphasis on public access and leisure, on the margins and sometimes at the heart of urban areas. The dreams of landscape-scale restoration, even if realised, will be remote for the majority of the population that lives in towns; yet here too there are growing expectations of access to green space. According to the City of Edinburgh Council, for instance, the waiting list for Council-managed allotment plots "increased by one third from 600 to 900 in 2005" (*Edinburgh Outlook*, spring 2006). Back in 1973, the critic Raymond Williams observed the extra-utilitarian value of such spaces, describing them as "important not only for their produce, but for their direct and immediate satisfactions and for the felt reality of an area of control of one's own immediate labour."

If the urban allotment is akin to the old commons, it benefits from continuing usefulness. The same cannot be said of England's heaths, which, having ceased to be of economic value, have also lost much of their cultural significance. For a majority of a population ignorant of the historical and biological significance of these unkempt "wastelands," they simply don't figure as places worth protecting. One of the solutions, busily undertaken by national and local conservation organisations, is to inform populations about the "meaning" of these habitats. But this is not enough, I fear, to secure the commons for the future. A modern equivalent must be found to the social role they once fulfilled.

Once again, Greenham leads the way. Its story in the twentieth century was not purely one of degradation, for the ideal of assets held in common persisted in the form of a national protest movement that greeted the installation, by the Thatcher government, of nuclear-armed cruise missiles in the 1980s. The feminist peace camp outside the base remained until the end of the Cold War, and it is perhaps the legacy of the peace activists that the land escaped new forms of exploitation.

When local government founded the Greenham Common Trust in 1997, its trading subsidiary, New Greenham Limited, established the Trust's main asset: a 150-acre business park on the site of the former airbase. Profits from the business park are not only ploughed into the ecological restoration of the common but also distributed to local groups and charities. In the first five years of its existence, Greenham Common Trust gave £690,000 to over 240 local organisations, as well as £770,000 towards habitat restoration and over £2 million to local hospitals and health foundations. Revenue from the business park also provides £200,000 each year in funding to New Greenham Arts. Nature, culture, and society all benefit from the mixed uses to which the old common has been put.

Greenham Common is not the only instance of capitalism adapting itself to "stakeholder" sustainability. The principles of the Brundtland Report, released by the U.N. nearly twenty years ago, of "development which meets the needs of the present without compromising the ability of future generations to meet their own needs," are slowly (too slowly?) nudging their way into the European mainstream, inspired to some degree by such pioneering community-based projects as the Sherwood Energy Village in Nottingham. Built on the site of the former Ollerton Colliery, this combination of low energy residential housing, green space, and business park (with profits, as at Greenham, returning to the Village and neighbouring communities), has attracted visitors from around the world. The voluntary eco-community, though laudable in itself, will never appeal to a majority of citizens. Projects like Sherwood Energy Village or Beddington Zero-Emission Development (BedZed) in south London, offer models for high living standards combined with low consumption. Such projects are at present a rarity; it remains to be seen if the London Olympic Village for 2012 will live up to its "One Planet" pledge. But with growing demands for sustainable design and the enterprise of people as diverse as former coal miners and Welsh hill farmers setting up community wind farms, it is becoming increasingly difficult for government and business to shirk their responsibilities. The rapidly worsening ecological crisis is doing much – though as yet not nearly enough – to waken a popular environmental conscience and recognition that the old "supply and demand" models of democratic capitalism are unsustainable so long as they ignore the true value of our global commons.

BIBLIOGRAPHY

Bate, Jonathan. *John Clare* (London: Picador, 2004)

Daily, Gretchen C. & Katherine Ellison. *The New Economy of Nature: The Quest to Make Conservation Profitable* (Washington: Island Books, 2000)

Mabey, Richard. *Selected Journalism* (London: Chatto & Windus, 1999)

Rackham, Oliver. *The History of the Countryside* (J.M. Dent, London, 1984)

Williams, Raymond. *The Country and the City* (Oxford and New York: Oxford University Press, 1973)

WEBSITES

Greenham Common:
http://www.greenham-common-trust.co.uk/
http://www.greenham-common.org.uk/

Rewilding Project in Holland:
http://www.oostvaardersplassen.biofaan.nl/

Community Forests:
http://www.communityforest.org.uk/
http://www.nationalforest.org/

Sherwood Energy Village:
http://www.sherwoodenergyvillage.co.uk/

Beddington Zero Emissions Development:
http://www.bedzed.org.uk/main.html

Community Wind Farms:
http://www.baywind.co.uk/
http://www.ailwynt.co.uk/

Justice: Four Windows

JANE HIRSHFIELD

"I say more: the just man justices…"
GERARD MANLEY HOPKINS, "As Kingfishers Catch Fire"

"Justice? – You get justice in the next world,
in this world you have the law."
WILLIAM GADDIS, "A Frolic of His Own"

I. EVOLUTION & JUSTICE

The mineral world stands apart from the axis of justice. A mountain rises and erodes, sandstones form and harden, granite decomposes to gruss, rivers change course without the possibility of outrage or protest. What happens cannot be put on the scale of morality, cannot be felt as right or wrong. It is simply what happens.

The vegetable world also seems innocent of justice's negotiations. Light comes and goes from a field. Heat, cold, rain, drought come and go and are, as we say, simply weathered. If the color-changed light cast onto one tree's leaves by those of another shows they are approaching too closely, the branch quite frequently turns away, in a gesture described as "crown shyness." Some experience of suffering may accompany the competition for soil nutrients and water, but if so, it is suffering of a kind beyond our human grasp.

Recognizable conceptions of morality and justice begin with the rudiments of a sense of a separate self and of self's place in relation to others: that is, with the social birds, fishes, and mammals. The experience of a correct order, or of dismaying disorder, becomes possible only if order is first present. The whiplash of inequality – its enforcement, its possible correction – becomes possible only when there are compacts of behavior between those who live in the context of a larger whole.

Hierarchy in herd, flock, or troupe is the acquiescence of others, won, maintained, or lost. Discomfort over who eats or mates first, last, or not at all is precursor to our ideals of "inalienable rights," to our feelings that each human being should know freedom of body, spirit, and mind; know security from arbitrary power; know love more than hunger, curiosity and ingenuity more than fear. Among social animals is also the beginning of visible mercy; the body language of submission is a surety that injury will end. Social animals (with a single exception – ourselves) rarely kill their own kind, and among the few species that do, almost never within their home community unless that community is stressed past bearable limits.

Primates, recent experiments show, possess both a sense of fairness and the impulse to collaborate and assist. A capuchin monkey, rewarded for some trained action with a bit of cucumber, sees a neighbor rewarded for the same behavior with a tasty grape and goes on strike, sulks in a corner, refusing clearly inequable wages. The capuchin's ostracism of the experimentor is a communication as telling – and, in the wild, as strongly repercussive – as a bite. Conversely, another recent experiment revealed that chimpanzees (and 18-month-old human infants) will hurry to bring a dropped item back to the researcher's hand – though if the clothespin or book is deliberately thrown down, it will be left where it landed.

This innate impulse toward helpfulness offers one alternative to the order of punishment and force. Altruism, empathy, and mutual nurturance – the evidence of a basic tenderness between fellow creatures – carry the survival strategies of symbiosis into the social world. Red foxes bring food to other, injured foxes who are not their own young. Elephants bring edible branches to dying elephant elders unable to rise. Scientists have videotaped a humpbacked whale repeatedly lifting another, dead whale to the surface, the same way a new-born whale is lifted to the surface for its first breath; the whale carried the corpse for five hours before giving up. These acts, which might be rightly named acts of empathy, of compassion, extend interspecies. Traditional stories in many cultures tell of animals adopting and suckling orphaned young of a different kind, including the she-wolf's suckling of Romulus and Remus. One man who attempted suicide from the Golden Gate Bridge in San Francisco was brought to the surface by a seal (a circumstance so unnerving he spoke of it to no one for three years). Newspaper stories, most recently one from Australia, report dolphins forming a circle around human swimmers to protect them from sharks.

These examples may not at first seem to center on issues of justice, yet they underlie our faith in the possibility of a life not ruled entirely by chaos, force, and fear. Simone Weil described the hope for justice in this way: "At the bottom of the heart of every human being, from earliest infancy until the tomb, there is something that goes on indomitably expecting, in the teeth of all experience of crimes committed, suffered, and witnessed, that good and not evil will be done to him. It is this above all that is sacred in every human being."[1]

Weil rooted our most fundamental sense of rightness in what transcends both personality and the personal, yet is also independent of the changing whims and fashions of collective life. She called this the realm of God, and it seems that in every human culture, the laws of right behavior (the Latin *ius*, "law," underlies the English word "justice") are first attributed to the divine. Yet given how often divergent ideas of the sacred seem to lead us to bloodshed, it may be a usefully calming corrective to acknowledge the creaturely acts of discipline and kindness that underly our human sense of justice and injustice, of compassion and ruthless force, and to acknowledge that even among the social animals, the individual matters and is cared for beyond practical exigency,

---

1 from "*La Personnalité humaine, le juste et l'injuste*," as translated in "Human Personality," in *Simone Weil: An Anthology*, edited by Sian Miles (New York: Grove Press, 1986).

beyond mere usefulness to the group. Civil society is older, and larger of heart, than is generally imagined.

That these concepts are primal in us – innate, pre-verbal, pre-human – explains no small part of the strength of their grip. That the desire for justice is seated in the friction between selves and their differing desires – in communal and not individual life, that is – remains a binding truth. A workable sense and measure of justice bestows on all social animals, including humans, no small part of our basic survival, both of body and spirit. The failure of justice lacerates because it is, at bottom, an injury to life itself.

2. AESCHYLUS' Oresteia

I asked a friend – a lawyer who specializes in the final appeals of death penalty cases – what he might have to say on the subject of justice. He answered with a quote from William Gaddis: "Justice? – You get justice in the next world, in this world you have the law."

Justice in animal life is simple – the customs of right behavior don't often change, or do so at the almost unobservable pace of evolution. Nor do they conflict with one another because of different conceptions of the meaning of right. In human life, the complexities tangle and entangle. We recognize injustice by the uprising of outrage within us. Yet those – whether the empowered or the almost powerless – who act in ways universally decried as "inhuman" claim themselves warranted, claim they have no other choice, that their actions are necessary, done for justifiable "reason." Reason: the double-edged sword in our human relationship to justice. Rational mind can harden the heart, strip it of the capacity for compassion, prevent it from reeling back from the commission of horrors; it does this by overpowering the recognition of outrage with manufactured rage or manufactured complacence. Equally though, rational mind can temper the heart's loosed fears and angers, which would equally perpetuate horror, if allowed.

To see the conflict of emotion and ideas in action, we need only read Greek tragedy, a body of work that explores the most difficult collisions of heart and mind and allegiance to conflicting values. Taken as a whole, these plays attempt to work through the question of what it means to act well, to choose well, in a human life amid human straits and dilemmas.

In Sophocles' *Antigone* (ca. 440 BCE), the issues and their resolution are both basic and comparatively simple. The king, Creon, forbids the burial of one of two brothers – the one who attacked rather than defended his city – as punishment for treason. Antigone, sister to both and also betrothed to the King's son, defies the command: to leave a brother unburied defiles an order stronger than any decreeable by kings. By the end of the play, the brother is buried, and the offended gods have stripped Creon of everything he loves: son, wife, and power. Antigone too is dead. It is a tragedy of the most straightforward form, in which no one survives intact. But the hierarchy of justice and right behavior is also clear – Antigone defends her desire to bury her brother with a simple statement: "I share my love, not my hate." Forgiveness, fidelity to blood kin, respect for the dead – these are presented as transcendent values, which must be honored.

Aeschylus's slightly earlier trilogy, *The Oresteia* (458 BCE), presents a story both more extended and more complex, one that is also, in no small part, an account of justice's evolution, in the face of irresolvably divergent claims, from private to public realms. That these Greek plays were created in the context of ritual – enactments intended to be repeated – is not accidental. Questions of justice – or any other genuine dilemma – cannot be answered in static or absolute form; they will continually be refound, recreated, renewed, and reformed.

The curse on the House of Atreus precedes both Atreus's own crime and the segment of the story recounted in the three plays. It stems from an alternation of parricide and sacrificed children (more than once then served up to their father as a vengeance-meal) that recedes into the past to the earliest gods. Vestigial from that first world of overthrown gods are the Erinyes, or Furies. Primordial forces of vengeance and the outward embodiment of inescapable inner guilt, they defend "right order" of the most fundamental kind: its roots in the love between kin. The story of their transformation and domestication into the Eumenides, or Kindly Ones—their inclusion, that is, into the world and order of human-centered affairs—is the end point of the Oresteia's tale.

The events explored in Aeschylus's trilogy begin with the sacrifice of a daughter in order to go to war. Then follow the killing of a husband to avenge the daughter, the murder of a mother to avenge the father. The core question of the Oresteia plays—a question that has resurrected itself, in new places and forms, throughout history—is how such a succession of vengeance and guilt might ever be ended. The god Apollo has demanded that Orestes kill his mother, Clytemnestra, who has killed Agamemnon, who has killed Iphegenia, also at the demand of the gods. Orestes does so. But even Apollo cannot then release Orestes from the pursuing Furies, whose cry is that the murder of a mother is a crime so scalding not even a god's command provides excuse.

It is the Furies' role to preserve horror at such an act, both within the community and within the self; their role not to allow the unforgivable to go unnoticed, let alone be forgiven. Orestes himself has played the role of a Fury against his mother, as powerless not to act against her for having killed his father as the Furies are powerless not to act against him. The insolubility of human grief before injustice stands at the center. In the Greek world preceding the Oresteia, a primal crime can never be undone or redressed. It can only become a new basis for the current condition of existence. And so there is further murder, for generations.

Northern Ireland, Iraq, Palestine, Darfur, Afghanistan, Argentina, Rwanda, Lebanon, Guantanamo, Bosnia, Chechnya, Haiti, Cambodia, Kashmir, Burma, Korea, East L.A.—loosed Furies move through them all. One religious disciple murders another, and a millenium later the act remains a reason for carnage. A people displaced from its homeland displaces another people from its homeland, and a child watches a house bulldozed while his mother weeps. An outspoken daughter is made to disappear without any accounting. A farmer is tortured because someone hid in his barn. A woman gathering wood for cooking is raped and visibly branded as having been raped; she returns home and is killed for shaming her husband. A gang member's young brother is killed, a nation knowingly left to starve. Gift blankets are seeded with smallpox, conquered fields with salt, and suffering leaps from victim to victor as invisibly and inevitably as a plague flea.

The Furies speak for the outraged dead from beyond the grave. They are pure vengeance, creatures beyond placation or reason. They are, themselves, for all who see them, terror.

Yet what the *Oresteia* proposes as a resolution is not the Furies' rejection. Pushed away, they goad harder. It is the courteous acknowledgment of them in the final play that makes possible a remedy beyond the cyclical continuance of bloodshed and revenge. Orestes has been sent by Apollo to Athena, goddess of wisdom, to establish his innocence or guilt. Athena listens to Orestes' story, then listens to that of the Furies. She is the first to treat them with honor, and her offered respect changes them from harrying, outcrying hounds to creatures who speak and explain themselves, who can stand within a broadened circle of communication. There is another step as well: Athena declares the decision of Orestes' fate too difficult for her to make alone. The full community must be drawn into the process. A representative group of citizens will listen and vote, with Athena herself, if necessary, breaking a tie—which she declares in advance will be a vote for mercy.[2]

What we see in this final play, The Eumenides, is the invention of what remains recognizably our own system of justice: trial by jury, in which even today, a hung jury results in retrial or freedom. The Oresteia proposes that private daemons can be softened by deeding them over to the realm of the communal—if, at the same time, the community is deeded in turn to the defense of fundamental values. The Furies are promised a decisive place in the fate of every household, and the first portion of every tribute to the gods, in return for entering into the compact of civil adjudication. The trilogy's resolution addresses more than Orestes' personal torment: individual impulse, uncountered by a communal desire for good, is disastrous for all.

From The Oresteia come the truth and reconciliation trials of South Africa, the gacaca trials of Rwanda, the opening of the Stasi files of East Germany and the mass graves of Argentina and Salvador; will come, we know, the opening of the gates and records of Guantánamo Bay. These processes bring the Furies to heel, allow the accumulated history of insurmountable grief and outrage to be spoken fully aloud and acknowledged by the community as a whole. Simple recognition, the admission and dignification of what has been suffered, the inclusion of all participants from every side—the Greeks' insight was to see that these gestures, in themselves, are aeration and healing.

---

2 To be complete, we must also note Athena's use of power as well as courteous invitation: she reminds the Furies that she alone, of all the gods, holds the keys to the place where Zeus' thunderbolt is stored. Yet the thunderbolt need not be interpreted only as literal force-threat—it can also be understood as light, an enlightenment overwhelming the darker and partisan aspects of our nature.

3. JUSTICE WITHOUT "JUSTICE": AN ALTERNATIVE VIEW

When Aeschylus has Athena arrange the participants of The Eumenides' story for trial, she instructs Orestes to stand by the Stone of Outrage, the Furies by the Stone of Mercilessness. The bare, high outcrop where this takes place, overlooking Athens, is a topography mirroring the inner sensations of justice. W.B. Yeats wrote, in "Easter, 1916" (his poem mourning and honoring the leaders of a failed attempt to win Irish independence by force of arms): "Too long a sacrifice/ can make a stone of the heart./ O when may it suffice?" By the time we find ourselves weighing the actions of self or other as right or wrong, we already stand in the hardening that rage and outrage elicit. The visceral awareness of justice, it seems, comes only when actual justice has already failed.

There may be a way to forego the realm of stones entirely. As with the transformation of Furies to Kindly Ones, it may be that justice's rigidities can give way to something more supple and more kind: to compassion. Might not the bond and acknowledgment of shared life — the very thing the Furies defend — already suggest the foundation for a coexistence less saturated with suffering? This is the path proposed by Buddhist views of the non-duality of existence, in which selves are not experienced as steeply divided and separate. In this seamless comprehension, harm cannot be inflicted by one on another. To harm anyone is to harm one's own heart.

Most people have had at least a momentary glimpse of what it is to experience the world as undivided — the narrow sense of self drops away, ego and its need to dominate drop away, proprietariness becomes the subject of laughter, as if left hand were stealing from right hand. The threads of one piece of fabric cannot argue with each other, and what happens to any part happens to the whole. The same description is given by mystics of every tradition: a simple falling into right relationship with all that is.

Generosity, patience, truthfulness, morality, equanimity, energy, wisdom, and loving kindness are not felt as exceptional; they are the fundamental qualities of human nature, present in us from the start. Within such a state of being, how can there be justice, how can there be injustice? Each encounter is intimate, each person is mother, child, "Buddha," "Christ," "Allah," self. "Do unto others as you would have them do unto you" becomes tautology, not advice. Yet the experience must not be understood as some sophomoric or saccharine "oneness." "Not one, not two," are the words used to describe it in Zen.

All spiritual traditions, including Buddhism, possess explicit moral components. Still, justice within classical Buddhism is not so much something imposed from outside as an understanding of cause and effect, operating from within. The Buddhist concept closest to the Western idea of justice is karma, in which the actions of each moment, or lifetime, are seen as influencing the circumstances of the next, in a continual opportunity for readjustment. Good follows good; evil is followed by further suffering. Moral sensibility emerges from self-observation and learning rather than fear of judgment by others.

Buddhism does offer as well guidance for virtuous behavior, in what are known as the ten prohibitory precepts—a person taking these precepts vows not to kill, lie, take what is not given, abuse sexuality, dull the senses by intoxication, and so on. A few of the precepts, however, are less familiar: "A disciple of the Buddha does not possess anything, not even the truth," one translation reads. This non-possession points back toward the nondual: part of what isn't possessable is self itself. Our sense of "self-worth," "rights," identity itself—each depends on making the distinction that I am I and you are you. Yet if the skin is felt less as barrier than as point of continuity and connection, no distinction between selves can be found. In this way, non-duality and compassion are inextricably linked—the second arises from the first, and the vow to relieve suffering immediately follows.

For practitioners of such Buddhist paths as Zen and Dzogchen, non-dual understanding is foundation ground, recognizable at any moment as where we already stand. In most Buddhist traditions, though, time is acknowledged as part of the karmic process – lifetimes may be needed for compassion to take root, for even the best of intentions to reach mature harvest. The intention, and its continual renewal, is what matters. When Gerard Manley Hopkins wrote (in the quote that stands at the head of this essay), "The just man justices," he reminded of justice's perennially elusive nature. Justice is not noun, but adjective, verb – attribute or action. It is either actively ongoing or non-existent. Folk Buddhism conveys the same comprehension, showing the need for a compassion of continuous reenactment. In the folk tales known as the Jataka stories, the Buddha, during many lifetimes, sacrifices himself for the sake of others. Seeing a hungry tigress with starving cubs, he gives himself to be eaten. Without identification in ego or attachment to a segregate and distinct existence, nothing can be lost. Still, suffering remains perceptible. Even if the fully awakened mind does not feel it as personal injury, an awake person, seeing suffering in others, attempts to end it. This is what Western conceptions of Buddhism as passive before suffering and political injustice miss. Acceptance of momentary conditions as momentary does not mean a failure to engage them.[3]

The Oresteia proposes that the solution to the unredressable lies in collective wisdom and the needs of the community as a whole for peace. Evolution would second this – altruism arises in animals, symbiosis in plants and biological systems, because the good of the whole is the good of the part. The Buddhism of non-dual awakening proposes that this can be so fully internalized, in

---

3 The misconception also disregards Buddhism's source: in a prince who, having learned the existence of poverty, old age, sickness, and death, could not return to his former life of comfort and palace.

each of us, that every vestige of self-seeking impulse is flooded by a deeper identification. Proposes it possible to say "we" without limit, to mean by "we" nothing less than "all."

4. KISSING THE MURDERER'S HAND: POETRY, RECONCILIATION, AND JUSTICE

When I began assembling these thoughts, I was staying briefly in a 17th-century coal-heated cottage in Northumberland. One night – March 26th, 2007 – I turned on the television. The reception was just clear enough to bring the BBC's report that Ian Paisley and Gerry Adams had, quite remarkably, sat down at a conference table and agreed that the future of Northern Ireland lay in just that: their ability to sit down at a table and speak, not on behalf of the partisan but for the whole country's wellbeing. This seems to me, as must by now be clear, the single through-line of genuine justice.

A few days later I was at a poetry festival in Dublin, and asked the poet Derek Mahon – born in Belfast, now a resident of the Republic of Ireland – what he might think about justice. He answered, "Justice? In Ireland, there's no justice." And then, "Justice has always got a bit of sadism in it, doesn't it, a taste of the urge to punish." The statement punctures, reminding of the inadequacy of absolutes before the actualities of human histories and lives, reminding that passionate ideals too often not only engender but also endanger.

Good poetry – allergic to the manipulations of slogan and propaganda – can bring to expression things inexpressible in any other mode. As we have seen with *The Oresteia*, it can not only hold the record of justice's inceptions but help create them. This is why, even now, cultures in trouble turn to their poets, singers, novelists, artists, filmmakers, and playwrights to find a way out amid conditions seemingly insoluble. Through those whose only allegiance is discovery and the recording of what is found, suffering can first be fully seen and acknowledged, then alchemized into a changed comprehension.[4] Art allows a moving forward because it invites the seemingly fixed to yield. It makes of the unbearable something that can be taken in and grieved, that can be healed by making it, quite simply, both hearable and heard.

Good poetry perforates our hard-shelled realities, allowing the seemingly fixed to yield. This is why it is so useful in times of duress. It complicates and unfastens the conceptual mind's black-and-white words and worlds. It defies the ego's wish for categorical statement and overly certain knowledge. It dissolves vitrification, at times almost unbearably well. If a poem is good, the solvent of compassion will also be in it, whether in visible foreground or as the subterranean murmur of counter-thought beneath the uttered words.

Because I have been thinking about both Ireland and classical Greece, of the many poems I looked at to see which might offer something otherwise unavailable here, I've picked a brief work by Michael Longley, another Irish poet who has witnessed the decades of sectarian violence and their grief-price. It describes and reimagines a scene from the Iliad, in which the Greek Achilles returns to the Trojan king Priam the dragged and dishonored corpse of Priam's son. The poem is a sonnet broken into four parts, whose rhymes are so tactful until the final couplet that they barely hold the balancing closures and reassurance it is rhyme's work to bring.

---

4 I am thinking here of Akhmatova and Milosz, of Coetzee, Gordimer, and Solzhenitsyn; but in subtler ways, innumerable works of art have changed their cultures: small measures that together work significant effects.

Ceasefire

I

Put in mind of his own father and moved to tears
Achilles took him by the hand and pushed the old king
Gently away, but Priam curled up at his feet and
Wept with him until their sadness filled the building.

II

Taking Hector's corpse into his own hands Achilles
Made sure it was washed and, for the old king's sake,
Laid out in uniform, ready for Priam to carry
Wrapped like a present home to Troy at daybreak.

III

When they had eaten together, it pleased them both
To stare at each other's beauty as lovers might,
Achilles built like a god, Priam good-looking still
And full of conversation, who earlier had sighed:

IV

"I get down on my knees and do what must be done
And kiss Achilles' hand, the killer of my son."

MICHAEL LONGLEY[5]

5   from *Collected Poems* (London: Cape Poetry, 2006); used by permission
of the author.

Justice is built on admixture: on the optimisms of altruism and awakened compassion mixed with the frictions – often ferocities – of personal and tribal desire for survival and power. Yet what "Ceasefire" (written, Longley has said, on the occasion of an earlier attempt at peace between Catholic and Protestant forces in Northern Ireland, and with his own father strongly in mind) brings into view is not insight into justice, nor anything about justice, really. It presents the pure necessity of actual life, and one possibility for how the unendurable might be endured: by entering it fully. The choice is either madness or softening, either mindless slaughter or replacing the concept of enemy with the knowledge that the father of the person we have killed could have been our own father, that the killed son could have been Achilles as easily as Hector.

The path to Ian Paisley and Gerry Adams sitting together at table, my Irish friends told me, was exhaustion: suffering endured too long. The people, they told me, had simply grown tired of death and hardness. Their leaders could either follow or be left behind.

And the hallmark and signal of this moment? A public act of conversation, of shared speech. An act that finds itself on a spectrum that includes the truth and reconciliation process in South Africa but also a play written and performed by a group of Turkish and Armenian children; the publication of a diary kept by a woman when the Allied forces entered Berlin, of the poems written in the Japanese-American internment camp of Manzanar, of the stories of the "comfort women" of Korea.

The Athenian Furies were put to ground for perhaps 50 years before they rose up again. It may be that no permanent justice can be negotiated among us while we remain unenlightened and human, gripped by the oscillant moods of complacence and partisan passion. It may be that the suffering everywhere around us – from the dispossessed and uncared for people of New Orleans's

Ninth Ward to those of East Timor—is too immediate to wait for awakened compassion. That what I've suggested here as an alternative to the sadisms and fixities of conflictual justice—the cultivation of non-dual understanding and kindness—is too rare and hard-come-by to count on, in any foreseeable future, as answer to cruelty, passivity, and strife. It may be that all we can hope for is ordinary law, ordinary justice, and the achievable, moment-by-moment ceasefire of Longley's poem. And to be held by his words' embraced knowledge, that all griefs will visit all hearts.

To see humanness when another person stands before us, to see the deep beauty of those we have wronged past any conceivable conception of forgiveness, the deep beauty of those who have wronged us past any conceivable conception of forgiveness—this is what Michael Longley's poem proposes. It is the most intimate description of what truth and reconciliation look like, lived fully through, between opposing soldiers and peoples, between neighbor and neighbor. The heart shattered, from stone-adamance to open.

On Justice, Memory, and Compassion

TONY EPRILE

PREFACE

I feel it is important, in seeking to understand another's argument, to have some sense of the ground upon which he or she stands and whence the argument proceeds. Here is a brief background on my connection to the theme of justice, to stand as preface to my paper on Justice, Memory, and Compassion: I come to this topic as a fiction writer who has written a novel with a central focus on memory, the narrative set in three crucial decades of South African history: the 1970s, '80s, and '90s. For the novel's purposes, the '70s is the period of "petty Apartheid" – the quotidian humiliations of legislated inequality – and of the protagonist's schooling, with the intention of showing how the authorities promote a falsified history in order to justify present-day actions and legislation. The '80s are the period of war (in Namibia, Angola, and the black townships of South Africa) and human rights violations – witnessed, and unwittingly participated in, by the protagonist. And the '90s are the period of the Truth & Reconciliation Commission and the protagonist's first tentative steps towards self-healing and a closer connection – both personal and metaphysical – to others in this transitional society. Among my goals in the book is to provide a nuanced exploration of individual responsibility in a society based on social inequality and repression, a close look at how memory can be a tool for oppression or for justice, and a portrait of how conflicting memories can be "accurate" within the context of different perceivers of a past "truth."

When I toured South Africa in 2005 upon the release of the novel there, I was often asked what I thought of the Truth and Reconciliation Commission. (My novel raises some questions about the absence of reconciliation hearings for rights abuses by the South African army while in Namibia and Angola.) The questioners themselves frequently revealed a sense of disappointment at the imperfections of the TRC process, a level of expectation that suggests a failure of memory too, since few people in 1989 would have anticipated the degree of justice and reconciliation achieved in this country within a mere decade. Noticeable, too, was the degree of South Africans' concern for how the rest of the world perceives and judges the TRC, as if ratification from outside the home context would help put their own qualms at rest.

Another orientation to the theme of justice arises out of my having at various times either taught creative writing in American prisons, or supervised students who were doing so. I recall from my first prison-teaching experience in Cranston, Rhode Island, how many of the prisoners—on learning my South African background—identified themselves as "political prisoners." I had grown up in an anti-apartheid family, a number of family friends had been jailed for their political activities, and we ourselves were both watched and our home raided by the police, and so my sympathies tended to fall more on the side of the incarcerated than that of the society that jailed them. Still, it struck me as ludicrous when a man who had forcibly detained and sexually assaulted 14 women in a laundromat referred to himself as a "political prisoner." Yet there was a peculiar truth to such statements in aggregate (and if one did not look too closely at a particular crime), since African-Americans such as this man were represented in disproportionately high numbers in the Rhode Island prison system. The longer a prisoner had been in jail, the more determinedly he adhered to the notion that society had rejected him for political reasons... suggesting, at the very least, that the system was not doing a very good job of encouraging a true sense of remorse.

As a fiction writer, I feel much more comfortable with the means that fiction offers to examine and describe questions of justice than with a position paper, since ambiguity and nuance are the lifeblood of fiction but all too often seen as "loopholes" in legal discussions. I offer here both a "position," and a brief fable.

JUSTICE, MEMORY, AND COMPASSION

Before going into the details of my thoughts on justice and its relationship to memory and compassion, it's best that I begin by discussing my assumptions and prejudices as to what "justice" should comprise, what its aims and effects should be. The assumption that underlies most of the laws in the Western world – in fact, of the world in general – is the close correlation between punishment for wrongdoing and official justice: i.e., "justice" is retributive, an eye for an eye, five years in jail for robbing the corner store, lifetime incarceration or hanging for war criminals and violators of human rights. This system is viewed to work through 1) discouragement before the fact ("if you can't do the time, don't do the crime"); 2) the chastened wrongdoer reflecting on his misbehavior during the many hours of boredom and physical and sensory deprivation that prison offers; and 3) "rehabilitation," which, increasingly in the United States, is left up to the criminal to effect himself, much like a child who has been rapped sharply on the knuckles is anticipated to improve his handwriting. This system is also expected to satisfy the victims of crimes and human rights violations by offering the consolation of seeing the wrong-doer so labeled and punished.

"We live in a moral universe," Anglican Archbishop Desmond Mpilo Tutu stated in an interview regarding South Africa's Truth and Reconciliation Commission, "and it is up to us to restore a balance that has been knocked askew." My own preference for a model for justice is one that seeks—perhaps quixotically, certainly idealistically—to restore that balance: i.e., *restorative* justice rather than *retributive* justice. The starting point for this view of justice is that both the victim(s) and the wrongdoer(s) have been sundered from society via an act of violence. The crime is one done by humans to humans, and both participants need to be healed for their own benefit and that of the community as a whole. Most extant justice systems take a more abstract position: that crimes are committed against the state or "the people," the individual(s) who have committed the offense being "perpetrators of a crime" who need to be removed from society.

The PFI Center for Justice and Reconciliation (Washington, D.C.) articulates the principles that form the foundation for Restorative Justice[1] as follows:

1) Justice requires that we work to restore those who have been injured.
2) Those most directly involved and affected by crime should have the opportunity to participate fully in the response if they wish.
3) Government's role is to preserve a just public order, and the community's is to build and maintain a just peace.

The website goes on to characterize Restorative programs by four key values, with attached definitions:

1) Encounter: Create opportunities for victims, offenders, and community members who want to do so to meet to discuss the crime and its aftermath.

---

1   See website: www.restorativejustice.org/

2) Amends: Expect offenders to take steps to repair the harm they have caused.
3) Reintegration: Seek to restore victims and offenders to whole, contributing members of society.
4) Inclusion: Provide opportunities for parties with a stake in a specific crime to participate in its resolution.

While there are ongoing programs of restorative justice in many countries in the world (including the U.S.), the largest, most sustained, and best-known program has been South Africa's Truth and Reconciliation Commission, which was mandated by the Promotion of National Unity and Reconciliation Act of 1995 and which presented its final report in October, 1998. The TRC began as a compromise solution as part of a negotiated change of government between formerly warring sides. A Nuremberg-style series of trials of human rights abusers was unacceptable to the ruling party (and would almost certainly have resulted in a military coup even if the Nationalist Party had agreed to it), while a blanket amnesty (as Pinochet of Chile had given himself, his ministers, and the army) was equally unacceptable to the liberation movements. The settlement offered amnesty on the basis of full disclosure of crimes and human rights abuses of a political nature (a policeman who murdered an activist could receive full amnesty for the murder but be prosecuted for theft if he stole the man's wallet for personal gain). It began as a political compromise, but its approach has been articulated as an ethical and moral response by its commissioners (such as Archbishop Desmond Tutu and Alex Boraine), the justices who mandated the program (Ismail Mohamed, Dullah Omar), and others. The TRC hearings fill five volumes, and it has been the subject of numerous books, papers, documentaries, and other films. I am going to just touch here on some of the TRC's connections to Memory and Compassion.

MEMORY

One of the remarkable aspects of the TRC has been the notion that publicly enacted and articulated memory (referred to as "truth," a more problematic term) is, in itself, an act of justice. Through telling one's story, the human rights victim is helped to again be part of the fabric of society. Through telling his story, the human rights abuser is set upon the path of rapprochement and healing.[2] In the case of the abuser, this disclosure has to be complete and without fudging of the facts... both to receive amnesty but also to fully partake in the process of reconciliation. Desmond Tutu said, "There's no future without forgiveness," but he also said: "Forgiveness in turn depends on repentance, which has to be based on an acknowledgement of what was done wrong, and therefore on disclosure of the truth. You cannot forgive what you do not know."

For the victim, articulation of devastating and irreparable loss, of indignities suffered, may allow a sense of return to society and a sharing of humanness. This process is movingly described by Pumla Gbodo-Madikizela, a TRC commissioner, in the following personal account:

> The Commission frequently held outreach meetings in different communities. In the course of one of these meetings I noticed a woman in the audience sitting defiantly with her back to the stage as my colleague delivered the official TRC message. I understood the meaning of her body language, but I went down the hall to find out why she was so distressed. When I approached her, she turned away from me, then got up and walked out of the hall. As she walked she started to speak, first

2   And also of punishment, since many of the policemen who described their violent and vicious acts found themselves shunned by their society, their marriages often foundering, themselves psychologically tormented by having held up a mirror to their own blighted souls.

muttering then blurting out, "Why did you come here? Why did you come here?" It was a brief moment of drama: everyone in the audience turned towards us as I followed her outside. She began to cry and gesturing with her hands said, "Have you come here to hurt us? Just tell me, have you come here to revive our scars?" She went on tearfully to tell me how she had forgotten, how she had "put grass over the past," using a Xhosa expression, and moved on. "And now you want us to remember? Is this going to bring back my son?"

We sat under a tree and I listened to her venting her anger at the Truth Commission, "a pointless exercise," as she called it, since the TRC was not going to bring her child back. I took her hand and held it between my hands, more to try and take her pain and cleanse myself of the guilt I felt for causing her such anguish, than to comfort her. I asked if I could take her home. As we drove to her house I felt the inadequacy of the word "sorry" and the frustration of being a messenger who would be here now and gone the next moment, who would not stay to pick up the pieces, but move on to cause more pain. It was an unhappy emotional responsibility.

She invited me into her home – two chairs, a table and a cupboard in the front room and a double bed in the small remaining room of the house. And this is where I saw the unpredictability of testimony as she started to tell her story with vivid detail and with amazing calm:

My son was eleven years old. He had come home during his school break at ten o'clock. I was sitting right there where you are sitting, just sitting exactly where you are sitting in that chair. He walked in dressed in his school uniform, went to the cupboard over there and opened the drawer to get a knife, and cut himself a slice of bread. He is doing all of this in a rush. He is like that when he comes home during break. He got some peanut butter from the top and spread it on his bread. He put the bread back, but there were crumbs left on the cupboard, and the knife – still smudged with peanut butter. He ran out. He is still chewing his bread and holding it in his hand. It wasn't long – I heard shots outside. Some commotion and shouts. Then I'm hearing, *"uThemba, uThemba, mama ka Themba nanku Themba bamdubule!"* [Here is Themba, Themba's mother, they have shot Themba!]. I went flying out of this house. Now I am dazed. I ran, not thinking. My eyes are on the crowd that has gathered – Here is my son, my only child. It was just blood all over. My anguish was beyond anything I ever thought I could experience. They have finished him. I threw myself over him. I can feel the wetness of his blood – I felt his last breath leave him. He was my only child.

This testimony is a compelling example of how witnesses remember the concrete details of the traumatic event: the crumbs left on the cupboard, the knife smudged with peanut butter. It is as if each image is etched in the mother's memory, taking on a new significance in the telling. "That chair" on which I was sitting, the jar of peanut butter that was always on the cupboard, all these items become symbols of the little boy's 'last act' in his home. Even the crumbs are treasured as a sacred memory. The tenses defy the rules of grammar as they cross and recross the boundaries of past and present. "He *ran out*. He *is* still chewing his bread. ... Now I am dazed. I *ran*..." The final moment comes when she recalls seeing her son's lifeless body: "*Here is my son*." With a gesture of her hand she transports the moment from the past into the present, as if the floor in her front room was the place where it all happened, as if her lifeless son's body were lying there at that very moment.[3]

Ms. Gbodo-Madikizela goes on to ask whether Mrs. Plaatjie was better off before she told her story than she was after telling it, answering her own question more broadly with the argument that "it depends on *how* the past is remembered. If a memory is kept alive in order to kindle and cultivate old hatreds and resentments, then it is likely to culminate in vengeance. But if a memory is kept alive in order to transcend hateful emotions, to free oneself or one's society from the burden of hatred, then remembering has the power to heal."

Elik Elhanan, a young Israeli soldier who became a conscription refusenik and member of Combatants for Peace following the murder of his sister by a suicide bomber, argues that seeking revenge for the murder of his sister would be "doing something very terrible to her memory also... My sister deserves better than to be confined to a dark place, as an object of sadness. Or to be limited to a reason to be angry, to hate, to fear."[4]

COMPASSION

Antjie Krog describes how she and other South African journalists covering the TRC hearings would often be in tears, earning

---

3 "Memory and Trauma" by Pumla Gbodo-Madikizela (from *Truth and Lies*, Jillian Edelstein, New York: The New Press, 2001)
4 Philip Weiss, *The New York Observer*. January 11, 2007.

them the mockery of foreign journalists for their lack of "professionalism." As a South African, Krog could not be dispassionate about the events she covered, and empathy was a necessary part of her own and the nation's healing process. What was not apparent to the journalists, whose profession had inured them (at least while working) to the sufferings of those they reported on, was that the entire process of the TRC would have been pointless if it did not elicit the empathy of its participants and onlookers. This point is thoroughly covered in a recent book by Lynn Hunt on the "inventing" of the notion of human rights. Hunt discusses the formative influence of the Third Earl of Shaftesbury's *Characteristics of Men, Manners, Opinions, Times* (1711) which presents the imaginative powers of sympathy as a means of distinguishing between right and wrong.5

It's worth distinguishing here between empathy and compassion. Jane Harris Aiken defines compassion as "a sympathetic consciousness of others' distress with a desire to act to alleviate it."6 Desmond Tutu argues similarly: "Compassion is not just feeling with someone, but seeking to change the situation.... If you are going to be compassionate, be prepared for action!"

Compassion is to be applied to both the victims of human rights abuses and those responsible for the offense, with the injunction that we, as members of society, do everything in our power to change, ameliorate, and end the circumstances that led to this disturbance in the moral balance of our universe.

I will end my comments with a brief fable that arose out of a statement I had heard Desmond Tutu make in a radio interview: that many of the interpreters for the TRC suffered mental anguish and breakdowns from having to speak in the first person for both violator and victim.

---

5 I'm paraphrasing here from Joanna Bourke's review of *Inventing Human Rights* in *Harper's*, May, 2007.

6 J.H. Aiken, "Striving to Teach 'Justice, Fairness, and Morality,'" *Clinical Law Review* 4:1, Fall 1997.

THE INTERPRETER FOR THE TRIBUNAL

Interpreter for Amnesty Applicant Major J. Herzbreek
MR. L.M. SPEKE

Interpreter for Witness Mr. Y. Inkululeko
MR. L.M. SPEKE

I was hiding in my friend's garage, a place no one would think to look. I had my informants, you see. We were boys together and I knew he'd never betray me. I waited until the time they usually brought him food and when he opened the door to my whistle, I was on him like a pack of wild dogs. He ground my face into the concrete, shouting horribly in my ear. The pain was terrible. I did not know what was happening. The trick is to disorient the prisoner right away. Get him off guard and he'll tell you anything you want to know. My arm was twisted behind my back and I could feel the ligaments tearing. I did not struggle but he kept twisting, his knee my knee in his back you bastard you're done now he screamed I was thrust from the darkness into the light, then into the darkness again like a sack of potatoes I threw him into the trunk of my car, I'm that strong. I could hear him thumping in the trunk as I drove and hit the brakes taking the corners hard I bashed my head against something hard and was thrown helplessly into the light of a two-thousand candle-power torch right in the eyes hitting him all the time the fists coming from nowhere and I felt a rib breaking, my nose breaking. The blood ran down his face and he didn't even lift a finger to wipe it off my glasses had come off when they got me and I had no idea where I was on the ground of that hut, and yes I sat on his back and pulled the sack over his head, the wet sack like I was drowning I could not breathe. He could not breathe, I pulled it off now you will tell me what I want to know because otherwise I could not breathe I told him everything it did not take long to get the names my friends who betrayed me the friends I did not know what I was saying what he was saying those were hard times and we had to be hard to live in them I just wanted the pain to stop but I have to live with who I am now who was I then it is too terrible to speak of it at all is to go mad.

BOOKS

Tutu, Desmond. *No Future Without Forgiveness*. The Archbishop's personal account of his experiences as head of the TRC, including his moral philosophy on reconciliation.

Edelstein, Jillian. *Truth and Lies*. The New Press, 2001. Excellent introduction by author, and essay on "Memory and Trauma" by Pumla Gbodo-Madikizela, along with haunting photographs.

Gbodo-Madikizela, Pumla. *A Human Being Died That Night: A South African Story of Forgiveness*. Boston, Massachusetts: Houghton Mifflin, 2003.

Krog, Antjie. *Country of My Skull*. Personal account of being a journalist covering the TRC. Made into the film *In My Country*.

Slovo, Gillian. *Red Dust*. Novel about the TRC. *Every Secret Thing: My Family, My Country* (1997), memoir about her family, including her mother, Ruth First, who was murdered by South African police who subsequently were granted amnesty by the TRC.

WEBSITES

www.csvr.org.za

Center for Study of Violence and Reconciliation (South Africa-based NGO) website. A considerable range of online resources relating to peace-making and issues of transitional justice, including links to the Truth and Reconciliation Commission reports.

http://www.csvr.org.za/papers/papstrg1.pdf

A paper on the efforts to promote peace in Mozambique by connecting former fighters from different sides of the conflict.

http://www.restorativejustice.org/

Most comprehensive website on the topic. Focus is largely on criminal justice issues.

Poetic Justice:
A Shared Irresponsibility?

MOHAMED MAGANI

Science is based on observation, or so have we always been taught, its concepts closely tested, confirmed, or refuted. If, in today's world, we subject the concept of justice to the same criterion, we would be hard put to observe any sense of justice among individuals or nations. What is to be observed, if we leave aside the philosophical questioning of justice, is no more and no less than injustice on an unprecedented scale, where the key word is globalisation. Can we truly, in all the disorders affecting the world, see a recognition and respect for the rights of the other, or a principle of equity guiding our fellow beings?

Not unless we choose to answer with something we, as writers, are accustomed to: i.e., abstract or poetic justice. That concept is, of course, not observable in international relations, not given the slightest significance, nor is it to be witnessed in the foreseeable future.

A word like "justice" is an abstraction so unreal and so utopian that there is no way to observe its indicators and attributes in the real world. Especially given that it is best accounted for, and defined by, its opposite. We need injustice to understand justice. Allow me therefore to dwell on the absence of justice, or injustice as an experience lived by the bulk of our fellow beings, for which there is much evidence in today's world, as it operates between the rich, affluent, and the hyper-educated societies, and the larger

part of under-developed countries – in other words, between the
West and the rest of the world. Even when one considers the
case of the future economic giants such as China, India and Brazil,
a gulf lies still between these two poles.

The first example of injustice, although conceived in intellectual
laboratories, is the profusion of theories bearing on the Third
World and their disastrous consequences. One can only, if one
wants, name a few from among the most notorious: "theory of
chaos" and "the clash of civilizations" and even "the end of
history." With the passing of time and the sway of their contents,
these theories have shifted human consciousness to some sort
of lethal indifference for the peoples subject to their scrutiny.
Not only do their proponents see ineradicable hurdles facing development and well-being in all facets of economic, psychological,
religious and cultural life; they in fact rule out any changes or
steps forward for them to improve their lot in the age of the new
paradigm called globalisation.

If we consider, with Edward Saïd, that there is no spider's web
without a spider, we can safely assume that theories, which at
one moment in history coalesce and point the way for further
theorising of a similar nature, are expressions of a higher intellectual and more powerful system. At the centre of the system is the
role of the State, with its servants and elites engaged in active
theorising, and to an extent resembling creative imagination
and creative vision. In 1986, PEN held its annual congress in
New York. The theme was "The Writer's Imagination and the
Imagination of the State." The bulk of the prominent writers par-
ticipating in the event denounced the "almost meaningless"
theme of the gathering. Among them, George Steiner termed
"The Writer's Imagination and the Imagination of the State" a
vacant phrase. "Its grammar limps." One notable exception, in
contrast, made a case for what had seemed an impossible theme.
Norman Mailer forcefully argued that if the State does not possess

imagination, then we are left with no need to write history.[1] Inasmuch as the State—an organism composed of many human beings striving in concert or in opposition—creates concepts, it struggles to empower and strengthen them vis-à-vis society and the world (the Third Reich, the Church in the Middle Ages, the military-industrial powers today, the resurgence of theocratic aspirations in parts of the Muslim world).

In its current phase globalisation is understood and made conspicuously visible only in terms of the economy, free trade, and the fierce competition among the big transnational companies, whereas nations of the South play a negligible role. In our poetic justice, we dare believe in a better world, free from economic domination. Yet taking the world for what it is, these nations are a long way from possessing the means and resources to develop. Adverse economic circumstances added to conflictual theories seem to reinforce each other to generate two kinds of reactions: either a return to all things past, a closing off with an aggressive stance, or a genuine, if somehow inaudible, will to dialogue, encounter, and communicate.

One legitimate question is to ask oneself where all the theories of economics of development have gone. These theories were high on the agenda of the underdeveloped and newly independent countries throughout the 1960s and 1970s. An entire field of study, knowledge, and research has vanished from teaching and from the academic curricula, its theories, concepts, methodologies, and prospective promises fallen in limbo. "What happened so that a promising field – the study of development – has become literally wiped out by... neoliberalism and its religion of the market?" asks Michel Rogalski, editor of *Recherches Internationales*, in his paper "The Return of the Economics of Development."[2] What these

---

1 Norman Mailer, "The Writer's Imagination and the Imagination of the State," *New York Review of Books*, 13 February 1986, p. 23.

2 Michel Rogalski, "Le Retour de l'économie du développement," *Recherches Internationales*. Available on www.gabrielperi.fr/

theories said in essence is that underdevelopment is the result of a long period of a multiform domination, often of a colonial nature, which brought about the integration of the *periphery* into the world economy through faulty and distorting structuring mechanisms, largely to the advantage of the *centre*.

Globalisation, says a researcher, broke into Algeria in the wake of its external debt – often referred to in Spanish as the "eternal debt" in many countries – and the accompanying intervention of the World Bank and the International Monetary Fund.[3] The same could be said of the four-fifths of human victims of unbridled globalisation. Wherever these two planetary institutions set foot, the consequences are far-reaching, and a sense of an inescapable "total crisis" leaves politicians, citizens, and intellectuals alike in a state of disarray verging on a zombie's walk in daylight. Globalisation is not a new concept, contrary to assertions in mass media. In the 1980s, the so-called "Washington consensus" put forward the criteria of "good globalisation": very little or no State, privatisation of all the economic activities, very little or no support to education, public health, and culture, neither customs barriers nor protection of national productions, and competition without restraint or limitations. Introduced into regions of the world unprepared for such an upheaval, the instrument of globalisation, the foreign debt, means permanent poverty and turns into "an immoral imposition, an illegal burden, a death sentence on future development and prosperity."[4]

The cost of globalisation is very high for its victims in many parts of the world. Its injustice knows no break or protections in the strongly marked tendency of a liberalising process imposed by force, whether political, economic, or military. More worrying yet is the fact that it looks as if conflicts and wars are the best

3 A. Nehili, "La Mondialisation s'est introduite par effraction," *Le Quotidien d'Oran*, lundi, 19 mai 2003.
4 Colin MacInnes, "The Pirate Who Inspired the Bankers," *The Guardian*, June 25, 2005.

ways to achieve globalisation, at least when one considers the regions of the world in turmoil today. In the name of freedom, democracy, and peace, unjust wars are waged against peoples thrown back into dark ages, their fate changed into permanent humanitarian crises. With theories like "clash of civilisations" on the one hand and hegemonic domination at work on the other hand, we observe the most salient feature of the new paradigm in world affairs: conflicts without end, as General Rupert Smith has it in his book *The Art of War in the Modern World*.[5]

In contemporary literature, the missing item is undoubtedly this new paradigm and its devastating consequences for millions of individuals. In the not-so-distant past, a keen sense of justice propelled writers to tackle, in their own way, inhuman conduct during the early industrial era, the long history of slavery, or the effects of civil wars. Lured by the phraseology of peace, justice, and economic growth expounded by forces above and over the individual, we have turned our back on the suffering that can so well be heard in books. Edouard Glissant sees two meanings of globalisation in the French language: *"globalisation"* and *"mondial-isation"* (sometimes translated as "worldness"). We certainly are in the first; as to the second we are not coming any nearer. Much determination and will to justice and understanding is needed on our part to achieve a truly lived and accepted experience of respect, tolerance, and recognition on a larger level. Our task as writers is to explore this new *frontier*, the new territory between *globalisation* and *worldness*, a vast sea of dangers, of powers of all sorts, of the good and the evil, of human frailties and greatnesses to be brought to light, so as to comprehend, measure, and build with words and emotions, harbours and bridges—something only books can build. Literature knows no *no man's land*, no forbidden territories.

---

5   General Rupert Smith, *The Utility of Force: Art of War in the Modern World* (New York: Alfred A. Knopf, 2007).

The second example of the absence of justice has to do with the past, a past strangely defined not for what it was but for its biased implication for the present economic, political, and, worse, racial supremacy. The tool for approaching it, history, is itself subject to attempts to simplify and instrumentalise it, reminiscent of the kind of theories and popular knowledge that anticipated colonisation in the early nineteenth century. The history of many Third World countries is revisited with the barely concealed idea that they are neither worth their independences nor able to evolve. Thus a new light was cast upon colonisation as exemplified by the 2005 February Law voted on by the French Parliament. What this law says is that colonisation had a positive role, glorifying it to an unthinkable degree. Exit the resistance of the subjected peoples, exit the spoliation of their natural resources and dispossession of their land, the obliteration of their identity, culture, and beliefs. An insidious construction of oblivion is in action, with the intention of averting the recognition of the colonial past and the subsequent act of repentance. Had it not been for the vigorous reaction of historians, social researchers, and citizens in both France and Africa, the February 2005 Law voted on by the French Parliament, albeit partially amputated of its most offensive clauses, would have not been abrogated, and history would have escaped historians. Minds captive in the nostalgia for imperial illusions and ruthless colonial adventurers have given themselves the assignment of hindering the conscious re-appropriation of memory, the sole way "to recognise the past as past, in other words not to live it as a present," says one historian.

A will to justice in history is as indispensable today as the recognition of the utterly unequal relationship between the North and the South. In the past, civilisations of the South had made great contributions to the world, as significant as today's accomplishments in the North. Self-image, self-esteem, and the right to self-definition are basic features of human nature. "If you believe," says the American historian William Lorenz Katz, "that a man has no history worth mentioning, then it is easy to assume he has no humanity worth defending." Truth about the past is one of the foundations upon which the right to justice at the level of individuals or between nations is built. The construction of oblivion is the surest shortcut to denial of justice. If historical justice is not taken into account, then the way is once more paved for renewed oppression. Without the struggle of the workers in the nineteenth and twentieth centuries and their influence upon intellectuals, historians, and writers, without the struggle of women and immigrants who have influenced historians, without the wars of liberation throughout the twentieth century, we would not have the multitude of historical studies available today.

To bring about justice in the historical affairs of our globe is a relentless effort. The recent publication of the *Dictionnaire de l'histoire de la colonisation française* (Dictionary of the History of French Colonisation)[6] is one of those contributions that massively document the reality of an unjust system and at the same time alert us to the insidious construction of oblivion. The latter is fed by the fear circle we live in, by the culture, politics, and rhetoric of fear constantly instilled in our minds. And fear, in turn, is nourished by lies as a form of political communication. "The lie belongs to the beginning of the twenty-first century," noted a political analyst lately, during a worldwide reading of the report on Chechnya by Anna Politkovskaya, the journalist and critic assassinated on October 7, 2006.[7]

Obviously, he referred to the invasion of Iraq. Before that, in the last quarter of the twentieth century, in the wake of the fall of the Berlin Wall, the lie was a nosy background rumour, a

---

6 Claude Liauzu, *Dictionnaire de la colonisation française*, (Paris: Editions Larousse, 2007).

7 Ulrich Schreiber, "The second anniversary of the political lie – in memoriam Anna Politkovskaya." Available on www.peter-weiss-stiftung.de/index_en.html

harbinger of the taste to come for manipulative theories and of the subsequent economic, political, bellicose experiments in the real world.

In our age, that of a huge planetary supermarket, we resent the fact that even cardinal values such as justice, dignity, respect, mutual recognition, solidarity, and compassion with the downtrodden on earth have become mere commodities or, at best, poetic messages to sell in the ad row. Yet I believe it is incumbent upon the writer to define a free territory for himself or herself, engaged in that "celebration of human consciousness" called literature, which has as one of its greatest assets the capacity to look back on its own long history. In the most desperate moments of Humanity, writers did not let down the human, "with conscience wide as hell," as Shakespeare wrote in a different context. Their works survived, and remain inspirational, in spite of all the walls of China that oblivion erects all around them. They are still with us today, I believe, thanks to the fact that they teach us how to *unlearn* the wrong disguised as the right, the utterly unequal dressed up as democratic consensus, the unjust clothed in the rhetoric of justice.

American Labasha

DANIEL ALARCÓN

"Everyone in Paraguay has the same fingerprints. There are crimes
but people chosen at random are punished for them.
Everyone is liable for everything."
DONALD BARTHELME, "Paraguay"

While I was researching my first novel, I came across a passage
in Ryszard Kapuscinski's The Emperor that I've never quite been able
to shake. In it, he describes Haile Selassie's attempts to modern-
ize Ethiopia in the years immediately preceding the fall of his
government. In the more distant and isolated provinces of the
empire, there was, according to one of Kapuscinski's informants,
an antique ritual called labasha that took the place of a criminal
justice system. It worked this way: a community is confronted
with a crime – a theft, for example – and instead of making any
attempt to discover who is responsible, the people of the village
select a child, usually a boy, and stupefy him with a potent herbal
tea. Under the herb's hallucinogenic effects, the drunken child
stumbles about, and eventually, based on signifiers only the boy
in his altered state can know – the color of a woman's dress, a
man's posture, or the geometric pattern of his shirt – he identifies
the culprit. No further proof of guilt is necessary. This person, who-
ever it might be, is then punished according to whatever crime
she or he has been convicted of.

In the case of theft, his or her hands are amputated.

Naturally, this strikes those of modern sensibilities as particularly cruel, as deplorable and essentially unjust. And it is all those
things – to punish people at random for crimes they may not have

committed certainly offends our notions of right and wrong. We like to believe that power is not arbitrary, and indeed, in the best of times, under the best circumstances, it may not be. But as this passage lingered, and eventually insinuated itself into the novel I was writing, I decided it would be a mistake to think of *labasha* as foreign or strange. If anything, it is simply a corrupt version of something we see all too often: in many ways, in many states, punishment is random. And the more complex and troubled the political situation, the more random it becomes.

At the time I came across *labasha*, I was well-versed in the routine horrors of a state that had lost control of itself. The novel I was writing dealt specifically with the civil war and its aftermath in Peru, the country where I was born. In response to the violent attacks of the Shining Path, a Maoist insurgency, the Peruvian state launched a campaign of wanton violence upon the poor, indigenous, rural majority—the same people who were most victimized by the Shining Path in the first place. Thousands were imprisoned without trial, or tortured, and of course, thousands more disappeared, never to be heard from again. In writing the novel, I alternately immersed myself in this shameful history, recoiled from it, and tried above all to understand how a society could sanction this arbitrary implementation of power and then, at the first convenient opportunity, forget that it had done so.

The refrain one hears most often from certain sectors of a besieged society is that the political reality demands compromise: we shoulder barter away our freedoms in exchange for the promise of security. How many societies have made these bargains? It is hardly exotic. And so: when suspects are selected for questioning and punishment based on outward signifiers—their age, their ethnic group, their country of origin, their religion, their occupation—rather than complicity with any crime, this, too, is *labasha*.

✧   ✧   ✧

Growing up in the United States, Peru seemed like a rumor, or a dream, and my family's periodic trips back home only served to accentuate the strangeness of the place. If the U.S. was solid, Peru was still under construction, a place where rules were more obscure, where power felt no need to mask its essentially arbitrary nature. Bribes occurred in broad daylight. Politicians routinely performed gestures of corruption so baroque one could only marvel at them. The war, as it progressed, only deepened the psychological distance between Peru and the tidy American suburb where I was being raised. The fighting began in 1980, the year we moved to the United States, at a moment when Peru was emerging from more than a decade of military rule, when the re-establishment of democracy was a legitimate cause for optimism, but then the Shining Path launched its violent campaign, and the state went along with this ruinous dance for more than a decade. The bloated rich, in their fear, sought to insulate themselves from the chaos with more money. The craven politicians, ethically rudderless, leaned on their worst instincts to patch the holes in the sinking ship of state. The conflict wore on, and, far beyond whatever military victories or reversals may have occurred or the shifting lines demarcating territory under nominal control of either the state or the insurgency, the two antagonists were most successful when it came to the dirty business of degrading and eventually destroying the concept of justice. Or whatever remained of it. It was invoked too many times to rationalize barbaric acts of violence from either side. Justice – is there any idea more complicated or nebulous? – in war time was stripped of its complexity, whittled down to something simple, crude. It became swift, expedient, aggressive and without nuance. A car bomb, a missing activist, a murdered judge, a blackout. People punished at random for the crime of living. Because it is true: war, in the end, makes everyone liable for everything.

✧   ✧   ✧

In the last few years, as I have wandered from the United States to Latin America and back again, I've seen the ways the two places I call home collide, becoming more and more like versions of each other. This, perhaps, is what the optimists among us call globalization: Peruvian children with Anglicized names, shopping—or aspiring to shop—as Americans do, exchanging YouTube videos with peers from cities all over the world. The possibility of instantaneous, unmediated information exchange—peer to peer to peer—is nothing less than breathtaking, and even the most jaded Luddite must recognize that something extraordinary is taking place, something we never before could have predicted.

I'm not able to say, unequivocally, whether this is good or bad. Others have, and others will, and for now, I can only say that I'm both troubled and intrigued by it, that I find myself unable to denounce it completely as I am a child of it. And yet, there is one way in which the United States—the country that adopted me as much as I adopted it—now resembles Peru, and I wouldn't have guessed this was coming. A war like the one that marked the 1980s in Peru has come to the United States, and as a consequence, those things that I once thought of as solid have come to seem as obscure, as under construction, as they were in the Peru I recall from my childhood. There are multiple struggles underway now in the psyche of the United States, and the most important of all, I feel, is for the integrity of our justice system. I worry, now more than ever, that the so-called war on terrorism will be the death knell of what was an already beleaguered and flawed arrangement of statutes and punishments and enforcement. Though we may have grand traditions of law and democracy and human rights, without diligent maintenance they are simply dusty old mementos we keep around to make us feel good in difficult times. Totems to another era. And in this one? Make no mistake: there are those out there arguing for—and persuading many—of the necessity and desirability of American labasha.

✧   ✧   ✧

I left Paros not certain I felt more or less optimistic about the state of the world, or the ability of human beings to be kind or fair to one another. Over the course of the four days there, I heard and discussed various cases of man's cruelty to man, one and then another withering example of a world full of beleaguered, weary, and dispossessed people. If you're waiting for justice, it's like my mother used to say: *mejor esperas sentado*. Don't wait standing up. Go ahead and get comfortable, because you'll be waiting a long, long time. And still, when I recall those discussions on Paros, I find that one emotion was evoked again and again – outrage. With so much injustice in the world, where does all this outrage come from? If we can look back at history, at any stretch of recorded time, and we can find egregious examples of cruelty and callousness, enough so that one might reasonably conclude that this is simply the way the world is. But outrage is, in some ways, related to surprise. Outrage is more than just our ethics being prodded: outrage exists when something defies convention. Ordinary cruelty becomes outrageous at the point at which we are shocked by it – but given that this bloody history is endless and repetitive and cyclical; that heinous crimes are eclipsed by even greater crimes; that a people can have their land taken from them, and then are condemned to wandering for a generation, or two or three; that they themselves took that land from some other people back in the pre-history that no one is ever quite able to forget; that this has been going on forever and will continue for the foreseeable future – given all this, why is it that we are still able to manufacture outrage? Shouldn't we be used to it all by now? Inured to it? Why are we still moved by these stories, and is there a point after which we will no longer be able to process another sad story?

If there's any reason for hope, it's the continued existence of this specific type of anger. This outrage is all we have left. At times, I feel very tired walking through this world, and then something hits me, and I feel it again, like emerging from a dream. Or a nightmare. Yes, these things happen all the time. Yes, they are ordinary, even mundane. Yes, we have lived in societies for thousands of years, and no, there is no real reason to believe in progress. But still, we are able to summon outrage, to say *this is wrong*, to clench our fists and weep on behalf of others, and when we lose that, if we lose that, we will have lost everything.

Dear God, if You exist: please don't let that happen.

The Writer in Search of Justice

HELON HABILA

An essay on justice should logically begin by asking: What is justice? Books have been written on this subject, philosophical careers launched. Everlasting fame has been achieved in the pursuit of it – an example is King Solomon's famous judgment over the case of two disputing women, "Cut the child in two." I wish our definition could be that easy: cut the child in two and discover justice. I am going for a simpler, more predictable definition: Webster's dictionary describes justice as a noun, its etymology as Middle English, from Anglo-French *justise*, from Latin *justitia*, from *justus*. One of the many definitions is given as: the administration of law; especially: the establishment or determination of rights according to the rules of law or equity. Another one is: the quality of being just, impartial, or fair, the principle or ideal of just dealing or right action, conformity to this principle or ideal.

The problem with the first definition, "the quality of conforming to the rule of law," is obviously the question "Whose law"? And so the most promising definition will be the second one: "the quality of being just, impartial, or fair, the principle or ideal of just dealing or right action, conformity to this principle or ideal." Here justice is raised to the level of an ideal, i.e. something we pursue, but which we never really catch hold of. That is how I see the writer's vocation: a ceaseless search for justice. Since there can be no justice without truth, the writer is also in search of truth. By truth of course I don't necessarily mean the truth of mere facts. I mean a higher, moral truth, a poetic truth. Speaking on the nature of this poetic truth, an essayist in the *Guardian* quotes Jean Cocteau on writing: "I am a lie who always speaks the truth." The essayist goes on to say:

> To go beyond mere facts, to record a true history that takes account of the unseen as well as the visible, Cocteau saw that the writer must create something that, on the face of it, is a fabrication. This is what art does; this is what any narrative must take into account if it is to succeed. The artifice is there for all to see, but is not the criterion by which a writer is judged: what matters is whether we accept the truth that Cocteau's "lie" reveals. If we do, authors can gain an authority that allows them to challenge dishonesty at the highest level – and, in doing so, remind us that the pen can be mightier than the sword.

It was the Romantic poet Percy Bysshe Shelley who described poets as: "the institutors of laws" or "universal arbiters." This is an attempt to show how exalted the call of the artist is. He is a giver of justice; under his pen the mighty is made equal with the commoner. It is no wonder then that the symbol for justice is a blindfolded woman holding scales and a sword. Truth is blind. I see a metaphor for the writer's craft in the Greek play *Oedipus Rex*. The writer's obsessive quest for truth leads him to stop trusting in forms and appearances, to look inward, just as Oedipus is forced to look inward by losing his sight; only then can he see the truth. As T.S. Eliot says, the true writer should never be blinded by his own personality – in fact he shouldn't have any personality.

Let us pursue this point further. If we have to attenuate our personality, or our ego, in order to be just, then does it mean that we all are capable of knowing what is just, or what justice is, but it is our intrusive or obstructive egos that stop us from applying it? The British, when they established colonies all over the world, believed that they were doing the colonized peoples a favor. They killed and raped and looted, they burned and pillaged, and yet this people, ordinarily very civilized at home, eager for justice in their own communities, saw nothing wrong with what they were doing in these new communities. In Zimbabwe for instance, Cecil Rhodes and his horde of settlers hoodwinked the chiefs into signing agreements which they then promptly announced as giving them the right to take over the lands and cattle of the Shona and Matabele. Clearly their egos failed to see that what they were doing was unjust – and yet they continued to talk of justice within their own communities.

So justice entails not just seeing, but seeing everything equally, beyond personality, beyond ego.

The writer's concern is not so much for right or wrong, but for righteousness; he answers to a voice inside him, an inspiration, a voice that speaks to all artists when they sit to produce their art. It is clear that this definition is leading us in one direction – towards the religious – and in this Shelley was ahead of us. He goes on to describe poets as:

> legislators or prophets: a poet essentially comprises and unites both these characters. For he not only beholds intensely the present as it is, and discovers those laws according to which present things ought to be ordered, but he beholds the future in the present, and his thoughts are the forms of the flower and the fruit of latest time.

The question is: do we, as writers, writing now, still see ourselves as searchers after truth, or is such a preoccupation considered old fashioned, something ancient poets amused themselves
with? In an essay in the *Observer*, Robert McCrum sees that trend
in current writing. He says of contemporary writing:

> ...The novelist has become a cross between a commercial
> traveler and an itinerant preacher...: in just over a gener-
> ation the novel has gone public in the most astounding
> way. In the process, the genre has sold out and become
> big business, the preferred medium of self-advance-
> ment and self-promotion... and almost unrecognizable
> to fiction-lovers raised on the literary names of the
> Forties and Fifties.

In short, he is saying the novelist is in danger of losing his soul,
his original vision. It is clear that today the search for profit, for
self-actualization, has displaced communal concerns. We see the
same thing the British did to their colonies being re-enacted on
the Iraqis by America. This is the story of empire, the dream of
empire builders. The frontiers of empire must always advance
outwards, and they do so by plundering other people's territories.

But let us retrace our steps to establish clearly what exactly
those "earlier" writers did that the present generation is losing
sight of. I will use the African writer in particular to explain.
When the first African novels in European languages started to
emerge in the '40s and '50s and '60s, critics were quick to notice
that they all shared one element: the political. True, they did
pay attention to language, they did weave beautiful plots, and
described beautiful characters, but over and above that, they
spoke the minds of the millions of voiceless masses trampled
under the boots of empire. By doing this, they gave voice to the
voiceless, they brought into relief millions of invisible Africans,

and for the first time readers all over the world saw that, contrary to what empire wanted us to believe, these masses are being oppressed and denied justice, and mainly because they are the "other."

The African writer was clearly being what Shelley described as "a legislator and a visionary." He was challenging the unjust laws that exist and presaging a better, more equal law. But to do this the writer had to put his personality in the background – he didn't speak for himself, but for the community. To understand the need for justice, one has to first understand injustice, and one understands injustice by suffering injustice, or by being able to empathize with those suffering injustice. It is like gold being purified by fire – that is why the world's greatest works of literature often emerge from the pen of those who survived extreme hardship. Because of the extreme suffering around them they had turned their gaze inward, and like Oedipus, they saw truth.

One of the best examples of this lack of empathy I have seen recently is in the report by a body called the Commission for Africa. This is a group of eminent individuals invited by the British Prime Minister, Tony Blair, to look into causes of poverty in Africa and to recommend ways to combat them. And some of the findings of the Commission are that the poor are poor because they were born into poverty and because they occupied unproductive geographical regions. This is the kind of blind, limited language and reasoning one sees more and more, especially in the media today. Why are the Palestinians refugees in their own land? Oh, because they are Palestinians. Why is there so much violence in Iraq? Oh, the Iraqis are terrorists. Why is there poverty in Africa? Oh, because Africans were born poor.

The only antidote to this zombiism is true art. Only the writer can bridge this gap, unveil the veil of complacency and ignorance and, in some instances, of malice. The writer's pen can demystify the mysterious, and unmask the pretender. The writer questions the easy assumptions and convenient answers power always presents so as to numb the minds of the people. The writer urges us not to be easily satisfied with these answers. If we are easily satisfied, and undemanding, our writers and thinkers become unchallenged. We get the kind of writers we deserve, just like a people often gets the kind of rulers it deserves. We must push our legislators to be just if we are to get the kind of justice we deserve, and when they go to war in our name, and plunder and dispossess innocent peoples around the world, we must stand up and loudly say: not in my name.

One novel that raises this issue of injustice regarding the individual versus empire in an original, unremitting way is J.M. Coetzee's *Waiting for the Barbarians*. It is the story of empire's unfeeling, unseeing way of extending its borders. It is the story of how one servant of empire dares to question the means and tools of such expansion. It is a story about ways of seeing the other, and putting oneself in the place of the other just in order to understand. The main character is an unnamed magistrate, administering a remote, sleepy border region of the empire. But one day his easy life is shattered when Colonel Joll, a member of the Third Bureau, the empire's secret army, arrives from the metropolis to investigate rumors of barbarian invasion. The barbarians are the people displaced by empire in its drive for expansion. The magistrate, who is the first person narrator, is faced with a dilemma as he watches the violence grow daily, unleashed by Colonel Joll. It is interesting how Joll is described in the very first page of the book: "...two little discs of glass suspended in front of his eyes in loops of wire. Is he blind? I could understand it if he wants to hide blind eyes. But he is not blind"(1). The magistrate's first reaction is to turn a blind eye to the new developments; he says:

> If I resolved to ride out the bad times, keeping my
> own counsel, I might cease to feel like a man who
> in the grip of the undertow, gives up the fight, stops
> swimming, and turns his face towards the open sea
> and death. (21)

But of course he isn't able to "keep his own counsel." There's
something inside him that refuses to keep idle while Colonel Joll
is out rampaging. One day he visits the prisoners incarcerated
and tortured daily by Joll. What he sees changes him forever: "I
ought never to have taken my lantern to see what was going on
in the hut by the granary. On the other hand there was no way,
once I had picked up the lantern, for me to put it down again"
(21).

The magistrate finally breaks rank with empire and becomes a
prisoner of empire himself. Colonel Joll throws him into the same
dungeon he uses for incarcerating and torturing the barbarians.
And only at that moment of final severance from injustice does
the magistrate finally feel free, happy: "I am aware of the source
of my elation: my alliance with the guardians of empire is over,
I have set myself in opposition, the bond is broken, I am a free
man!" (78)

Perhaps the profoundest passage in this book is where the
magistrate, after his incarceration, contemplates the meaning of
justice:

> Justice: once that word is uttered, where will it all
> end? Easier to spout No! Easier to be beaten and made
> a martyr. Easier to lay my head on a block than to
> defend the cause of justice for the barbarians: for
> where can that argument lead but to laying down our
> arms and opening the gates of the town to the people
> whose lands we have raped? (80)

This points us neatly back to the issue of ego and personality. By being just to others we are acknowledging that we are all the same; no one deserves better than another person just because of how he looks or where he comes from. The magistrate is saying here that if the powerful will decide to give justice to the powerless, then the world as we know it now will cease to exist. And that is a scary prospect for many – it is the writer's job to show us that though it may be scary, it is the only way forward, and at the end, both the strong and the weak will benefit from it, till at the end there will be no strong or weak. There will be only people.

REFERENCE

Our Common Interest: Report of the Commission for Africa, (2005)
Coetzee, J.M., Waiting for the Barbarians, (1980)
Eliot, T.S., "Tradition and the Individual Talent"
McCrum, Robert, "Has the Novel Lost its Way?" The Observer, May 28, 2006

Justice and its Image

ANASTASSIS VISTONITIS

The companions died in turn,
with lowered eyes. Their oars
mark the place where they sleep on the shore.

No one remembers them. Justice.
GEORGE SEFERIS, *Mythistorima*

The most difficult thing for a writer has been and continues to be to control his emotion of anger. If we leave aside all that is included in an undisputed masterpiece such as Flaubert's *Education Sentimentale*, we shall see that such is, in reality, the central theme of this overwhelming novel: maturity, the coming-of-age of emotion, the blunting, in the end, of the sharpness of experience which makes it possible to see life retrospectively. With resentment? With nostalgia? With everything entailed in the inevitability of assumptions? Wherever it is we arrive, nevertheless, there is a single conclusion: the emotion of anger, wherever, however, and whether it makes its appearance, is due to an absence of justice, which appears more marked at moments of historical tension.

For that reason every transgression involves the element of deprivation, a stolen truth whose consequences for the emotions we hardly ever understand. "My brain was clouded," says the perpetrator of the crime of passion. And this is reminiscent of Milton: the brain is calmed when the emotions become inert, when a man enters into that phase of ageing of the spirit when the only image he sees before him clearly is the exit, the gate of the grave.

Man is born with a sense of injustice, since an awareness of death stigmatises his life indelibly. In any event, it is for this reason that great art monumentalises the sense of the eternal and the sacred. The religious content of these concepts, however, covers only a small part of their semantic field. Eternity is the great ocean of the memory, as immortalised in Homer's *Odyssey*, where the return of Odysseus is nothing other than the setting right of a longstanding injustice (of ten years' duration). By extension – and as this is given expression in the texts of the world's peoples – when there is an injustice, the balance of the universe is disturbed, the societies of this world collapse and are followed by ashes, disasters, and ruin, allowing us then to proceed to catharsis, which will open up a window on the future. This is why the symbol of justice in Greek poetry, and in religious texts, is light, the triumph of the visible, the end of interminable night.

Justice, however, is not a decision. It is an act, or, otherwise, the execution of a decision; it is complete only when it is administered. In its pure form it cannot be dragged behind the chariot of political power, which it checks and, if necessary, represses. Consequently, the executive power in democratic societies serves as an extension of justice. In other words, justice is under an obligation to control political power, because it is only by controlling it that it judges its own omissions, acts, or weaknesses, and is then able to correct them.

The safeguarding of the independence of justice, which in modern societies is an *acquis* of the Enlightenment, is the only effective way of controlling political power – or power more generally. There have been more than a few occasions when independent judges have saved the honour of democracy, as was the case a few years ago in Italy, or in the 1960s in Greece, when a young examining magistrate, Christos Sartzetakis, did not hesitate to bring to trial the leadership of the Thessaloniki police for the murder of the deputy Grigoris Lambrakis by agents of the para-State.

The sense of justice is directly bound up with the desire for a better world that will not find its balance through doctrines of power but rather through the rendering unto each of that which he deserves for his acts, and his omissions. Thus the penalty in the legal system goes beyond the meaning of punishment pure and simple, bringing about the making good of the damage caused by the criminal, not only to others, but also to himself. Whether the penalty then functions in many cases not as a corrective act but to fuel crime and injustice is a different issue. In any event, crime begins where people overstep limits. Crime is the secular version of the ancient *hubris* – but this applies only in those countries where democracy operates. When under tyrannies men rise up, the resort to force is an explosion of oppressed sensitivity, giving expression to a sense of injustice in an extreme form. This is no more than opposition to the fact that some suck out the life of others and deprive them of the air they breathe.

In the ancient world, the sense of the sacred was the only thing that could legitimate man's secular expression of himself. Justice was a goddess, she was a person, a living presence even in the courts of law, where behind the judges and the jury the shadows of the gods rose up. The court was not anonymous and vast as it is in Kafka's *Trial*, where it includes the whole of society.

Any lack of justice is, nevertheless, expressed today as a trauma of the individual and of a society as a whole, and may lead to an uprising against injustice, seen as an impersonal state of affairs, a polymorphous – or, rather, amorphous – totality of acts, omissions and quasi-ideologies. Thus justice, judgment, and the Last Judgment, as these find expression in Christian doctrine, express as a rule an inability to deal with the cosmic monster of injustice, which dominates the greater part of the planet.

However, society's inability to reward, or acknowledge, what is just because of its various social and political inflexibilities is made good by popular wisdom, which supplies its own answers. "Everything here has its price," the people of Greece say when, by coincidence, disaster falls upon someone who has blatantly done wrong and has not been punished. "Divine Justice," we say at other times, echoing a memory from ancient times.

We Greeks have shed our blood innumerable times. If there is no justice, the dead do not rest easy, our tradition tells us. Hubris always has to be paid for, otherwise all concepts lose their significance. In the fifth century BC, the Athenian Democracy, before laying Melos waste, asked the Melians to surrender unconditionally. The Melians replied that the gods did not want this injustice. The Athenians responded that the gods always take the side of the strong, and wiped out Melos. A little later, the Athenian fleet was destroyed by the Spartans at Aegospotami, and this meant the end of the Athenian Democracy and its hegemony. The speeches of the Athenians and the Melians, as recorded by Thucydides in his History, are among the most astonishing and most political texts ever to have been written on justice and injustice, presented as a narrative of power's arrogance and of the punishment that always falls upon the arrogant.

Justice is blind: here is another definition of eternity, where all are equal before the law because apart from human time there is universal time – the Latins thought of it as horror vacui – in which no distinctions are made. Justice is, according to Elytis, a notional sun that sheds light into dark corners of History, and of conscience.

For the artist and the intellectual, however, the sense of justice always precedes its actual occurrence, beyond and above its institution, because it determines our sensitivity and our attitude not only towards organized society but towards life itself. In order to create a society it is necessary to legislate, to set limits on individual behaviour – but the starting-point for any form of institution, for any legislation is freedom. This is what the charter texts of the world's peoples, the declarations of the rights of man and of the citizen – everything that provides the foundations for today's democratic societies – take first and foremost into account.

How many centuries have had to pass for us to progress from the right of the strong to equality of all before the law? The transition from the Middle Ages to the Renaissance and from there to the Enlightenment took place in leaps. From then on, it could reasonably be said, no substantive moral or political progress has been made. The right of the stronger continues to determine events in very many regions of the planet, and it is no accident at all that it is applied in countries where there is no democracy, even while being refuted by the societies of the West. When the latter do apply it outside their own societies by adopting the "logic" of war, they violate every principle of justice and, circumventing the charter principles of their own societies, become agents of *hubris* in our own time.

Insofar as this logic continues to prevail in contemporary politics, civilisation is imbued with the poison of contradiction. We refer constantly to human societies and regard justice as their connective tissue, yet in spite of this we do not cease to maintain mechanisms of external violence. These mechanisms exist, of course, and are reproduced, because their chief property is the negation of the other, derived from our inability to accept as a factor for cohesion that which differentiates us, or else to accept those things that we are fundamentally unwilling to cede to political authorities.

To live in an organised society entails ceding a percentage of one's individual freedom for the good of the whole. But what you cede you must receive back in another form many times over – and, in any case, the gesture of giving up must not be the result of imposition but of consensus. Every time the freedom of even one individual is ceded, or filched, without society's reaction, injustice sits enthroned, giving the tyrant the right to mock his unfortunate subjects – if not to send them to prison, into exile, or in front of the firing-squad.

In 1958, Isaiah Berlin gave his first lecture as Professor of Social and Political Theory at Oxford, in essence talking about justice. The lecture was entitled Two Concepts of Liberty, and defined these concepts as *positive* and *negative* liberty. How is it that what for one person is just, is unjust for another – and how does the extension of the individual liberty of one person rob his neighbour of a percentage of the air which he breathes? The principles of the Enlightenment, the separation of powers and the safeguarding of the rights of man and of the citizen are all supposed to have supplied answers to these questions. We are unfortunately forced to use the qualifier "supposed," because the experiences of the twentieth century have been far from encouraging. We believed, for example, that the extension of the gains of the Enlightenment at the social level would correct the injustices created by unequal distribution of wealth. The outcome was exactly the opposite: not only were these injustices not eliminated, but in the name of setting them right vast masses of human beings were deprived of their individual rights, millions were sent to jail, hundreds of thousands faced the firing-squad, and innumerable others found themselves in forced labour camps.

We are frequently surprised by the iniquitous paths followed by the human mind – that fairy transformed into a Minotaur, adapting every now and then the logic of war and force. What happens when man, though knowing what is good, does evil? What is it that makes us fail to see the self-evident? At a mature age, Arthur Koestler, following paths of parapsychology, arrived at the conclusion that some mistake occurred in the first stage of the creation of the world – hence all our tribulations. And so, since the seed of evil is latent in civilisation, society, culture, and individual behaviour will continue to be Manichean. In any event, almost all our systems, even down to the binary logic by which the computer functions (0-1), can be seen to be Manichean.

Nietzsche wrote a whole book, *Beyond Good and Evil*, to decry the bipolar nature of a civilisation that he most profoundly abhorred and denounced from the heights of his passion – but a way out of this civilisation is not meaningful, nor does it exist. A mediocre society can destroy a man of genius, particularly when in his work its conventions and ordinances are reduced to their constituent atoms. A way out of conventions means a game with paranoia and death. All convention, however, entails suppression, and suppression means only one thing: deprivation of freedom. Just as in the jails of totalitarian regimes the prisoners do battle with the ghosts of freedom, so in our own societies we have to battle with the ghosts of injustice.

The battle is unequal – absurd, Camus might say. It is not possible for human nature to be interpreted and described convincingly because the phenomenon of death goes beyond the forms of understanding of the real that man has created. But it is worth the effort, because otherwise morality loses its meaning, as does civilisation, which is for the scrap heap unless it corrects the weaknesses of human nature, or at least makes that be one of its primary aims. In the present instance, the reiteration of a commonplace would not seem inappropriate: worthwhile creativity cannot be other than a constant quest for freedom through individual or collective expression. This alone has the power to bring us to a level beyond good and evil, that is, to a poetics of freedom.

The conviction that we can explain, shape, or even correct the imperfections of human nature and bridge the gap between individual objectives and the collective interest by means of compulsory social schemata leads inevitably to totalitarianism. Since we are mortal, it is not possible to eliminate from the life of society every imponderable factor; we cannot approach – still less achieve – happiness through voluntaristic structures.

Democracy has proved to be the best political system because it is based on the relativity of things and on the importance of equilibria emerging from the constant movement of ideas, individuals and groups, from the ceaseless interaction of the things the human spirit creates. To repeat another commonplace: creation is unthinkable without the existence of the human factor, but the latter's special quality in each historical time stems from its ability to constantly subvert these equilibria. Consequently, how, when, and to whom the derivatives of civilisation are awarded – from material to non-material goods – has a close connection to freedom and justice. But it is the state in which the general population of any country finds itself that gives us the true measure of the justice its citizens enjoy, or else are deprived of. A just man is thus one who recognises the right of the other, even when – or particularly when – this right conflicts with his individual interest. And justice is a product of civilisation – it does not exist in nature, where the law of the stronger holds sway. The theory of evolution itself tells us that.

In human society, however, the strong and the weak must co-exist and enjoy the same rights. The genius and the mediocre, the creator and the performer, the visionary and the plodder – all contribute to a society remaining cohesive and so improving, so that each generation enjoys a better standard of living than the preceding one.

Faced with injustice, the creative artist has only one option: to stand with the victims and against those in power. In dictatorial regimes, no form of ideology can replace the major injustice: the deprivation of freedom. No promise for the future is of greater value than what the mechanisms of suppression take away from the present. In these cases, the imposition of silence is the greater

form of injustice. Deprivation of speech is a negation of civilisation, because through discourse and expression man not only
takes part in the social and historical process: he also – and above
all – learns to think.

A free man is someone who does not negotiate his right to
express himself and to judge, or one who – regarding as a personal benefit what is no more than a shared and inalienable
right – cedes this right in order to circulate in an environment
controlled from above. Consequently, justice means refusal of
force or resistance to it – and particularly when force takes on the
forms of a regime. The acceptance of any violent or totalitarian
regime means quite simply the ceding of rights, and a consent
to injustice; and this monster feeds, of course, on toleration –
which, when it is long-lasting – inevitably ends in collusion.

In Western democracies, we consider much of this more or
less self-evident, and thus talk all the time about ancillary issues
in an effort to *understand* why the same view does not hold in
the rest of the world. Yet with disturbing frequency this verb is
used euphemistically. It is, in any event, fashionable to examine
repressive societies in the Third World in the light of cultural
particularities, so that we supply with an alibi those tyrants who
use the "tradition" of their country (a so-called "tradition" whose
real name is stagnation) as an ideological weapon in order to keep
their citizens in a state of hypnosis and aphasia. The defence of
democracy is interpreted – as a rule by those who enjoy its benefits in their own country – as an attempt at cultural and political
manipulation.

In this way the old principle, which says that to understand
another person does not mean to grant that he is right, is circum-
vented. Subjectivity is an endemic disease of post-modern thought,
and *interpretation* the alibi for the formulation of various arbitrary
theories and for speculations turned into doctrines. There can be
no doubt that in confusing the subject with the object of the

law, we serve only despots. And despots do not support societies of justice but rather those of penalties, which are established not as consequences of the implementation of law but for the opposite reason: laws come *ex post facto* to shore up a system of penalties based on strength, acting as a shell or an alibi for the system of punishments upholding the repressive society. When cultural or religious beliefs are regarded as above the law, the sense of justice is constantly blunted; in the end we arrive at societies that are static, outdated, and barbarous.

Manifested in one of its worst cultural forms, that of specialisation (which leads to the demise of a rounded education and of cultivation, something Robert Graves already discerned in his *White Goddess*), barbarism is far from extinct in our own time. There is a lot of ground left for us to cover before we emerge from prehistory.

Justice on the Waiting List for the Burmese

MA THIDA

The value and the essence of justice are not different for the Burmese than for others all over the world. We don't, of course, have very much justice. Yet most Burmese believe that it can be achieved not only through the courts but also through the natural cause-and-effect process. According to natural justice, no one will be able to avoid the "effect" of their own action, its "cause." But how about legal justice?

Twenty-four-hour neon lights wreath Nay Pyi Daw, which means "the royal kingdom," a city of less than a million people. It is here all military giants and ministerial offices have just recently moved, away from the 5 million living in Yangon, established in 1755 and a capital ever since, through colonial days and the post-Independence period. Since Nay Pyi Daw was established, electricity in Yangon functions irregularly and sometimes only 6 hours per day. For nearly two decades, Mandalay, the second capital in Upper Burma where most civilians live, has had totally unpredictable home electricity and nearly absent street light. The rest of Burma, especially for provincial towns and villages where most civilians live, has always had even less.

Soon after the 1988 coup, the Ministry of Defense built its own vocational universities and other educational, health, and social infrastructures. Most new resettlement areas beyond the old town's suburbs were occupied by poor and displaced civilians, while the most convenient places of those resettlements were reserved for military officers who never live in that town, or around it. An average military officer can own several rental properties in different towns, while most local civilians lose their land and are displaced out of town. Most business opportunities are reserved for military families, with civilians becoming their modest employees.

Most Burmese living in rural areas usually don't have any idea about how much better they could be treated by the government. The various regional, racial, and religious groups feel that they are unjustly treated but don't notice carefully enough that there is no equality and equity in their social, economical, educational, health, and political opportunities.

Some Burmese were quite surprised to learn that privacy advocates protested when President Bush claimed the right to open personal mail without a warrant, or when Republican Governor Arnold Schwarzenegger offered a plan to provide health insurance to all Californians. Why? Not only are print and electronic media scrutinized by the Information Ministry; all mail is opened, read, and resealed, without notice, by a special bureau within the Home Affairs Ministry. Web-based free email is banned, internet access is limited and restricted. In contrast, young military officers can get uncensored Internet access at special places. Most high-ranking military officers are unbelievably rich and usually get their health care in Singapore or Bangkok, even while the majority of civilians cannot afford to use even the cost-sharing national health care which charges every patient for surgical blades and gauze bandages. Though the regime newspapers printed once that no one was above the law, the rule of law is established differently for the military and the civilian populations. In that way, present-day Burma practices "one land, two countries," much like China promotes "one country, two systems." Burma's military country has custom-tailored law and order while its civilian country has corrupt judges and repressed media. Justice is different for Burma's military population and the civilian population.

I myself experienced, and practiced, this differential justice in the Insein prison in the 1990s. As my own experience as a political prisoner shows, I was able to demonstrate to the military and prison authorities how one can practice justice even under custody. My own good and justified acts, based on Buddha's Vipasana meditation, were always a threat to them. What follows is the account of my prison experience.

In 1993 I was accused of endangering public serenity, of being connected with illegal political organizations, and of printing and distribution of illegal pamphlets. My only crime was reading a weekly journal published by an illegal political organization abroad. I was sentenced to 20 years imprisonment in the notorious Insein prison in Yangon. This was a very small compound, with only six cells; in it were six people altogether, all of whom had been given a death sentence because they killed someone during the 1988 uprising; the other two were communists. My environment was thus not very good for meditation. Our compound was inside a big ward, one intended for detention rather than for those already sentenced. Every two weeks we could meet our family members for 15 minutes. Every time we were to meet our family we had to pass through the whole compound to the interview room. Because of our isolation in the small compound, it was not every day we could see people living in the ward. Off and on, passing through the entire block, I could notice how badly the criminal prisoners were being treated. Every time I walked through there, I noticed how afraid I was of becoming one of them. For, according to Buddha's teachings, every effect has its cause: the bad treatment those criminals were receiving might have been pay-back for misdeeds in their previous lives. According to Buddha's teachings we can't be free from the eternal universe without practicing meditation, without enlightenment.

Mostly we tend to neglect the practice of meditation in our daily life. That is why monks set an example. When you see a child, a patient, or a prisoner, you notice how they are unable to do anything by themselves; depending on others to attend to them, they can't change their future by any action in the outer world – except for meditation. That was the beginning. Having just finished my tuberculosis treatment and being in recovery from it, I decided to meditate nearly the whole day. Even when everything is taken from us, we still have this one last action available. That is why I started to meditate. I might be released after my twenty years' imprisonment but without meditation I cannot be released from the eternal life-cycle. In twenty years' time I might be released by those who have the keys to the door of the ward, and they are thus the owners of my freedom; but if I meditate, it is me who has the keys. I need to meditate upon all my past misdeeds and to conquer their effects in my future life. My real fear is of an endless life-cycle, of being born again, of dying again. Once we meditate upon that first fear, we get the right perspective on what our task is inside the prison walls as well.

I wanted to show the other political prisoners, and also the guards, how one can be just even while remaining within the ruling law. Moreover, it seemed to me that resistance within the prison wouldn't be of any use because as long as I was jailed, the military government could not be at ease. I never felt myself to be a victim; even though I was a prisoner I never felt under any authority. My premise was that nobody could hurt me; the only one who can hurt me is myself. That is why I tried to not betray myself. I was the one responsible for my thoughts and deeds – that was why I had always tried to do the right things, and think the right thoughts; I also tried not to hurt anyone else – including the guards and the officers – except when I needed to protect myself from being hurt.

In 1995 I contracted severe lung tuberculosis, and began suffering from a gynecological problem. I had 6 consecutive months of fever, and my body weight was down to 80 pounds. The medical officer in charge of the women's ward was very uncooperative when it came to treatment. When my health condition deteriorated, I was sent out to the general hospital, but was discharged from there after 12 hours without any treatment by request of the prison's medical and administrative authorities. As soon as I knew I was going back from the hospital to my cell without any treatment, I warned the staff that the consequences would be the responsibility of the prison authority, not mine. Then, soon after I was returned to my cell, the medical doctor on duty asked me to give up all of my own medicine.

I went on a hunger strike. I posed two demands: to give me back my medication, and to release me from the care of the ward's woman doctor, who had been both unjust and unprofessional as far as my condition was concerned. By this action I was not hurting anyone else. I was not hurting myself; rather, this was the only remaining way of protecting myself. The authorities were afraid that I would commit suicide, a crime against the system, while in reality they were about to commit murder. I found the only solution where dialogue was still possible. I showed them that if their intention was to keep me alive, they had to trust me – not the assigned doctor. Thus I showed myself in command of my own situation, and theirs – for unlike them, I really understood my true physical condition. My general thought was that it did not matter whose the intention was: if the intention was good, to protect life for example – in Buddhism we do not approve of suicide since it does not solve the task of freeing oneself—I must go along with it. The only thing to watch for was where the intention went wrong, where the misdeed or a crime could be committed. And as long as we recognize some good and some truth behind the actions of others, even if they are our executioners, we are able to do real justice and not commit injustice.

I didn't hate those who kept me in prison; I felt sorry for them. For I could always follow the route of justice while they could not: the key to their freedom was always in the hands of their superiors. In my case, after forty-five minutes of discussing my hunger strike and my treatment, they gave up everything. I had all of my medicines returned; I in turn gave up the hunger strike since all my demands were met. What I had done was simply point out what my demand was, why I made it, and how they could negotiate with me to solve this problem. At the end of that debate, one of my wardens said: "Thida, you are free, but we are not." At that moment I was standing right in front of my locked cell. I knocked on the door, showing that it was closed. "How do you mean, I'm free?" I asked. I knew what he meant, but wanted him to confess it. "You are free in your thoughts and words, but I'm the government's employee, I do not have that kind of freedom." This was equal to saying that it was I who obeyed the law and it was they who could not obey it; that it was I who was outside the cell and they who were inside, and even that it was I who was the jury and they the criminals.

I think that the problem of my country lies not only in the fact that we have an unjust government, but also in the fact that the religion of the people, their daily practice, is not at all based on what they claim it is—on Buddhist meditation and its attempt to liberate us. We do not have to be in prison cells to practice justice, that is, to be not committing crimes. Passive acceptance is not enough. We need to practice goodness, and to understand where evil comes from. Then what was happening to me in my cell would be happening to everybody in a country that has become a prison for a large proportion of its people. The government resembles wardens and a prison more than a citizen's representative. On my way out of jail, after I had been saved by many international organizations, and by the desire of the government to look just in the eyes of the whole world, I left a note of thanks to the military intelligence staff: "Thank you for giving me the opportunity to meditate twenty hours a day." I also thanked myself for taking advantage of the opportunity they gave me.

The Burmese value justice in their unjust nation. The majority, whether they are Buddhists or not, accepts the fact that every action has a reaction reflecting it. As the Burmese society is very small, and Buddhism and Buddha's teaching have spread among young people, most Burmese have generally heard of, and accept, the cause-effect theory. Therefore, as non-violent Theravada Buddhists, most of us are reluctant to take up any type of violent action, even against those who have treated us callously and cruelly. Since we accept that any cause will have an effect accordingly, we rarely want to react or act violently against anyone in order to prevent a similar effect upon us. The cause-and-effect natural law will make a doer suffer as he or she did to others, whether in near or far future, the present or a future life. That is our Buddhist understanding of fairness or justice. So, even if nobody would be punished by another, a wrongdoer could still suffer from his or her own past action. That is why, for Buddhists, justice can be achieved not only through the courts but also through this natural cause-and-effect process.

According to this theory, every action can produce a symmetrical reflection. The military believe for instance that they can obtain merit in exchange for their donations, so as to overcome the negative reflection of their wrongdoing, and donate a lot to Buddhist monks throughout their time in power. In fact, however, no reflection can be avoided, nor can anything be deducted from any reflection. Right and meritorious deeds will cause good reflection, while wrong and de-meriting deeds will cause negative reflection. Someone who has committed both meritorious and de-meriting deeds will not receive "a sum of all reflection," the total of the good subtracted from the bad, but rather will definitely bear both the good and the bad reflection.

So, could someone be saved by the strictly legal model of justice? Could something be faded out, undone by legal justice? According to the principle of natural justice, no-one is able to avoid the effect of her or his own action, her or his cause. But what of legal justice?! Nature is nature, and a human being is a human being. Nature makes natural law. So too human beings make legal justice. The Burmese do indeed worry about legal justice in Burma for now and for the future. Will military officials be put in front of a legal court one day, and made responsible for their wrongdoings and crimes? And even if they were accused in front of a court of law, would justice prevail for the civilians? I am also worried whether ordinary people would be able to practice justice under unjust conditions, to protect themselves. At the present moment, justice is still on the waiting list for the civilian population of Burma.

On the Images of Justice

Ksenia Golubovich

When people begin to talk of justice, I grow silent. Coming from
a childhood permeated and embittered by this grand theme,
having passed through an adolescence in which it was wholly
discarded – and now nearing my early middle-age – I face a difficult but timely requirement: how do I rediscover for myself the
idea of justice?

The Soviet Union as a country hurled an accusation in the
face of all mankind. Historical justice was finally to be done and
executed in this one part on the globe. The classes that had so
unjustly enjoyed the fruits of all human labour were wiped out
of existence, and the poor peasants could finally afford oranges,
as one of the old revolutionaries – who had spent 25 years in the
camps and still was a true believer in the system – used to say.
Yet when the historical accusers faced accusers of their own for
the crimes they had committed in the name of justice, this leading social theme was totally erased from people's minds, and em-
erged instead reformulated as the theme of freedom, completely
separated from the sense of "true measure" and "punishment
equal to one's deed." The *ethos of* raw individualism that characterized the initial post-Communist era did not admit "true measure,"
nor did it see itself as committing any crimes: it simply did what
it deemed necessary – no questions asked. As soon as you heard

someone mention the word "justice," you knew right away that the person "belonged politically to the 'undemocratic' wing." Russia may seem a simple country but, it has enormous historical experience when it comes to witnessing the rise and fall of big political issues, and seeing both ends meet in a full circle.

Circle or wheel: can this be the symbol of natural justice, bluntly glossed by W.H. Auden as "Those to whom evil is done do evil in return"? We could say that in this sense the history of the Soviet Union and its post-*perestroika* deconstruction is, too, an example of just such "return." Those in whose name the evil was done have experienced the return of justice upon them, while those who robbed them have in the process themselves experienced an appropriate justice, whether by killing or by being killed, or else by having to feed with bribes those higher up in their own criminal hierarchy or in the enormous state apparatus. The mechanism is only too familiar. And does not immigration into Western Europe, being the direct return of colonial politics, bear witness to the inevitability of historical debts and payments? Or the fact that the very same people whom the U.S. used to nurture and train against its enemies have now turned their weapons against their former mentor? If justice is a circle, then it is a full circle of guilt and accusation, of attempting to get one's share and of constant complaints for not getting it. In which case the circle of justice is, at its bottom, the round of injustices we perpetrate, and must tolerate in return. For if full and final justice is to be accomplished, and each is to get what he deserves, then in the end we shall all be exterminated. Sometimes one thinks that the atom bomb – as Stanley Kubrick so convincingly showed – is the central and final image of the world's justice. Our mutual tolerance of the injustices we commit against one another is our last resort against the Big Justice we all deserve. Not very appetizing. How on earth do we get from here to scales and a beautiful blind-folded woman with a sword – that emblematic image which has for such a long time haunted our classical imagination, and suddenly seems so... refreshing?

Was it not Plato – the first political thinker – who raised his voice against relevance and a fixed point of view in relation to truth? Yes, it may have taken the Sophists to name man as the measure of all things and to put the relativity of our judgment into focus. But was it not Plato who placed before the newly-discovered man a difficult task – the task of knowing himself? I know that I know nothing, said Socrates. Yet it was this famous method of not-knowing that ultimately laid the foundations for our procedures of evidence, of witnessing, and of the presumption of innocence. Furthermore, this method underlies the notion of gradations of guilt, because one cannot punish the "whole" human being for partial guilt. Only very simple societies impose death as the sole punishment for any and every transgression. Justice must be just in its every detail. It is an art of cutting and measuring, proportioning to the minutest stitch, like that of a tailor. (The connection between Western fashion and law – the measurement of decency and indecency – must be left to another day.)

The great machine of justice, its mighty chariot: this is another image one could turn to. We know we are only human; we do not know; we may be wrong; and this is precisely why we have to work so hard at justice. "I beseech you, in the bowels of Christ, think it possible you may be mistaken!" another less than appetizing historical character, Oliver Cromwell, once said. Such doubt forces us to focus on the idea of the value human life is allotted. Only societies which take human life very seriously, and consider its each individual extermination *as* extremely dramatic, even tragic (as much theatre, that is to say, as one can possibly bear) – only these societies take justice as their working mechanism. Was it not Plato who berated Athens for one unjust death – that of Socrates – turning it into an age old drama? Christianity, following the Athenian tragedy, brought centre-stage the mysticism of Jerusalem and an unjust court-case as the horrible precedent for centuries. Such justice does not *have the shape of* a wheel, or an atom bomb, or even a medieval skeleton with a scythe. What it does look like is a perfectly-proportioned human body with scales and a sword, eyes closed by a blindfold, one not serving any warring factions, nor competitive complaints.

It took Phidias' sculpture, Socrates' method, Rome's imposition of laws and roads, Jerusalem's historical feeling and messianic expectation, Egypt's ascetics, and the whole Christian era (with Aristotle preserved in the Arabic world, then brought back to the Christian) to work out the concept of justice we have today – the concept that *deems* it extremely problematic to take human life. I do not really think there is any other justice save this – except the atomic bomb, of course.

It took the flourishing of both East and West, North and South to create this concept, and to pose it at the core of the world's drama – and there is no way we can think it alien to anyone. The more any man or woman is seen as just a human being, the more *impartial* the law is, and the larger the part of the "whole human body" covered by its protective shield. Coming from a country of great literature – a literature which raised to its front concern the question of the "little" man, reduced, short-changed of his due, witness to the never-ending wheel of injustice, mutual complaint, and corrupted victory – I cannot say that Russia does not *know* about the "scales and the sword and the perfectly proportioned body" representative of the notion of justice we just talked about. Any more than I can say it of any other country. Everyone knows, as long as he or she chooses to "know thyself," i.e. chooses to doubt and think, to pay attention to what is going on. And we can be certain that the principle functions even when *the human being as such is not getting his or her due.* For in these cases the ancient mechanisms of bribery and corruption, vendetta and suppression will surely continue their work – promising people a lower compensation for their absent share. Justice is *the same as* a Human Being: it sticks its sword in the wheel, cuts clean, and so prevents the starting of yet another cycle. Remember how, after the signing of the unjust Versailles Treaty, the very people who pushed it through said: "This is not a peace treaty. It is a temporary armistice." Being far from naïve, they *knew* they were begetting a new war. Nor do I think the way the modern Balkan pie has been sliced up will solve anything for long. When decisions are made by siding with someone, the vicious circle begins its course again. I strongly believe that we needed the International Court at the Hague before – not after – the war, and that we should have brought the Balkan drama into the courtroom, not onto the battlefield, so as to bring into play every art of right proportioning we had at our disposal in order to avoid bloodshed.

Faced with two women at odds over a baby belonging to one of them, King Solomon made a just decision. Since it was impossible to prove whose the baby really was, he suggested slicing the baby in two. The real mother objected; the false one agreed. The one who wanted the baby to live even if it meant rejecting it was the true mother. This ancient riddle teaches us that real justice is not about splitting things up (like military loot). On the contrary, it is about knowing how to see where humans are being partial, and insisting they stick to the whole. Justice is a paradoxical art which should be taught alongside poetry, psychology, and philosophy. And the real basis of this art is human love, our love for each other, which Dante Alighieri (and Isaac Newton) so strongly believed to be the sole power that "moveth Suns and Planets."

If the image of a militant female seems too Victorian, heavy with bad associations, then at this late stage of civilization, perhaps, when it is not the essence of justice but its representations that lack universal character, we can try to choose something less burdened by symbolism. What image would I choose for justice today? The answer is, the same as Dostoyevsky once chose – a child, born naked and in want. For is it not only natural to give it shelter and warmth? It is as innocent of crime as the human condition can allow. Is it not only natural, too, that all injustices will show up for what they are in its presence? It attracts our love and care – no matter whose it is. There is no other creature capable of such suffering from the wars of egoism; and a happy child is the measure of things well tended. If Earth itself, this little old orb, be a symbol of our existence, then a child is the symbol of the Law that truly governs it. Was this not the intuition expressed by Stanley Kubrick in the final sequences of A Space Odyssey, and by his colleague Andrei Tarkovsky in his "more Russian" Solaris and Sacrifice?

AFTERWORD TO THE PAROS CONFERENCE

For some reason writing for people from so many different countries seemed to be pushing me (and not only me) to think of justice in terms of politics, international and domestic. Although in my essay, I tried to use the word more as a guiding principle and focusing on the well-known poetics of its main symbols (scales, woman, sword) – the real referent of everything I was thinking about was "politics." The idea that a developed concept of justice is aimed at cutting clean the cause, ending things right there, taking us to no future chain of consequences and effects, escaping the oscillations of blind revenge – that idea was mostly aimed at modern-day political issues. Yet suddenly, through the conversation with other writers from so many different countries, the concept began to "grow," building into a language of its own. The idea of "ending the circle" came very close to the Buddhist religious world view as expressed in the wonderful and touching account of Ma Thida of her days and labours in the Burmese prison. Deep within the core of the Buddhist meditation she opened up a space of true and just action, the domain of non-violent yet strict response, one that draws a sharp line between doing something without violating the other and mere passivity, a criminal acceptance of crime. Thus my previous concept of justice was amplified by Ma Thida's concept of freedom, lifted from the domain of the political to the domain of the spiritual. Justice is the practice of a free mind and a free will fighting for an open future (be it the future of one's historical self or one's ultimate future in the afterlife). It remains a practice of the spirit even when its actual application is reduced to the span of a four square meter prison cell, and when its subject-matter is brought to a seeming absurdity. Take Thida's story of "four mangoes" (which she insisted be returned to her parents if she herself couldn't have them). While in my essay I did eventually arrive at justice as the highest intellectual practice of humanity, its principal "idea" (as Plato puts it) thus leaving the domain of the political, I didn't think I would meet such concrete and enriching equation in another culture, a culture that has no swords and scales to represent the same concept, and which reminded me that freedom is the basic link between justice and us.

Another direction of the development of the idea awaited me in South Africa, in Tony Eprile's piece, which linked this idea to memory. It did escape me at first that to have justice in any way at all you need to have a memory of what happened, you must tell a story. I had altogether missed the act of narration which lies at the foundation of justice. Oblivion, not wanting to tell or speak, entered here into direct connection with the ways of injustice, at the same time reviving the old idea of True Speech as the core of a more archaic definition of poetry itself, of poetry at the heart of our moral universe and self-creation. What touched me most was the idea that justice is about trying to open a free space not only ahead of oneself but also behind, in what is to follow one. Stratis' memory of his heroic father "dying for nothing" because justice was not done, and his testimony to the final arrival of justice in Greece many years later was part of the same discussion for me. Only through admitting the Truth of what one did, or has done to oneself can one enter a new society, enter the future. This more "medicinal," "poetic" aspect of justice aims not at punishment but at change through narration, when the work of justice, its final sentence, lies in the symbolic (legal and personal) death of those identities we used to see as our own, and in our rebirth once we exposed ourselves to the judgement of others. Thus the new nation is born by immersion into one common Poem that will execute its healing powers over history, undoing, cleansing what has happened in the very act of commemorating it. This semi-utopian experiment of the Truth and Reconciliation Commission in South Africa, so close to psychoanalysis as well as to the Christian practice of confession, brought my mind back again to the inner potential of art, and to the new task of the story-telling in the modern world.

One last thing. There was a moment of surprise, of real eccentricity. During the discussion of the term *labasha* in Daniel Alarcón's deeply interesting essay, where the concept was used negatively, we found ourselves to be in favour of that archaic execution of justice without any legal procedures whatsoever, one which chooses its victim randomly, by some chance circumstance. A strange archaic sense, deciphered by those present at the symposium as saying "if something bad has occurred in the community, we are all guilty no matter who really did it, so let's trust the most innocent of us, in the shape of the most unconscious (the intoxicated child) to choose any of us to pay the debt to gods" – this scene suddenly struck a chord. My own essay, ending with an image of a child, suddenly acquired for me a somewhat sinister turn. Daniel Alarcón meant it only as a metaphor, so as to navigate his argument towards modern-day American politics, but this surprising pause at, and attention to, the archaic metaphor, convinced me that despite the discursive ideologies successfully fuelling our own texts, what we here really are close to, and perhaps drawn into, is the darker, more uncertain side of human experience, a side that will never fit into any of the concepts, even our own. Not for nothing was Antigone a recurrent symbol in the conversation. And the question of whether or not a person can rise up to practice justice in the dark hour of his own *labasha* was, it seems, the most crucial for all of us, for this was the question of the "hero," one that has haunted poets since time immemorial.

Odysseus Goes Home

Jeffrey Carson

PROLOGUE

Since 1970 my wife and I have lived year round on Paros. Not exiles, we are citizens of both Greece and the United States. We live here, not because we dislike our former home, but because on Paros we can be authentically ourselves. The home of place is weaker in Americans than in Europeans; my childhood suburban neighborhood might have been anywhere (luckily it was at the edge of New York City). But when we first looked long at the Aegean, from a terrace on Paros, we recognized it, and here we still are, gazing at azure, at foam froth, at island shapes of myth and history, still learning what we meant when we called it Homer's sea all those years ago.

I

Home is a chief theme in the *Odyssey*. All three main characters, King, Queen, and Prince, seek it and find it. Telemachos must undertake a risky circular journey from his mother's supervision, that takes in two of Hellas' loftiest kings, Helen-tamed Menelaos and venerable Nestor, and return a master in his father's palace. Penelope, the cleverest woman in ancient literature, must find a way to readmit, to the island palace she is in grave danger of losing to louts, an equal and balancing masculinity to her wily and

captivating femininity. And Odysseus is seven years inactive on
Calypso's somnolent isle, where he is served dainties by fetching
handmaids, lives resistless after years of strife, and has for bed-
mate a smitten goddess more beautiful than his human wife
could ever be, as he admits. Encountering nothing but effortless
pleasure, he longs for home, his real home. But

> Calypso in her cave constrain'd his stay
> With sweet, reluctant, amorous delay;

and what's a mere mortal to do, longing for the bed of his imperfect wife?

So Odysseus' voyage in the *Odyssey* is an escape from what is
wholly alien to his nature: Calypso's logy land, her cave that
reeks of drowsy poppies and lacks the salt tang of wild mountain
thyme. At the start of Book V Hermes, persuaded by hero-loving
Athena, has been sent by the gods to secure Odysseus' release
from Calypso at last; Homer's description of the messenger's
journey and of Calypso's home – Odysseus' prison – is an exquisite
set piece of nature writing, rare in Greek literature. We first
encounter the hero walking disconsolate along the alien seashore,
where constrained Calypso seeks him:

> The nymph, obedient to divine command,
> To seek Ulysses, paced along the sand,
> Him pensive on the lonely beach she found,
> With streaming eyes in briny torrents drown'd,
> And inly pining for his native shore;
> For now the soft enchantress pleased no more;
> For now, reluctant, and constrained by charms,
> Absent he lay in her desiring arms,
> In slumber wore the heavy night away,
> On rocks and shores consumed the tedious day;

There sate all desolate, and sighed alone,
With echoing sorrows made the mountains groan.
And roll'd his eyes o'er all the restless main,
Till, dimmed with rising grief, they streamed again.

Odysseus is a hero unlike his peers in battle, Achilles, Ajax, and Diomedes: they do not pace the shore alone, longing for their loving wives and children. Unlike him, they think almost entirely of glory, honor, their legacy of fame, their *kleos*. Odysseus, who hardly seems a bronze-age hero, pines for home. To get home, he is willing to brave the violent, unchartered sea in a rickety raft. If we feel lost, Odysseus Elytis says in "Ad Libitum," it is because we are "the other Odysseus/upon a raft/centuries now."

II

Mythology suggests that home has always been on Odysseus' turning mind. Unlike the other heroes, who move in with their richly dowered wives, Odysseus has brought his to his capital Ithaca, a poor island, unfit for horses, on the extreme edge of the civilized world. When Agamemnon's emissary, Palamedes, arrives to draft him for the Trojan war, the wily young king tries to evade it with a ruse, and ploughs the sandy shore near his infant son as if he were mad. In Troy, while the heroes fight duels and vaunt their reputations, he spies, takes practical measures, chats with grateful Helen in her love-nest, and hopes for home. When after the impious sack the royal Trojan women are distributed as prizes, he accepts aged Priam's aged Queen Hecuba for his trophy, and prudently leaves her behind, avoiding Agamemnon's vainglorious insult to his wife Clytemnestra when he returns to Mycenae with the lovely, silent princess Cassandra beside him on his groaning war chariot. Penelope is home, and home is everything.

Escaping the debilitating inanition of Calypso's paradise, he is again offered a home in Princess' Nausicaa's refulgent utopia, Phaeacia, where the men are fleet of foot and the women graceful dancers and grisly war over the horizon. Mythology, aware of his temptation, lets Odysseus marry Telemachos to her. He compares the royal girl to a golden palm he saw at Delos, and so we may fairly imagine his black ship sailing by our Paros, a mere fifteen miles from Leto's sacred rock.

Athena reports to the gathered gods that he yearns

> To see the smoke from his loved palace rise,
> While the dear isle in distant prospect lies

When foolish Agamemnon warns him in Hades not to trust a woman, he is polite to the great king, though Penelope is the only one he trusts. And when aided by Aeolus' fresh, following zephyr, contrary winds bound in a bag, he sees, as Tantalos sees fruit, home before him, in Homer's percipient exaggeration. Home is where he can be Odysseus, husband, father, man of action, man of thought, king. The meaning is, then, that home is where we can be ourselves most fully.

III

In a fine bit of irony, when in Book XIII Odysseus arrives on Ithaca at last, exhausted, asleep, tended, and is placed in an olive-shaded cave with his booty (such caves in Homer symbolize rebirth), on awakening he doesn't recognize where he is.

> Disconsolate he wanders on the coast,
> Sighs for his country, and laments again
> To the deaf rocks, and hoarse-resounding main.

We are only half way through the poem. For most of us the sea-faring adventures are the best part, but for Hellenes it is politics; for the same reason Dante stuffs traitors into Satan's Cyclopean maw.

One part of home is achieved. And when he meets his son, who resembles him, at loyal swineherd Eumaeus' hut, another precious part is in place.

Soon after he arrives at his own megaron in his beggar's rags, Penelope sends for him, to get news of the world. Homer, who is usually more complex than he seems, claims she does not recognize him before the suitors are defeated and she can set him a test. But does he mean this? As we have seen, Penelope is the cleverest and most observant of women. Is she really so captivated by a beggar as immediately to invite him into her chambers, where her personal maidservant Eurycleia, once his nurse, bathes him? When Eurycleia notices the childhood boar's tusk scar on his thigh, she cries out, and is shushed (many great heroes, e.g. Jason, Achilles, Perseus, have an imperfection in the left leg, as deference to the feminine). Penelope is quivering with awareness. Her conversation then becomes more intimate. She devises the ruse of the axes, which would be inappropriate did she not know him, and he agrees. Odysseus has made plans with his son; now he makes plans with his wife, likely spied upon by disloyal maidservants so that they dare not speak openly. If I am right, the next great piece of home, Penelope, is being set in place, to her joy. She insists that he sleep outside her bedroom door, a preparation. And she sets about inflaming the greedy passions of her suitors with her charm and beauty, partly to show her husband that she retains her erotic power, as he does his (every female in the book falls for him).

> Meanwhile Minerva with instinctive fires
> Thy soul, Penelope, from Heaven inspires;
> With flattering hopes the suitors to betray,

> And seem to meet, yet fly, the bridal day:
> Thy husband's wonder, and thy son's to raise;
> And crown the mother and the wife with praise.

When Telemachos reveals he is able to string his father's bow, and does not for the sake of strategy, he has completed his journey and is fully his father's son.

Penelope's ruse of the bed is a fitting conclusion to his reinstatement as family man. After the slaughter, she keeps her distance, though Telemachos wants them to embrace. But Odysseus understands her deliberate pace: they have not embraced for nearly twenty years. When she says she has moved the bed, his flaring anger proves to her that he is worthy of it, and is fully her husband. For he built the bed with his own hands from a living olive tree, and it is the center of their married life, and the silver flash of olive leaves lights it.

> But if o'erturn'd by rude, ungovern'd hands,
> Or still inviolate the olive stands,
> 'Tis thine, O queen, to say, and now impart,
> If fears remain, or doubts distract thy heart."

His reinstatement in his marriage bed, as it were in another olive-shaded cave of rebirth, causes Athena to lengthen their night two hours. And in between bouts of love he tells her his adventures, as he has never told another. As Aristophanes points out, a man and woman joined aright in love compose a whole, and to be whole is to be home. Were the epic a Romance, it would end here.

IV

But there are two more books, for the Greeks were, and are, a political people. Odysseus has killed, however justly, the sons of his kingdom's aristocratic families, and civil war ensues. He must again don his panoply. When he fights together with his father and son, and is granted victory by Athena's intervention, he is fully king again. To fulfill your proper communal rôle is to be home. Now he is father, son, husband, and ruler: a wise man of action who is home at last.

> "Descended from the gods! Ulysses, cease;
>   Offend not Jove: obey, and give the peace."

This is as far as it is possible to come from Calypso's dreary bower.

V

The Classical Greeks, dazed by the glamour of Achilles, saw Odysseus as sly and guileful, and not a man who desperately wants to go home. Dante, exiled from home, a descendant of the Trojans who became Romans, sees him in Canto XXVI as hubristic, but also full of Renaissance individuality. Ulysses' sin, councilor of fraud in war, doesn't interest Dante (he also doesn't quite accept the sinfulness of Paola and Francesca, of Brunetto Latini, or of the unbaptized). His Ulysses expresses Dante's own intellectual restlessness, and is a proto-Renaissance man.

> Nothing – not sweetness of son, nor piety
> To an aging father, not the promised love
> That would have brought joy to Penelope –
> Could overcome in me a burning wish
> To experience the entire world
> And learn of human vices and of worth.

For Dante, exile meant he could not engage actively in the politics of his polis, his home, that continues to fill his thought. But he would not return home unless all charges were formally dropped, and the Florentines still send oil to his tomb's lamp in Ravenna.

Ugo Foscolo, who was born in Zakynthos, an island in Odysseus' kingdom, was also an exile, owing to his politics of liberation and his roving eye for women. In his sonnet "To Zakynthos," he envies Odysseus his success:

> Ulysses, beautiful with bane and fame,
> Returned to kiss his rocky Ithaca.

He feared a foreign grave, for which rhyme was scant compensation. For Foscolo your land is your mother, in the archaic circularity of womb and tomb.

Contrary anxieties frightened Tennyson; lacking adventurousness, fearful and uxorious, he stayed home. Atremble at mutability, he assigns his indomitable Ulysses an impossible last voyage, to discover the anti-home of death. However you explore the world, worries Tennyson, the world remains unknown.

> How dull it is to pause, to make an end,
> To rust unburnish'd, not to shine in use!

The familiar is an inadequate home for the timorous.

Cavafy, the first poet anywhere to write in the modern style, after a childhood in Constantinople and London (English was the language of his education), spent most of his life in provincial Alexandria, which he rarely left. He cynically quipped, not untruthfully "Where could I live better? Under me is a house of ill repute, which caters to the needs of the flesh. Over there is a church, where sins are forgiven. And beyond is the hospital, where we die." Believing in nothing but a dispersed Hellenism, he redefined home in his "Ithaca":

But you must always keep Ithaca in mind.
The arrival there is your predestination.
Yet do not by any means hasten your voyage.
Let it best endure for many years,
    until grown old at length you anchor at your island
    rich with all you have acquired on the way.

For Cavafy, home is the place whence your mind can soar.

Nikos Kazantzakis wrote an epic longer than Homer's about the hero. An extremely restless man himself, he could not imagine Homer's home, where you seek to stay, whither you strive to return (though even Homer assigns him another journey). His Odysseus says, "My soul, your voyages have been to your native land." A Bergsonian vitalist, he thinks like Cavafy that the voyage is the meaning, and like Tennyson he thinks that death is its ultimate goal, which his Odysseus embraces.

Penelope's olivewood bed means little to these poets. But Joyce thinks Homer got it right: "At rest relatively to themselves and to each other. In motion being each and both carried westward, forward and rereward respectively, by the proper perpetual motion of the earth through everchanging tracks of neverchanging space."

EPILOGUE

As a slow caïque took us south past Delos,
The sea transparent and inscrutable
To signify what god is out of sight,
A pair of dolphins suddenly finned out
Between us and the sunken ancient harbor
Whence boats would ferry the dying and the birthing
To Rheneia opposite for a Sister's care;

Their blue backs shedding sudden silver, they
Stayed with us as we angled through the strait:
We had our glimpse – it's all that we may get
And blue enough to say: "Perfection is here
Also; for a moment we were home,
And spoke the fearsome language faultlessly."

NOTES ON THE TRANSLATIONS

Homer's lines were translated by Alexander Pope; Elytis' and
Foscolo's by Jeffrey Carson; Dante's by Louis Biancolli; Cavafy's
and Kazantzakis' by Kimon Friar.

Home/lands

NICK PAPANDREOU

Alex, a young Iranian, was arrested nine years ago by the "religious police" of Iran on charges of homosexuality. His incarceration lasted for forty-five days, and included all sorts of torture (beating his feet, rape). Homosexuality in Iran is considered a crime punishable by death. Twice he was led in front of the firing squad. Allowed to attend his mother's funeral, he succeeded in escaping to Turkey, and then on to Greece. Once in Greece, he was tested by the Greek Medical Center for Torture, which certified his allegations. He claimed he had a right to be allowed into Greece on the grounds that he was a political refugee and required asylum. The Ministry of Public Order said no. It worried that accepting him would open up a window and create a new category of political refugee: being gay. Gaydom as freedom. Gaydom as a category of abuse.

Another Alex, Alex Meshiesvili, son of a single Russian mother living in the small town of Veria in northern Greece, is far more famous. He allegedly witnessed a child pornography ring run by traffickers of human beings, in the import-export business of people. They killed him to cover their tracks. The pictures of him that dominated the news in 2006 reveal a shy blonde boy with glasses, crooked teeth, reeking of adolescent awkwardness that renders him harmless, a "good" foreigner. He was eleven when he disappeared. His mother has appeared repeatedly on Greek television requesting help to find him or his body. She speaks Greek with an accent familiar to Greeks by now, the Slavic one. At first, she failed to report her son's absence because of fear of deportation. Now she is so famous nobody dares touch her or bring up the question of her "papers." Questions about whether this could have happened to a "true Greek boy" are part of the subtext, never mentioned openly, but always there. Would the traffickers have dared execute a full-fledged citizen with Greek parents or was it easier to get away with this little boy, a weaker version of the full citizen? Is Alex of Greek descent, perhaps? Who after all is a "true Greek?" Should non-Greek students be allowed to carry the Greek flag at student parades celebrating wars against Turkey and Germany?

To get to Corinth from Athens you have to drive by the shipyard town of Elefsina. Smoke stacks, cement factories, and hundreds and hundreds of ships make up this town. A homeless old man with a grizzled face named Pharmakis once lived there. For a hat he wore his coat. You could find him in the parks, hanging around sites under construction, or along the shore. His sole occupation was to search for ancient bits of sculpture. Elefsina used to be a major port in ancient times, and the relics in the earth are abundant. When he found a piece—a statuette, a coin, a bit of an urn, an old olive press, he would dust the item with a small brush. The smaller pieces he carted to the museum yard. The large pieces he piled up in an empty space nearby. He was the keeper of the stones. When archeological sites were covered up by cement, he wore a black armband for weeks. When he died, the few locals who attended his funeral called him "a true Greek."

An Albanian hijacked a bus a few years ago, requesting money to "get his life back in order." The bus drove along the highway towards Albania, along with seven other passengers. It was stopped at the Greek border. Reality TV. The man insisted on crossing the border. When he arrived in Albania, despite Greek entreaties, he was executed by the Albanian police. A Greek was also killed. The incident inspired a Greek movie, The Hostage, which did poorly in theaters but quite well on the festival circuit.

Most European countries don't grant asylum just because the applicant is a homosexual. In 2003, "Alex," the Iranian who had been living in Greece with his Greek boyfriend Phoebus, made a second request for political asylum. This too was rejected by the Ministry of Public Order. By that time, Alex spoke Greek quite fluently. He was pretty much a free man, although a death sentence seemed to be hanging over his head in his own country.

A hundred thousand Muslims live in Thrace, next to the Turkish border. Some of them call Turkey their home. None of them want to live there, however. They prefer their "special status" in Greece. They don't like the law that obliges all Greek citizens to attend school up until the age of fourteen, which means their Muslim girls have to attend as well, instead of getting married.

This being the age of the Internet, little Alex's mother, Natela Itsouentse, with help from local organizations, set up the FIND ALEX website:

A MYSTERIOUS DISAPPEARANCE FROM THE CEN-
TRAL STREET OF THE TOWN OF VERIA OCCURRED AT
7 O'CLOCK IN THE EVENING. FIVE JUVENILES CON-
FESSED TO HIS MURDER. THREE SUBSEQUENTLY
RETRACTED THEIR CONFESSION. TWO CONTINUE TO
CONFESS TO MURDER AND ALSO IMPLICATE THREE
ADULTS WHO HELPED THEM. DESPITE ALL THIS, THE
POLICE ARE INCAPABLE OF SOLVING THE CASE, WHILE AT
THE SAME TIME OBSTINATELY REFUSING TO SEARCH FOR
THE BODY OF OUR SON. ALL THIS IS HAPPENING IN
A COUNTRY WHICH IS A MEMBER OF THE E.U.! WELCOME
TO WONDERLAND!

The Socialist party, heading up the opposition in the Parliament,
is led by a Greek who was born in Minnesota in 1952, grew up
in the States until he was in his mid-twenties, and worked as an
immigrant worker in Sweden for a few years. His proposal for
citizenship is simple: anyone born in Greece is automatically
a Greek and by extension a European citizen, with all rights
and privileges that accrue. Any person who attends three years
or more of elementary school in the Greek school system is
automatically eligible to be a citizen. Today you must prove that
you have lived (legally) in Greece for a minimum of ten years,
and even then the result is not certain. The Socialist party has
the most immigrants and regularly allows them to vote in its
primaries and referenda. Look at its national convention roster,
and you'll see names from across the globe. When George enters
emigrant's clubs, he is called "our man in the Parliament."

The most powerful union of immigrants is the Filipino one.
They know their rights, and they demand them. Middle and
upper-class Greek families seem unable to do without "Filipino
help." "Do you have a Filipino in your home? Isn't she just the

best?" is a typical point made at an upper-class dinner party in Athens. I can imagine similar discussions across the developed world. "Omigod, the Georgians? Educated but lazy. Sri Lankans? Sheer heaven." A generation of young Greeks speaks Greek, English, Filipino, Russian, Albanian, and Kurdish.

Marwan Akkawi, a Syrian filmmaker who fled Lebanon in 1975, has two kids born and raised in Greece. He has lived and worked here thirty plus years. He is still not a Greek citizen. His multiple applications for citizenship have been rejected because he once spoke out against the application process on television. Some bureaucrat, under orders from above, then put him on a blacklist as a "possible Palestinian terrorist." Getting on that list is easy. Getting off is impossible. His kids now have citizenship. They are thinking of "adopting" him as their father, a circuitous route of getting him automatic Greek citizenship. A real father converted to false fatherhood.

Aegean Coast Guard sailors dress up like cousins of Rambo. They prefer black short-sleeved T-shirts, with the Hellenic Coast Guard logo across their backs, tight-fitting sun-glasses, cropped hair, khaki military pants, pistols and knives at their hips. Machine guns atop the fore and aft of the boat give it a look of a pending shootout. They are working class men who bench-press in their free hours and swagger knowingly when they stop the rich yachts of rich Greeks. They are usually invited aboard for a beer. They believe they run the Aegean. They are responsible for halting the flow of illegal immigrants from Turkey. They have been told to treat them well, the whole world is watching. The Greek ethos of *philoxenia* still manages to surface, even among the Rambo set. And they often go out of their way to save men

thrown overboard in the tempestuous Aegean, rough looks
notwithstanding.

On stormy days bodies of aspiring immigrants wash up on the
shores of the easternmost Greek islands. Nobody knows their
names, their home, their place of origin, their customs. Are they
sent "back" or buried in Greece?

Refugee camps now exist near traditional Greek villages on
Kos, Lesvos, and Chios, large islands that are a stone's throw
from mainland Turkey. The locals usually do what they can
with their own supplies to clothe and feed the newcomers.
Buildings have been constructed for them. For the duration,
they are considered stateless, nameless, homeless. Each refugee
is processed and his reasons for emigrating ticked off on the E.U.
chart of allowable reasons to live here.

The ancient port of Lavrion, to the southeast of Athens, hosts
a major refugee center. It is populated mainly by Kurds fleeing
Iraq and Turkey. From the rent-free apartments fly flags with the
Communist Party emblem. There were also many pictures of
Ocalan, the Kurdish PKK leader now in jail in Turkey, the same
jail that Trotsky sat in many decades ago. The Turks want to
execute Ocalan. They also want to be part of the E.C. They aren't
sure whether to go East or West.

The recently arrived Russian mafia drive mainly black
Mercedes-Benz. They live primarily in Glyfada. That's where the
Americans used to live when the Sixth Fleet was docked here.

My Greek-British nephew, when still a kid, attended a camp
for Palestinian and Israeli children called Seeds of Peace, in
Maine. When he turned 18, rather than attend Boston College
as expected, he fled America and moved his butt to Norway,
because Norway, he said, was the closest thing in the world to
Socialism. Now 27, he lives on the island of Crete, where he

wants to create something in agro-tourism, make money, and save the environment at the same time.

Picking olives with me on our small plot of land in Corinth last November were five Greeks and three Albanians. When I saw one Albanian cross himself I asked him if he was Christian. "Yes," he said, "and I am your brother. We are all Greeks." A Greek woman working the tree kept muttering under breath, "I hate Albanians. I hate Muslims. They should go back to Albania. They are pretending to be Greek. They don't speak Greek, not really."

The Pakistanis have their own rural community in the ancient town of Marathon, thirty kilometers from Athens. They tend the lush land there and grow mainly vegetables. They take their kids to school. A teacher there told me about a run-in with one of the fathers. She gave one Pakistani student a low grade, and the father came to school. When he saw the teacher was a female, he went into a rage. He showed her his son's report card and then tore it up in her face. "A woman cannot grade my son. Only Allah can grade him!"

How is a country represented abroad? By its famous home-growns: Maria Callas, Aristotle Onassis. The musician otherwise known as Vangelis.

By its immigrants, or children thereof: Jennifer Anniston. George Michael. Spiro Agnew. Pap(anikolaou) smear. There is something chauvinistic in the home country's need to show off its successful emigrants and their descendents. There is something else in it too, fundamentally human.

On the beach last year, on the small island of Aegina, a man in his late forties, his hair held back in a pony tail, asked a little boy of about six a provocative question. "Little boy, you know what? Are you Turkish?" The boy stared back, eyes full of fire. "Turkish? Just the opposite! I am Greek!"

It seems the opposite of Greece is Turkey. Just as at one point a hippie in the U.S. was, to an "enemy" construction worker, supposed to "go back to Russia!" The opposite of a Frenchman, a German; of a Brit, a Frenchman. India—Pakistan. Ethiopia—Eritrea. It depends on which war has gone on, and where. Which ethnicity killed your prime-minister.

The small province of Kosovo was recently pronounced a country by the powers-that-be. In the heart of the Balkans, the large powers have created a new country, one based solely on ethnicity, Muslim ethnicity no less. For most people living in the region, this is a bad sign. One more border to cross, one more bureaucracy to fight. For the citizens of Kosovo, great happiness.

How is a country represented abroad?

Souvlaki, gyro, moussaka. Tzatziki, bouzouki, feta.

Cavafy, Elytis, Ritsos, Zorba.

In Porto Heli, a summer resort in the Peloponnesus, the local women have formed an association to win their husbands back from the imported females that dance at the Babylon Club. The "imports" are mainly from Eastern Europe. "Women against Imports," they had thought of calling it, until one of them pointed out that it sounded too much like an anti-globalization movement, and they weren't against that, were they? Their association remained untitled. Titled or not, they did succeed in getting at least a few husbands back.

Go to the Church of Saint Constantine, in the heart of Athens. On any given weekday you will see a motley crew of women in their forties and fifties, dressed in dull colors, all of them Eastern European, talking excitedly, exchanging stories. Every now and then someone walks up to them, and they go off to one corner to speak. That person is a middleman, an emissary. The women are too old to entice Greek men into marriage – a sure way of getting a green card and eventual citizenship. Yet there are many old widowers, Greek men in their seventies and their eighties, who are looking for companionship in their final years. They send their paid emissary, something like a real estate agent, to the church of Saint Constantine, and he/she bargains with the women: stay with my old man for three years, and he will marry you and leave you half his will. No, I'll do two years, but let's start with the citizenship papers. Screw the will. What's in his will again? The haggling goes on. A deal is struck. The women are engaged in a very odd form of slavery. Marriage into cleaning-woman-dom. All in order to get a European passport and the benefits that accrue from that. And maybe half the will.

The Greeks who were forcibly removed from Turkey in the 1920s to Greece and the Turks living in Greece who were sent to Turkey are called "exchangeables." In Greece they are known as Pontians, from the Pontos. In Turkey they are known as Christian Turks, though they are Muslim. Their grandchildren in Turkey speak a bastardized Greek. A few of the exchangables still survive, only women (women outlive men), grand old dames in their early hundreds. "I'm an exchangeable," one of them said on a recent television interview. "I still remember what happened. Some call it genocide. Others call it 'The Wars.' I don't care what you call it. Won't bring back my home or my family. I'm exchangeable."

Liturgy: A Meditation on the Mississippi Gulf Coast

NATASHA TRETHEWEY

> Where you came from is gone. Where you thought you were
> going to never was there. And where you are is
> no good unless you can get away from it.
> FLANNERY O'CONNOR

When I think of the landscape of my home, Gulfport, Mississippi, what comes to mind first is the small tugboat anchored on land just across from the beach. In 1969, during Hurricane Camille, it washed ashore, crossing the highway and landing in an open lot. Not long after, someone renamed it the USS *Hurricane Camille* and turned it into a souvenir shop – a reminder of the storm, and a place to buy trinkets, the kitschy talismans of memory. It was still standing, in the same place, after Katrina – all around it destruction, the name of one storm emblazoned on its side in the midst of another. An ironic marker of an event in history, it stands as monument to my earliest recollections of the place to which I am native. Setting out to contemplate the idea of home and my relationship to my homeland, I am struck by how both are underscored by feelings of longing and nostalgia, as well as a kind of psychological exile rooted in historical erasure, and the ever-present possibility of disaster, like the two storms – Hurricanes Camille (1969) and Katrina (2005) – book-ending my past and my present.

Alongside the USS *Hurricane Camille* – the morning after Hurricane Katrina – hundreds of live oaks also stood among the rubble along the Mississippi Gulf Coast. They held in their branches a car, a boat, pages torn from books, furniture. A few people who managed to climb out of windows had clung to them for survival as the waters rose. These ancient trees, some as many as 500 years old, remain as monuments not only to the storm but to something beyond Katrina as well: stripped of leaves, haggard, twisted and leaning, the trees suggest a narrative of survival and resilience. In the past two and a half years, as the leaves have begun to return, the trees seem a monument to the very idea of recovery.

Such natural monuments remind us of the presence of the past, our connection to it. Their ongoing presence suggests continuity, a vision into a future still anchored by a would-be neutral object of the past. Man-made monuments tell a different story. Never neutral, they tend to represent the narratives and memories of those citizens with the political power and money to construct them. Everywhere such monuments serve to inscribe a particular narrative onto the landscape while – often – at the same time subjugating or erasing others, telling only part of the story. On the wall of a Civil War fort on the barrier island just off the coast of my hometown, for example, a plaque lists the names of the Confederate soldiers imprisoned there, yet no mention is made of the Louisiana Native Guards – the first officially-sanctioned regiment of African-American Union soldiers who manned the fort and guarded those prisoners. According to historian Eric Foner, "Of the hundreds of Civil War monuments North and South, only a handful depict the 200,000 African-Americans who fought for the Union." This is only one example of our nation's collective forgetting, and it serves to fill me with a sense of psychological exile as this proud story of my people goes nearly unacknowledged in so many places around the country and in my homeland. With such erasures commonplace on the landscape, it is no wonder that citizens of the Mississippi Gulf Coast are concerned with historical memory. And it is no wonder that the struggle for the national memory of the events in New Orleans – particularly the government's response in the days after the levees broke–is a contentious one. Political contests over the public memory of historical events under-gird the dedication of particular sites, the objects constructed, funds allocated, and the story that is to be told. These contests, rooted in power and money, under-gird the direction of rebuilding efforts as well—how the past will be remembered, what narrative will be inscribed by the rebuilding.

All along the coast evidence of rebuilding marks the wild, devastated landscape. A little over a year ago much debris still littered the ground: crumbled buildings, great piles of concrete and rebar twisted into strange shapes, bridges lifting a path to nowhere. At the rusted shell of the former public library a lone light fixture hung above what was the entry to the stacks, a stairway spiraled up to the sagging roof. Vacant lots broadcast one message—AVAILABLE—on sign after sign. Even now there are houses still bearing the markings of the officials who checked each dwelling for victims. It's an odd hieroglyphics—an X with symbols in each of the four planes, the number at the bottom a crude marker for dead. Not far away, new condominium developments rise above the shoreline, next to the remains of a gas station, its single overhang, the concrete stripped or gouged, revealing the steel frame, like bones, underneath. Here and there a sign of what's still to come: "South Beach" and "Beachfront living only better."

Still other evidence abounds of how slow rebuilding can be. Even now there are whole communities of FEMA trailers all along the beach road, the highway, the neighborhoods farther inland—nearly 10,000 of them still, many of them laden with formaldehyde. From a distance they seem, instead, the above-ground tombs of New Orleans' famed cemeteries: white, orderly rows bearing the weight of remembrance each time we see them.

People carry with them the blueprints of memory for a place. It is not uncommon to hear directions given in terms of landmarks that are no longer there: "turn right at the corner where the fruit stand used to be," or "across the street from the lot where Miss Mary used to live." There are no recognizable landmarks along the coast anymore, no way to get my bearings, no way to feel at home, familiar with the landscape. In time, the landmarks of destruction and rebuilding will overlap and intersect the memory of what was there – narrative and meta-narrative – the pentimento of the former landscape shown only through the shifting memories of the people who carry it with them.

Some time ago – before the storm – my grandmother and I were shopping in Gulfport, and we met a friend of hers, shopping with her granddaughter, too. The woman introduced the girl to us, saying her nickname, then quickly adding the child's given name. My grandmother, a proud woman – not to be outdone – replied, "Well, Tasha's name is really Nostalgia," drawing the syllables out to make the name seem more exotic. I was embarrassed and immediately corrected her – not anticipating that the guilt I'd feel later could be worse than my initial chagrin. Perhaps she was trying to say Natalya, the formal version, in Russian, to which Natasha is the diminutive. At both names' Latin root: the idea of nativity, of the birthday of Christ. They share a prefix with words like natal, national, and native. I write what I have been given to write, Phil Levine has said. I've been given to thinking that it's my national duty, my native duty, to keep the memory of my Gulf Coast as talisman against the uncertain future. But my grandmother's misnomer is compelling, too; she was onto something when she called me out with it.

I think of Hegel: "When we turn to survey the past, the first thing we see is nothing but ruins." The first thing we see. The fears for the future, expressed by the people I talk to on the Coast, are driven by the very real landscape of ruin, and by environmental and economic realities associated with development, but they are driven by nostalgia too. When we begin to imagine a future in which the places of our past no longer exist, we see *ruin*. Perhaps this is nowhere more evident than in my own relationship to the memory of my home.

Everywhere I go during my journey back home, I feel the urge to weep not only for the residents of the Coast, but also for my former self: the destroyed public library is my past – is *me*, as a girl, sitting on the floor, reading between the stacks. Empty, debris-strewn downtown Gulfport is *me* at the Woolworth's lunch counter – early 1970s – with my grandmother; is *me* listening to the sounds of shoes striking the polished tile floor of Hancock Bank, holding my grandmother's hand, waiting for candy from the teller behind her wicket; *me* riding the elevator of the J.M. Salloum Building – the same elevator my grandmother operated in the thirties; *me* waiting in line at the Rialto movie theatre – gone for more years now than I can remember – where my mother also stood in line, at the back door, for the *peanut gallery*, the black section; where my grandmother, still a girl, went on days designated *colored only*, clutching the coins she earned selling crabs; is *me* staring at my reflection in the glass at J.C. Penney's as my mother calls, again and again, my name. I hear it distantly, as through water or buffeted by wind: Nostalgia.

Names are talismans of memory too – *Katrina, Camille*. Perhaps this is why we name our storms.

When Camille hit in 1969, I was three years old. Across the street from my grandmother's house, the storm tore the roof off the Mount Olive Baptist Church. A religious woman, she believed the Lord had spared her home – damaging, instead, the large red-brick building and many of the things inside – and thus compelling her to more devotion. During renovation, the church got a new interior: deep red carpet and red velvet draperies for the baptismal font – made by my grandmother, her liturgy to God's House. In went a new organ, and a marble altar bearing the words Do This In Remembrance Of Me. As a child, I was frightened by these words, the object – a long rectangle, like a casket – upon which they were inscribed; I believed quite literally that the marble box held a body. Such is the power of monumental objects to hold within them the weight of remembrance.

And yet, I spent so little time in the church when I was growing up that it surprises me now that so much of my thinking comes to me in the language of religious ceremony. But then, when I look up the word "liturgy," I find that in the original Greek it meant, simply, one's public duty, service to the state undertaken by a citizen.

I am not a religious woman. This is my liturgy:

Liturgy to the Mississippi Gulf Coast

To the security guard staring at the Gulf
thinking of bodies washed away from the coast,
    plugging her ears
against the bells and sirens – sound of alarm –
    the gaming floor on the Coast;

To Billy Scarpetta, waiting tables on the Coast, staring
    at the Gulf
thinking of water rising, thinking of New Orleans,
    thinking of cleansing the Coast;

To the woman dreaming of returning to the Coast,
    thinking of water rising,
her daughter's grave, my mother's grave – underwater –
    on the Coast;

To Miss Mary, somewhere;

To the displaced, living in trailers along the coast, beside
    the highway,
in vacant lots and open fields; to everyone who stayed
    on the Coast,
who came back—or cannot—to the Coast;

To those who died on the Coast.

This is a memory of the Coast: to each his own
recollections, her reclamations, their
restorations, the return of the Coast.

This is a time capsule for the Coast: words of the people
—*don't forget us*—
the sound of wind, waves, the silence of graves,
the muffled voice of history, bull-dozed and buried
under sand poured on the eroding coast,
the concrete slabs of rebuilding the Coast.

This is a love letter to the Gulf Coast, a praise song, a dirge,
invocation and benediction, a requiem for the Gulf Coast.

This cannot rebuild the Coast; it is an indictment,
    a complaint,
my logos—argument and discourse—with the Coast.

This is my *nostos*—my pilgrimage to the Coast, my memory,
    my reckoning—

native daughter: I am the Gulf Coast.

Nine months after Katrina, I went home for the first time. Driving down Highway 49, after passing my grandmother's house, I went straight to the cemetery where my mother is buried. It was more ragged than usual – the sandy plots overgrown with weeds. The fence around it was still up, so I counted the entrances until I reached the fourth one that opened onto the gravel road where I knew I'd find her. I searched first for the large, misshapen shrub that had always showed me to her grave, and found it gone. My own negligence had revisited me, and I stood there foolishly, a woman who'd never erected a monument on her mother's grave. I walked in circles, stooping to push back grass and weeds until I found the concrete border that marked the plots of my ancestors. It was nearly overtaken, nearly sunken beneath the dirt and grass. How foolish of me to think of monuments and memory, of the politics of inscribing the landscape with narratives of remembrance, as I stood looking at my mother's near-vanished grave in the post-Katrina landscape to which I'd brought my heavy bag of nostalgia. I see now that remembrance is an individual duty as well – a duty native to us as citizens, as daughters and sons. Private liturgy: I vow to put a stone here, emblazoned with her name.

Not far from the cemetery, I wandered to the vacant lot where a church had been. Debris still littered the grass. Everywhere there were pages torn from hymnals, Bibles, psalms pressed into the grass as if they were cemented there. I bent close, trying to read one; to someone driving by along the beach, I must have looked like a woman praying.

Ain't Got No Home in this World Anymore: Notes on a Son's Homecoming

DAVID ST. JOHN

Some years ago I was asked by W.T. Pfefferle to write an introduction for his book, *The Poetry of Place*, a collection of interviews he'd conducted with American poets about the importance of place and local landscape in their poetry. In thinking of this essay, I re-read that introduction and came upon this passage that I had written then:

> We live in a world that is constantly in movement, perpetually fragmenting and re-assembling itself. Those places from which we come and those to which we've moved provide the ground against which the figures of our lives themselves move, change, depart. Poetry is forever looking to discover and then describe what we mean by a sense of "home." Is such a place located in an actual place, in the imagination, in albums of memory, or in some combination of them all? From the time we are young, we all fear that loss of home, of place, of belonging... [We all] know that the poetry of the human heart and the living mind always seeks residence in the available landscapes of the lived world. The poetry of American solace is the poetry of place.

Often, the summoning of place is an almost incantatory act against loss. In the same way that we tell stories of those who have died as an attempt in some measure to keep them alive, so do many poets tell—in their poems—the stories of landscapes they fear may be lost to memory or to progress or to any of those many erasures we gather under the rubric of "time." So, too, we recognize the intrinsic social and political natures of these poems of place, however personal they may at first seem...

Today, it is a soft April morning here in Venice Beach where I make my home. Looking out the long window in front of my desk, I can see the newly dense garden outside, the lavender stalks exploding, the widening bells of the trumpet vine eager to make some noise about the spring. Hanging in long clusters along the arbor trellis, the wisteria is shaking its soft violet blossoms along with the breezes that have been uncurling off the ocean all morning, as the early tides build just a few blocks away.

My son, who is visiting me, is still asleep after his long train and bus ride from my mother's house up in the San Joaquin Valley of California, in Fresno (the city where I was born). It is a house that my mother designed and had built, a house where I lived from the time I was six until eighteen. Last night, my son, who is also named David, reminded me that my house in Venice Beach is the place where I have lived longer than any other in my life. I was startled to realize that he was right, that I had moved here over fourteen years ago when my daughter Vivienne, David's half-sister, was only a few months old. We began talking about the fact that it was almost fourteen years to the month that, four days after graduating from the University of Southern California, the university where I teach, David boarded an airplane to return to Tokyo, to make a life, to find a life, in a city where he had already lived for two of his five years as an undergraduate in college.

As a young man, David had always been enviably adept at languages. He'd studied Vietnamese, Mandarin Chinese, and Russian as a teenager. At the University of Southern California his major area of study was Japanese. He'd learned Japanese so quickly and so proficiently that the department of East Asian Studies allowed him to go abroad and study at Waseda University as a sophomore, after only one year of work at USC. He returned to Los Angeles and USC for the next year but was soon back in Japan again for yet another year of study before finally coming home to Los Angeles to complete his degree.

My photos of him in his graduation robes holding Vivienne in the brilliant sunlight of May, 1994, became a reminder to me of the moment my son stepped from the shore of one life in America to the shore of a new life in Japan. David had always loved traveling to those places in Southeast Asia that fascinated him—Thailand, Indonesia, all of the islands in the Ring of Fire. While traveling, he designed his own tattoo of a dragon holding the globe of the world in its talons, to be etched onto his bicep by Jimmy Wong, a renowned tattoo artist in Bangkok. It always seemed to me his proclamation of holding the world in his own talons, his own capable hands. David had always felt comfortable traveling, taking his home with him in his backpack, in his mind, and carried along by his body. A body-builder since his teenage years, he was confident of his physical place in the world, of his ability to respond to any of the physical demands or threats his travels might present.

Perhaps here is the place to say that David himself lived from the time he was very young with the reality of having come from what is called a "broken" home, a home which broke into two pieces as the result of a divorce. He lived with his mother and his younger half-brother, Andrew, for some years in Fresno, where my parents' house (and my childhood home) remained a centerpiece of stability and continuity for the boys. Then, they moved to Minnesota, where David lived until his senior year of high school, when he returned to Fresno to live with my parents. During those years he would spend time with me in Baltimore, where I was teaching at Johns Hopkins University, and later, in Southern California – Venice – after I'd moved there to teach at USC, the place he would also move to begin his college education.

Yet I'd always felt that David's sense of "home" seemed consistently – and admirably – portable, fluid, attendant less to a particular place than to the weather systems of his being and his tireless curiosity. His urge to travel, to see something he'd never seen, to explore what was unknown, wasn't simply that of a restless and reckless young man (though he may have been both). Like any young person "on the road," he was, of course, enacting an important coming of age drama; but I believe he found that travel in some way – or many ways – suited his temperament, suited his physical, emotional, and psychological rhythms. I know this to be true because, in him, I recognized all of these same characteristics that I'd first found in myself as a young man as well. He was the embodied mirror of that calm I had always felt while traveling, that peace that comes with one's movement across cultures and borders, that consoling sense of the world's expanse and its infinite varieties of experience.

And so, after graduating from college, David had gone to Japan to make a life. He founded an English Language School and then moved into advertising, writing copy in both Japanese and English, working as the art director on some campaigns as well. He edited a magazine for teens published by Sony. He helped design the first Citibank website for Southeast Asia. He met and married a beautiful young Japanese woman who was a competitive ballroom dancer, a woman whose life seemed to have been lifted intact from the great Japanese film, *Shall We*

Dance? They had three children, Michael, Rachel, and William. They lived in Chiba, in the suburbs of Tokyo where his wife, Yoshie, had grown up. After ten years, wearied by the advertising world, David began to look toward the natural world, toward the ideas of permaculture and sustainable agriculture. He took his family first to a rural farmhouse in the Nagara region of Japan, a house so rustic, he said, his wife blanched. Then, they found an exceptionally capacious and warm house to rent on the eastern coast of Japan, near Shimoda at the southernmost tip of the Izu peninsula. On a large piece of land, surrounded by trees, set against a hillside, and a short walk to the ocean, it seemed to them an ideal spot. It seemed like a place they could make a home.

Over the three years he was there, David turned the hillside into series of terraces in which he could plant. He moved over ten tons of rock from the surrounding fields and mountains to build stone walls in order to create planting beds, bringing ages-old humus from the nearby forests to turn into the earth to make these beds. From the local fishermen he was given hundreds of pounds of kelp; from the local stable he brought over five hundred pounds of horse manure. Among the many things he planted were: grape vines, inter-planted with peas and beans and wild blackberries; tomatoes, green peppers and eggplants; cabbage and broccoli; spinach, mustard, buckwheat, baby greens, turnips, radishes, and daikons; a field of four varieties of potatoes bordered by more lettuce and radishes; another field of corn, beans, and pumpkins; blueberry and strawberry plants; two cherry trees, fig trees, mulberries, and goumi (a relative of the olive); and lastly, apple trees, a lemon tree, and a tangerine tree. Still, it would not be the home that he had imagined.

In fact, this would be his last house, the last home he would have in Japan before coming back to the United States. After more than two years of struggle, his marriage came apart for good.

As in all such difficult and wrenching separations, the reasons were many and deeply personal, and to some degree long-standing. I'd followed the oscillations from a distance, offering the little wisdom and counsel I could along the way. Now, he had come back, first to a homecoming in Fresno, in the Central San Joaquin Valley of California, to see my mother, his only living grandparent, and to see Andrew, who'd moved back to Fresno from Minnesota and bought a home only four houses from my mother's. For Andrew, who had at times lived in my mother's house to help take care of her while building his own life in Fresno, to have found a house so near the gravitational center of his emotional past-life, a house so close to the place he had always thought of as home, echoed exactly David's sense of return. Although David and his family had visited the States many times over the fourteen years that he'd lived in Japan, this was a different kind of visit back to Fresno. In fact, it wasn't a visit at all; it was an actual *return*. It was in every sense of the word, a homecoming. And now, as he is sleeping in this house, my house, here in Venice Beach, I have been thinking about his being here, of his homecoming to this place, to his father's house. When he awakens I tell him that I have been writing this essay, that I have told the story of his last house and his memorable garden, and of how proud I am of him and all of the work he put into making such an extraordinary place, such a powerful sense of home.

Having listened carefully to what I'd had to say, David looked at me and said, "Under Japanese law every rental house must be returned to exactly the state it was in when one moved in. My last weeks in that house in Izu were spent uprooting all of the trees and vegetables I'd planted, moving the ten tons of stone back to the hillsides. Before I left, the wild boars came through and devastated whatever was left in the fields." He continued, "When I arrived in Japan fourteen years ago, I arrived with my backpack, a few books, and almost no money." He looked at me with a wry smile, understanding that I knew he'd given all of the money he'd made from advertising all of those years to his ex-wife, all of the gold he'd shrewdly bought and saved at a time of an uncertain economy, and said, simply, "And I left the same way."

I wonder now about the place my son will next call home. There are many possibilities, of course, and he is taking his time. He wants a place where he will know his children will feel comfortable when they come to stay with him over the summers. Like many of us, he now carries with him the sleek, portable home of his laptop computer, a reliable link to his extended community of friends and family. Email has become the echo-location device that can home in on the place or places he is or will be, wherever in this world that happens to be... and wherever he is now, is as likely as not to be at least a momentary version – however temporary – of home. Then, he will again find that place that feels like the place he might belong, a place he can imagine that he truly belongs.

A few days ago, sitting with David and Andrew and Vivienne in a café looking out over the ocean, I said that I didn't know if I could ever live anywhere else, that I love Venice Beach and being by the ocean. I began to add that I loved it in part because... and then David interrupted me with a huge grin on his face, quoting me from an interview I'd given to a magazine once, repeating something he must have also heard me say at other times as well, that I "loved those places that were at the end of the road, where the land ran out and there was nowhere left to go, places like Key West and Venice Beach," places where all varieties of human life had washed up on its shores. To me, those were always the places that felt like home.

One summer in the late 1970s, back seeing my family in my old home in Fresno, I decided to drive down to Laguna Beach to visit my friend, the poet Charles Wright. On a gorgeous California night, we sat on the deck of his home in the hills above Laguna, the stars overhead and the lights from houses across the valley all competing for our attention. He'd put on the record player—people had record players in those days—a collection of his beloved Carter Family tunes, including one of my favorites, an old Baptist hymn called in some versions, "This World Is Not My Home." As tunes about salvation go, it's a catchy, buoyant song, and I loved the Carter Family's version of it. It was also a song that Woody Guthrie had heard in the migrant labor camps he'd visited in the late 1930s, a song that Guthrie had taken exception to, a song that had in many ways angered him, as he knew it was asking the migrants to accept their worldly fate and wait for their reward in the next life. To the same tune as the original hymn, Guthrie had written in 1938 a revised version that, as his biographer Joe Klein says, "stood the [original] song on its head...." Woody Guthrie called his song, "I Ain't Got No Home," and it's final verse is:

Now as I look around, it's mighty plain to see
This world is such a great and a funny place to be;
Oh, the gamblin' man is rich an' the workin' man is poor,
And I ain't got no home in this world anymore.

I love the dark humor of Guthrie here, contrasting the heavenly salvation of the original song with those more common and earthly struggles we all share; I also love his witty insistence upon the grace of being in this world, not beyond it. We all are used to living in several places at once, half in one place, half in another—in the past and the present, with loved ones and utterly alone, in Japan and America, even heaven and hell. Which, the question often becomes, will one day be thought of as our final "home"?

In these past few weeks since he's returned from Japan, I've been reminded that David was never anyone to do something half-way, never someone who could live half-way in any regard. When I asked him what the most difficult thing had been about living for those fourteen years in Japan, a look of sadness passed over his face, a momentary flash of defeat, then he said that the most difficult moment had been realizing one day that, however long he lived there, he would always be seen as being unalterably *other*. And I knew he felt this dilemma of being "other," of "half-ness," most profoundly when it came to his children. David himself had grown up with surprising ease with two families, two half-brothers and two half-sisters. In his heart and his life, he'd made sure that those halves had always been held and made whole. Now, at this distance, he would need to do something even more difficult – to provide a sense of completion and whole-ness to the identities of his children, Michael, Rachel, and William, who were half American, half Japanese. He would have to be sure that they knew always they were and always would be, even divided by an ocean, wholly his children.

We are all, at different times in our lives, made aware that we are simply not at home, that we have become simply "other" in our circumstances, whether we've crossed the borders of other countries or perhaps just the borders of the heart. Those pro-found feelings of alienation, loneliness, exclusion, and judgment can occur throughout the world and in our own homes, of course, even in our own "homes," those very places we have built and created to counter that solitude we so often experience in the world, that larger world which unfolds so constantly and complexly around us. More and more these days, it seems to me that the job of every one of us, whatever our occupations or pro-fessions, is to try and make this world a slightly less lonely place, to help make out of those clusters of individual "homes" scattered across the planet some more elaborate and connected conversation of hope, by which I mean a joining of voices, some alignment of possibilities, and the claiming, person by person, nation by nation, of our fragile, worldly home. I speak only for myself of course, but I'm weary of singing Woody's final, ironic line, "I *ain't got no home in this world anymore.*" I want a home as large as the world, and a world that might one day become as safe and as tender as a home.

The Sacredness of Home
My Question is:
Who Deserves a Home?

KAVERY NAMBISAN

The great advantage of a hotel is that it's a refuge from home life.
BERNARD SHAW, from *You Never Can Tell*

Give a young child some crayons and she will draw you a home with a red-tiled roof, a door and a window, a little garden, and the sun smiling overhead. Observe that drawing which comes so easily to the fingers of the five-year-old. Is the door meant primarily for shutting oneself in or for stepping out? Is it to be thrown wide open for guests? Are the windows meant to let in the sun and air, or to flaunt one's possessions? Are they curtained to protect intimate moments, or to hide private miseries? Ask that child and you might even get to hear the truth.

Two years ago my husband and I purchased our home in a small town in western India. It stands on 600 square feet of land and has everything a couple needs to feel comfortable and secure. We call it *Nemmadi*, meaning contentment. To own a house is a middle-class dream. In India we give our homes names like *Shanti* (peace), *Kailash* (the abode of God Shiva), *Nirvan* (salvation), *Abhilasha* (hope). Or *Nemmadi*.

As for that five-year-old with the drawing, I think she will want the window open and the curtains drawn back at all times because the world outside is one continuous spectacle, and the *kulfiwallah* – or the ice cream man – may come by. Her mother will want it shut because of the dust, the stray dogs, and prying neighbours. Her father comes after a day at work to shut himself

in, for he has had enough of the outside world for the day. Her
seven-year-old brother will open the door, leap across the door-
way, and run off to meet his friends.

When we learned to enclose ourselves in caves or a hutch of
leaves or within four walls, we became self-centred. Along with
security and shelter came the possibility of acquiring objects of
comfort, ostentation, and enjoyment. Seclusion provided the
space for solitude and reflection. Home became a private haven.
(Interestingly, our intimate body parts – more or less hidden from
public gaze – are called the "privates," and in Hindu religion the
Lingam,* which symbolises the creative and destructive powers of
Lord Shiva, is enshrined in temples and worshipped.)

How private is home, I wonder. The Guest is God, say our
Hindu scriptures. No one, not even a beggar, may be turned away
without being offered food and drink. Of course, caste might
determine whether the visitor comes in through the front door
or the back. Right up to my teens we were used to having some
distant relative stay at our home for weeks while he hunted for a
job or battled with a personal crisis. He used the spare bedroom
and was served the best portions at meals. He stayed until he was
ready to go. Such traditions of hospitality rarely exist anymore.
The same relative will stay at a hotel. Maybe he will call or visit
us. Maybe he won't.

I have often wished I were a man because it would give me
the physical freedom to wander. As a woman, I have enough male-
ness in me to make it happen in little ways. But little is not enough.
Maybe because of this, for me, the most exciting place to be is in
a hotel room. Of all the attractions of a holiday, the most enjoy-
able is that I get to stay in a new, strange room, sometimes alone.

My requirements are a clean, airy room in which I can measure
ten good paces, quiet, safety, and cheap food available within a

---

* Lingam (sanskrit) : the male sex organ especially symbolising the powers
of Lord Shiva.

kilometre. I can quickly make the impersonal personal and escape the homely preoccupations of cooking, washing, and worrying about the spider on the windowsill quietly putting up *her* residence. A hotel room also happens to be the best place to write in.

This is perhaps because a hotel for me has always been a transient residence. Home is where I find true contentment. It is where I feel wanted, and that is enough. I want to be cemented to the land, to the chair on which I sit, the bed I sleep on. I am filled with a profound and glorious laziness that comes with belonging. I welcome the ossification. My wanderings are of course an expression of a certain smug belief that I can belong anywhere.

I have hungered for the security of a home and, on getting it, felt indescribable happiness. My concept of home has changed with time, though. I wonder if home deserves to be considered something sacred. It is only a shelter, an address to which you lay claim, a dwelling place to crawl into. As for my homeland, I do not feel any pride that one is expected to feel. Being Indian is not different from being Swiss or Syrian or Sudanese. If my ancestors did achieve something worthwhile, I feel happy for what has been achieved.

My own ancestors did not achieve anything special. There are no histories written about them or statues built in their honour. Ours is a small community of ancestor worshippers, one among several tribes who live in the foothills of a mountain range in southern India. My people grew paddy and hunted. When I was young, besides the farm produce there was bison, boar, wild fowl, and partridge meat. In my father's youth it was still tiger country, and any man who shot a tiger was "married" to the beast in a mock wedding ceremony. Many families display their tiger skins even now. Every family has its spears, country pistols, and rifles preserved through generations, every other woman her tiger-claw brooch. We escaped the ritual forms of major religions until the seventeenth century, when invasions from neighbouring states brought the Hindu religion to us. Then we got our temples, our Hindu gods, the temple priests, and a caste. But, strangely, while we became hinduised and later, when the British came, westernised in conduct and deportment, we did not cut ourselves loose from tradition. We follow our old customs, eschew the Brahmin priest at our festivals, and make offerings of food and liquor to our ancestors.

Living now near the west coast of India, for me, homeland is a memory and a reality I visit every year. I have worked as a doctor in my community and met people who have retained the dignity and simplicity of their past. At rare moments of connectedness I feel a physical and spiritual intimacy with them. Homeland is the connectedness of memory.

This—the happy reminiscence of a plain and dignified ancestry—is what I would like to believe. The truth is somewhat more nuanced. My brave and honourable ancestors subjugated the smaller tribes of the area, kept the land and its riches for themselves, and used these men and women to work for them. These utterly innocent people built their hutments near the land they worked on. Their children did not go to school, the men and women came under the spell of country liquor. One can argue that we were a genetically stronger and somewhat smarter race. The truth is also that we exploited the smaller tribes which have remained uneducated, impoverished, sick, and landless. If ill health does not take them away in the next ten or twenty years, alcohol surely will.

The right to possess also comes with the right to dispossess.

Large populations are attacked, evicted, threatened, or butchered so others can benefit. Governments displace entire village communities in order to build bridges and megadams. No choices were afforded to the black people from Africa shipped westward as cheap labour, or to the British convicts transported to Australia, or to the Indians who worked as indentured labour in South Africa, or to the Jews killed in Nazi Germany. In India, there is a big political movement which claims that we should be a nation of Hindus and that all others – that is, roughly 200 million people – had better behave.

What is it like not to be wanted? Have not some of us, at some time, entered a home and breathed in the air of rejection, indifference, or hostility?

Is there such a thing as total unwantedness?

Yes, there is. In the housing colony where we live, one thousand homes like our *Nemmadi* are being built. There are as many homeless families living all around us in their makeshift shacks built out of discarded plastic and tin. They are the workers who build our homes, so we must tolerate them until the thousand homes are done. Then we can push them out: the land does not belong to them, and the label *illegal migrant* can be pinned onto their rib cages. They will move without question to another place where another thousand middle-class families are fulfilling their middle-class dream. I look out of my window and see the little children squatting right across from my home, and what thought comes to mind? They'll mess up our neighbourhood, these filthy people.

Migrant labourers, as we contemptuously call them, are rural folk in dire need of a livelihood. Thanks to the diminishing returns from agriculture, their land no longer yields enough to feed them. They come, uprooting their children from village schools and leaving their old parents behind.

Our homes are legal, but the men and women who build them are illegal. In India we refer to these people in millions. Only in millions, who matter at voting time when our leaders salute them and make incredible promises. A few hundred or a few thousand of such people – like the homeless who live right next to my home – go unnoticed.

I understand the word illegal to mean against the law. When this is applied to a person who is moving within his own country in order to make a living, it can only mean that he has no right to live. This is not some garbled sentiment but reality. A few years ago, in Bombay, a group of "pavement-dwellers" agitated for their right to die. Their argument was that if the right to live is denied them, they should be allowed the alternative. Ironically, in the last few years, at least a dozen pavement dwellers in Bombay have been mowed down by speeding vehicles.

To belong somewhere safe and to be allowed basic physical comforts should be a fundamental right.

Having been a migratory person – of a different sort, because as a professional I do not face the indignities I just spoke of – I wonder where my home is. Is it my place of birth, which has changed beyond recognition but is distinct in memory? I let my thoughts sweep back to when, as a young girl, I waded through fields of paddy, pulled the leeches off my feet, and did all the crazy things normal to a village girl. I go further back to my mother's home in a nearby village, with its small dark rooms and colourful bed linen made with the remnants of old clothes. When my father was nearly seventy he shared with me his secret of having peeped in through the bedroom window when my mother, assisted by two women, brought forth their third child. I felt so privileged to be told this, to be home-born and to be fathered by that young man who cared enough to risk censure from his in-laws.

The ultimate memory would be to slip back into that first home in which I floated for nine months. But the womb too is a temporary dwelling place we climb out of to begin our wanderings. The legs are meant for it. Our distant vision is meant for it.

In the 1970s, the Hippies who came in droves to live in "exotic-and-poor" India were rebelling against the concept of home. We in turn were treated to the spectacle of foreigners who abandoned Western comforts in exchange for a wrap-around length of cloth, a flower in the hair, some brown crystals in the palm, and homelessness.

Large populations have moved and will move, risking peace and contentment in favour of the unknown. In prehistoric times, man looked across the seas and at the hills in the distance and wondered, What happens there? He was bitten by the deadly wasp of adventure. He moved alone or in a group and overcame risks, or he succumbed. Globalisation is only a faster pace of the stirring up of societies which began when humans seriously started to leg it.

Nearly a third of the population of this world is insecure, penurious, drifting. We deprive others constantly, unthinkingly. I'm not a pessimist but I feel certain that such unfair outcomes of power and greed will not be redressed any time soon. The tragedy of shifting homelands will decide the frail and uncertain futures of all of us. Who will win, and for how long?

A few weeks ago, Indian newspapers brought us this story: A fifty-two-year-old man who was incarcerated in one of our prisons for thirty-four years without trial had been acquitted of the petty crime for which he was jailed. When he came out, he could not remember the name or location of his village. Home itself was wiped from memory. He belonged nowhere but in the few inches of space within the skull. Those few inches of real home that no one can take away.

Home and Places

Eiléan Ní Chuilleanáin

We travel in order to return, but, before returning, to pause, to turn through a hundred or so degrees and survey – what? A larger world in which the place we left glows in its setting. Not only the relocating of home, but the verification of distance now between ourselves and home enables us to think and to create. When we remove ourselves from that daily intersection of competing demands we can see a home that does not exist in a single moment but is a summary of its past meanings. And it is the other-place where we find ourselves, indeterminate, away and outside, that captures the energy of the present.

Firstly I should admit that it's as a poet that I speak and that I perceive a division between the poet and the writer of most kinds of prose when it comes to place. I find in much prose an emphasis on the usual and, even when it is resisted, a gesture towards the communal. It's as a poet that I return, as often in my own past, to talk about my native city of Cork.

Cork is a fine place, founded by Vikings, walled and defended for centuries. It sits on an island, on a clutch of islands rather, in the river Lee. Over the centuries its pile-driven foundations bit into the wet soil, its walls hemmed in an oval in the surrounding marshland, it was pinned at either end by a pair of humpy stone bridges of which one still remains. It was occupied, reclaimed, then besieged and colonised by the English. The newest buildings on the main street – itself once a branch of the river – were built with the compensation money paid after British soldiers set the town on fire in 1920, destroying the centre including the City Hall. (That wasn't the first major fire; the city had been badly damaged in 1622.) Between the new stone facades of that latest reconstruction are the older eighteenth-century houses which still predominate in a couple of elegant streets. The warehouses of the merchants from the same period, who made it a prosperous place (in part by provisioning the slave ships on their way to the French West Indies), are made of the characteristic and beautiful combination of red sandstone and white limestone sourced from local quarries. I'll get back to the stone later.

There are gestures at consistency. But much of the city is a haphazard succession of buildings dating from a mixture of periods, still following the medieval pattern of streets and laneways, crammed on their island site, churches, markets, and houses. On the hills that surrounded the town, suburbs grew up: some respectable, terraces with British Army names recalling Wellington and Waterloo, inhabited by the officers from the barracks higher up again; some grim and filthy with names like Brandy Lane, Spudtown, Cat Lane. I still remember the smell of the lanes and tenements, the public houses and their truculent customers, the shadowy shawled women making off down an entry clutching drink or money with equal desperation.

Is it clear that I am attempting to describe this place with love? Love aroused by the inexhaustible mystery of a place, by the acute nonchalance with which its history was worn, by the extreme oddity of its features. Let me pause and consider why the oddity was so marked. And why it might be of interest in a discussion of homelands.

The sense of home and of place must be, irrespective of genre, very largely mediated through the consciousness of a child, that is to say a consciousness where the notion of "normality" has not yet established itself, because a child lives in a world of arbitrary, uncontrollable change. The child's mind rapidly understands why the poor woman clutches her whiskey, why the poor families live in crowded flats, why the broken and distorted parts of cities are still there, as if forgotten when a bigger child moved on to a new game. The child may understand the ruined better than the new. The child is poor and often afraid, and is an expert at constructing temporary retreats. Thus, the strangeness of a street that was once the back entrance to a stable, with a featureless stretch of wall between two stable gates (which is in fact the last remaining vestige of an illegal eighteenth-century monastery) is the strangeness and hiddenness that makes sense to a child's mind. Its uniqueness incises it in memory.

My native place was experienced by me as unique, but also as invisible, unnamable. This wasn't just because it was a provincial city in a country which had a hyperactive cultural identity but had partly shut itself out of a particular international connection known as "the English-speaking world." It was because my childhood was a time of cultural transition. As a precocious early reader I could see that both the English-speaking connection and the newer Irish national culture included expectations that a place would define itself as "an English-speaking city" or "an Irish city," to which this obstinate, self-centred, poor, and largely ignorant place would not conform. After the departure of the soldiers of the Crown, the renaming of King Street and George's Street, some members of the generation who had taken part in the founding of a new state produced a realist prose which reflected the disarray of the city. I grew up as an apprentice poet who sensed the absence of a specifically poetic tradition which would express its invisible reality as a place that had been at least partially erased.

The erasures of history were powerful. The Anglo-Irish war of 1919-21, the fire, the murder by British soldiers of one Lord

Mayor, the death of another on hunger-strike, were notorious, in Ireland and beyond, but on the spot they sank out of sight. I haven't mentioned the erasure of the Irish language, or the persistence of the geography which laid down that the oldest churches of any but the Anglican denomination, the ones that dated back to the time when the dominance of English was established, were still cramped on lanes and back streets or what the *Parliamentary Gazetteer of Ireland* in 1846 refers to in this connection as "squalid and irregular alleys."

The short story writers were not I think bothered by these historical irritants. They had a tribute to pay to the typical and provincial; the genre naturally positioned the city at a distance from a cultural centre. A story by Frank O'Connor described a Cork child reading a friend's copy of a British school story in which upper-class English boys frequented a school that was a romantically Gothic building, looking "like the lunatic asylum with us." A borrowed text, a powerless child reader, an imperial theme viewed from a provincial angle, an architecture borrowed and debased.

O'Connor's story showed the place's prose existence as multiply limited and occluded – this because of the rules of its own genre, which tended towards the "scrupulous meanness" of the French and Russian masters as well as Joyce. The poet must I think have an unscrupulous approach: like the graffiti writer the poet must change the reality that is there, must appropriate and proclaim, create a new centre. In 1960 I discovered the poetry of Patrick Galvin, a working-class emigrant from Cork writing in London who had the authentic sense of how the meaning of the city needed to be resurrected. He makes the street names of large thoroughfares and unregarded back lanes sing out; inadmissible in realistic prose because of their sheer oddity, they are a kick-start for his apocalyptic poetry.

In Patrick Street
In Grattan Street
In Ireland Rising Liberty Street
The Kings are out.

Along the Mall
The Union Quay
In every street along the Lee
The Kings are out.

With knives of ice
And dressed to kill
The wine flows down from Summer Hill...

A decade later I and my friends got to know Galvin, by then
back in Ireland, and presently the magazine of which I am one-
quarter editor published poems of his. In an issue from 1976
I find his "Ballad of Sister Mary"; he writes:

When Sister Mary rose from the dead
And walked through Cork, the children fled
And mothers tucked them up in bed
And locked and barred the doors.

But Sister Mary issued fire
From mouth and eye and wrinkled bone
And neither cross nor earthly moan
Could save a single child.

From Ballinlough to Spangle hill
She hacked and chopped till all were slain
The flesh she hung in Blue Boy's Lane
The hearts she spiked in Douglas...

The fury in the poems is the fury of history alive in a place; as in the same poet's "Statement on the Burning of Cork." These are proclamations that life does not consist only of the quotidian, and yet their surreal imagery keeps them far away from the kinetic vulgarity (to quote Joyce) of political agendas. In Galvin's poetry the resurrected past is often feminine as well as fierce, and the wrong that is avenged can be political or sexual. In Ireland, especially in the 1970s, we were being told we were too interested in our own history, but we have continued to excavate, often social and sexual wrongs; and there is a poetry, and I include my own, which can only be written out of the sense of the absolute proximity of the real past and the place which is home, from which history can be seen.

The real past is there everywhere—in landscape and cities, in every stepping-stone across a stream, and planted tree, and roofed shed. The city is constructed by soldiers and politicians, but, underneath what we think we see there is the layer of actual work, the work of carpenters and plasterers and electricians and stonecutters who polished and planed what had been drawn, who discovered the reality of the seasoned wood and the quarried limestone and the marble fetched from far places. The best book about Cork is by a sculptor, Séamus Murphy, who recorded the lives and sayings of the craftsmen in stone with whom he had worked in his youth. He wanted someone to take over from him, to celebrate the other craftsmen, cabinetmakers and plasterers, bellfounders, smiths, glaziers, and their materials, among which the citizens still dwell unawares. Perhaps someone will add to his work some day.

In the same copy of Cyphers where I found the "Ballad of Sister Mary," I happened on a poem of my own, called "Barrack Street" which celebrated those crafts, as we moved into the age of wholesale demolition:

Missing from the scene
The many flat surfaces,
Undersides of doors, of doormats
Blank backs of wardrobes
The walls of tunnels in walls
Made by the wires of bells and the shadows
    of square spaces
Left high on kitchen walls
By the removal of those bells on their boards,

The returning minotaur pacing transparent
In the transparent maze cannot
Smell out his stall: the angles all move towards him,
No alcove to rest his horns ...

As imaginative writers we have the advantage of never ever
having to say more than we mean. The corollary is that we are
tied to what we have really known – in terms of a knowledge
so authentic that it allows us to imagine without claiming to
own the experience of others. A static provincial experience can
offer an arrow-slit through which the mobile and the nomadic
can be glimpsed. To return to the theme of travel, perhaps all
wandering is a search for a lucky view. The wandering around
the house looking for the moment when we see the far window
reflected in the glass door blazing in afternoon light. I found
such a view when I was asked to write a poem to celebrate the
fiftieth anniversary of an association founded to assist the victims of polio in Cork. I wanted it to be a poem about care and
freedom:

The Polio Epidemic
No hurry at all in house or garden,
The children were kept from the danger –

The parents suddenly had more time
To watch them, to keep them amused,
To see they had plenty to read.
The city lay empty, infected.
There was no more ice-cream.
The baths were closed all summer.

One day my father allowed me beyond the gate
With a message to pass through a slit in a blank wall;
I promised I would just cycle for two hours,
Not stop or talk, and I roamed the long roads
Clear through city and suburbs, past new churches,
Past ridges of houses where strange children
Were kept indoors too, I sliced through miles of air,
Free as a plague angel descending
On places the buses went: Commons Road, Friars' Walk.

A Small Home

Kei Miller

You will forgive the writer if his essay is ... well ... somewhat
tangential, because to write about "home" he would like to write
about "nation" and "nationalism," which, you might say, are the
same thing, and perhaps what you expected him to write about
anyway. They are not exactly the same, but both have to do with
a sense of belonging, and both we like to pretend are solid things
– like walls and floors and windows and land and trees. But they
are, neither of them, so real – not as real as houses or countries.
They are powerfully imagined things. And his tangents don't
stop there – because in writing about his own nation – Jamaica –
he would like to write about patties – a pastry you might be
unfamiliar with, a flaky turmeric-flavoured envelope filled with
the not-so-nice parts of beef. In the writer's experience, a beef
patty is what Jamaicans are almost always homesick for (... well,
that and the desire to live again in a country where they can
beat their children soundly without the little brats threatening
to call 911). Do you see what he means about a predilection for
tangents – the parenthetical? So – back to our narrative – in writing about foods and the way they can become symbolic of
nations, he would like to discuss hamburgers and America and
McDonalds, and all kinds of ports: lost passports, Jamaican air-
ports, the question of what we import and who we deport. He

can only ask you to trust that these tangents are crumbs scattered in a wood; follow them, and he will try to lead you back to the topic at hand – home.

✧   ✧   ✧

The writer was a child of the '80s. In Jamaica, this was the time of Edward Seaga. In the wider world it was the time of Reagan and Thatcher and Gorbachev, the Cold War and its end. The writer witnessed on television the biggest symbol of what was widely perceived as an American victory in the impasse: the opening of a McDonald's franchise in Moscow; the two-mile queue waiting for the glass doors to open; the record-breaking figure of 30,000 customers being served in one day. It would always seem to us, unbothered by the nuances of international politics and attracted to fantastic metaphors, that it was the weight of those golden arches that had squashed communism. And so when, years later, that very symbol of neo-American imperialism finally reached to his own Caribbean shores, you will understand his and his countrymen's wary sense of the inevitable – the belief that resistance was futile, that as fat as they would become on all that foreign fast food, they were still too small to fight it. And you will understand then, their great surprise when they won. A modern day David and Goliath. The little ones who were without breastplates or helmets, armed only with the exactness of their taste buds, the love of pimento, scotch bonnet pepper, and healthy servings – they did what no other country had ever done: they forced McDonalds out, out of business and out of their islands. In Trinidad, in Barbados, in Jamaica it was all the same story: the corporate giants had to slash prices, they had to switch management, they had to launch extravagant promotions – but none of it worked. Caribbean citizens who for a long while had no idea they were even fighting or resisting, ended up winning. And most amazing is this – that in Jamaica, wherever Ronald McDonald left a vacant storefront, it was taken over by a patty shop.

Like many Jamaicans this essay's writer also stood on a viewing deck, watching with delight that crazy clown climb the metal steps into American Airlines flight 462 back to Miami, and from there, who cared? It was the clown's leaving that became the fulfillment of his motto and song – though I'm not sure on this occasion that it finally happened – that he loved to see us smile. The writer was one of the celebrants, waving green and black and yellow flags; he was one of those caught up in the euphoria – this feeling of sudden significance – not that he and his people were larger than they had imagined, but rather that they were more powerful even in their smallness. It was nationalism that the writer had been swept up in, and in reflecting on that now, he does not feel proud. He is not sure how he feels. This is an essay of unsurety. Perhaps, most significantly, the writer is unsure of that line where nationalism ends and where fascism begins.

Considering the celebration that ensued when McDonald's left, this is the conclusion we might reach: homes or nations are always defined by doors and walls and borders. They are just as equally sites of exclusion as they are of inclusion. It is only a firm sense of who a home is meant for, a sense of nationalism as it were, that can celebrate so rapturously a climate that was unwelcoming enough that the unwanted had to leave, this feeling that the home had been disinfected, purified. To reflect responsibly on home is to reflect on the two spaces that its walls create: the cozy warmth of inside, and the cold severity of outside.

The writer must now state categorically that he does not want to enter into that most expansive and dull realm of liberalism that cries foul and responds with knee-jerk homilies to every instance that the world proves itself to not be some kind of utopia. The writer does not in fact have any problem with homes being necessarily exclusive and necessarily small. Indeed, to his mind, they are a celebration of smallness—a place where we are relieved of the global burden to always be big and broad and expansive. At home, we can be small beings with our small thoughts and our small rituals and we can hold on to the small beliefs that sustain us—that one day might reveal themselves to be bigger than we thought. (Perhaps this is why the writer is drawn to parentheses—a clearly bordered home within the expanse of a paragraph, where a smaller thought can reside.) And dare he say this—about home and what it celebrates—that it is a place where we can even live with our small-mindedness and our small prejudices. That is what home means.

It must be obvious then, why this troubles the writer—because small prejudices can expand quickly; they can become intolerance and hatred and crowds and stones and bullets and murder. Sometimes the writer does not know how to celebrate homes or nations, when by their very nature, they have the potential to become something so wrong—even evil. And when—let us be honest—the things a nation chooses to hate and chooses to love can be so arbitrary.

The essay would like to return to the topic of food. The writer shared with you the story of McDonald's collapse and a patty shop's triumph. He must now add another story to complicate things. The writer, having a predilection not only for tangents, but also, unfortunately, for losing passports or having them stolen from him, found himself, three years ago, being interrogated by immigration officials when he had landed again in Jamaica, coming from England. He was traveling on an emergency travel certificate, and the immigration officer wanted to be sure that he was in fact Jamaican (as if there are people who smuggle illegally into developing countries that don't have a surplus of jobs or opportunities). The immigration officer posed this question to the writer: What is the national dish of Jamaica? The official answer would have been "Ackee and Saltfish." Perhaps "beef patty" would have sufficed too. The writer, however, answered, "Kentucky Fried Chicken," to which the immigration officer laughed heartily and said, "Yes—you truly are Jamaican. Only a Jamaican would know that."

How arbitrary is this sentiment called nationalism, this construct called nation—that in Jamaica it can, on one hand, throw out McDonald's as imperialist American plastic-posing-as-food, and, on the other, embrace KFC as its own. Things are not always as clear as they seem.

This essay has not been as clear as it could have been, but now that we are finally talking about the things a nation imports and claims as its own, and what it tries desperately to deport, the writer will broach a topic his essay has been conscious of from the beginning but never mentioned—and it is this thing of a hyper-Jamaican masculinity, and conversely, Jamaican homophobia. If you've observed the island's culture at all, listened to the music, watched How Stella Got Her Groove Back, you might be familiar with this almost iconic image of the ultimate man from Jamaica. Jamaicans would gladly have the world believe that our primary export is not reggae, or ganja, or sunshine, which we haven't found out how to package yet, but rather male heterosexuality. It is as if Jamaicans believe that on the underside of every straight man's phallus is a little cotton tag that says: "Made in Jamaica; wash carefully." The fact and extremity of Jamaica's homophobia hardly needs to be rehearsed here. On writing this very essay, the writer had to pause to converse with a friend on MSN messenger whose new display pictures were of bruises he had received the night before in a parking lot in Jamaica, given to him by men who had decided his behavior was too effeminate—not hyper-masculine enough—not appropriate for Jamaica. Stories like his have begun to filter through the doors of our small home and have made their way into the wider world that has been sufficiently shocked, and has risen up to say, "Oh No! This is an awful thing that is happening in your country. We demand that this stop!" Perhaps, quite rightly, the world has been offended and has condemned not only the large acts of violence, but the small-mindedness and the small beliefs that are the seeds of such action. But did the world stop to think, could they have known, that to critique the ways in which a home is small, is to critique the very essence of that home?

The backlash has been tragic. Jamaica has also risen up, against all these "outsider" voices to say, "How dare you! Homophobia is our national right! It is who we are! It is what we stand for! We will not be dictated to by your imperialist, broad-minded beliefs."

And so it is, in direct response to international critique and pressure, that the home has fortified itself. The violence against men perceived as gay has gotten worse. In Jamaica, we import guns and the blueprints of the worst kinds of genocide, and we embrace them, over a meal of Kentucky Fried Chicken, and declare these things are intrinsically ours. We allow them to define who we are as Jamaican men. And in such a climate, we've made our home so uncomfortable and unsafe to certain men that they are continually deported – either to America or to England or to their graves.

All of this, it seems to the writer, is a consequence of home, of nation and nationalism. Where he stands in the midst of all of it is a place of unsurety. For this is not just any writer – he is a Jamaican writer. Some have tried to flatter him, saying such an identity might be smaller than his talent. Some have warned him more directly, saying that to be a regional writer is to place oneself in a box. (Oh but then what a large box Faulkner must have been in!) The point is, this writer does not mind from within a warm space – from within a home. It is the sounds from that space that he is trying to capture on the page; it is the small beliefs that he celebrates and that sustain him. He is committed to the national, to the homeland – but is aware, always, of its walls, the cold severity of outside, and of those who should have every right to stay in, but are cast out. Perhaps all this writer can hope to do is to write a literature from within that is so large it begins to push the walls and doors and the roof – slowly, slowly – that it begins to expand the territory of his home.

That ascerbic critic, Harold Bloom, states magnificently that Shakespeare invented us. That to think in a rhythm, in a vocabulary, in metaphors largely passed down to us from that bard, he has become the father of our humanity. This writer – I – I would like to believe this. I would like to believe that that is the power of writing – that language is a tool that we think and feel in, that when it is expanded, we too are expanded. Grand as it may sound, this is what I want to do to the inhabitants of my home, and to the home itself. Grand as it may sound, it is the only thing worthwhile I believe any home-writer can do.

I Land Home in the Waft of Sibyls with their Rueful Smiles

Stephanos Stephanides

Home like love is prone to disease; thinking of home can engender a pathological desire for somewhere when we know this is impossible. Medical wisdom in the eighteenth century designated the sickness for this impossibility of homecoming as the disease of nostalgia. Do we know that we will never return? If we do not go back, it is also true that we do not go forward either, or at least not straight forward. Medical science seems to have given up diagnosing it as a sickness but might yet suggest pills or other ways of alleviating the pain of a sense of loss. It is the task of writing to bring home what is lost, or what we feel is lost, to where we feel might be home. We are forever recreating Ithakas in multiple permutations, not simply in places of origin and end, but in the journey to somewhere we imagine we came from, or might be destined for. To get there, we make infinite transgressions and digressions, not always fortuitously or freely in our imagination, but pressured and constrained by the dominant powers that impose their boundaries on the places where they want us to belong. Homesickness is still with us, with some new symptoms and conditions, looking for new words and stories.

In recent years, there has been a surge in the poetics of migrancy, which has become a new literary cause célèbre. In the '80s Salman Rushdie excited me with his evocations of imaginary homelands. I found a voice for translated men like myself. Moving back and forth between languages and cultures of departure and languages and cultures of arrival, we are not just lost in translation, we may well find and bring something new in the process. Dorothy was relieved to get back to Kansas in black and white, Rushdie tells us, but in fact the magic and color of Oz beckons her to return to Oz, because the real meaning of this movie as a homily of home, Rushdie argues, is not that "there is no place like home," but that in fact home is in no place. But this cannot tell the whole story. Home is in place and out of place, and as we move in and out there is erosion, attrition, and entropy at war within and without, in the crosscurrents, and in the metamorphoses. You do not even have to leave your house to feel this melancholy. Pamuk still inhabits the house in which he was born in Istanbul, but in his memoir of the city he shares in the communal melancholy of its transformations, of its debris and decay. Home moves even if the house remains in the same place. A plantation-laboring guru descendant of Indian migrant indentured laborers in Guyana shared with me the wisdom of the elephant-god Ganesh, sensing that I felt faraway from home. Home is in OM, which consists of—A—U—M—waking consciousness, dream consciousness, dreamless sleep, and the silence before and after.

As poets of home, we may never return but we continually make turns—old turns and new turns in a chorus of strophes and epistrophes—from right to left through a multilayered melancholy with a bittersweet promise of an originary vision, not an ineffable origin, but a way of being in the world that we hope might not be forever lost. It tempts us yet with its possibility and elusive transience, our need to make it yield its fugacity and translate it into the sensuality of place, where we realize our being and becoming in the world, in the unforgetting words, images.

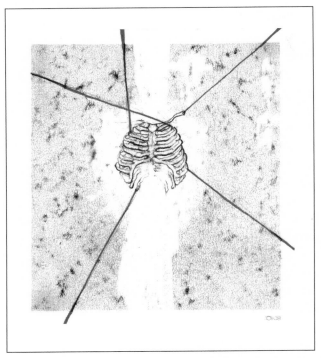

ELIZABETH HOAK DOERING

We create boundaries from its boundless meaning, bind it in and bind it out, make space a place, a room of one's own. And then if we bind it in too tightly it becomes inhospitable, inert and stultifying, or violently exclusionist for the privilege of one group whether it be ethnic or some other kind, and its original sensual mystery of home slips away and we feel out of place or a prisoner in our own place, if we have not already been violently displaced from that prison. Boundaries become alive where something begins, not where something stops, when a horizon of expectation opens, a dynamic unfolding, the gift of hospitality we give or receive by letting go. Or we sometimes lose and find home in forced or involuntary movement, flight or eruption, or a sudden dislocation. Then it is always more memorable for its aftershock, its post-memory. It leaves us wondering where we are or how we got there – like our first dislocation, pushing forward, hopefully head first between two legs, grateful for the midwifery ushering us forward when dispersion hits home in a sudden outburst, a big breath of air, a cry of light in the darkness, with a lingering memory of rhythm and water and taste like almond milk, the smell of blood and excretions. Do we remember that journey or how we made it out? In a distant echo of rhythm, water, light, and air? How did we get there in the first place before we had to force our way out? Is there a "first place" anyway or is home just a transition – from nowhere to somewhere now here – from the gestation from an unknown space into the vast and unruly plethora of differences that we weave into ourselves through layered dislocations?

Sudden eruptions and sedimentations, traumas and revelations, losses and expectations, anxieties and promises – to which we bear witness in an infinite rehearsal of our memory, our forgetting – an infinite rehearsal of home that is an imagined and unimaginable beginning before and after anything we can ever remember. We rehearse the possibility of home through its stories – rehearse it both creatively and involuntarily – stories retold, withdrawn, withheld, revised like a palace of memory, always in a process of construction with ghostly gestures of something that might have come before and after the chain of our remembrance.

In this my island habitat, the effort to shape a shared dwelling, a common habitation, has to emerge from the ruptures of multiple dislocations and fragmentations of the continuum of place, its contested stories and the inability of the collective consciousness to absorb it all. This process of reconstruction is an eternal negotiation. The island is an implosion and breach of the surrounding continents like a fractured vessel on the permeability of the surrounding seas, which are always in contradiction with its dry dusty plains and its internal borders imposed by the powers that be, resolutely dividing northern shore and southern shore. The island itself is like a womb distended by geology and history – an asymmetrical mandala with five uneven promontories jutting out differently into the sea, different densities and intensities of life as if seeking an exit from insular containment, the image of the world in its imperfect reflexive circularity and liminality, to be seized in poetic turns that mark the eruptive discontinuities in the interplay of continents and seas. How to write the revelation that will take us from and between the experience of space to its transformation into place and home? I think about how I too have been transformed from one island to two then three, and then a multitude of scattered islands, an entire archipelago, how I have been metaphored and dispersed.

I was lifted from the island as a child in what felt like a precipitated second birth – this time ushered with my father's midwifery as if pulled out by forceps from a maligned womb. A child in my new habitat, I became a denial of the past, a promise of the future, a perhaps unacknowledged incarnation of Mediterranean homesick blues, a rift in the soul joined by a hyphen, two islands separated by a continent (until I found an exit to a third). I now learnt the word home in another language, on another island – home was always somewhere else in a dialect fading in my memory, another language, whose traces were still with me, that did not have a word for home; there were only houses, villages, genealogies, secrets still untold. Before I knew it I was subjected to a semiotic invasion, overrun with the new language with its own ideas of home, its idioms, and refrains: hit home, home sweet home, home grown, home spun, home run, home base, home on the range, home on the prairie, home alone. The new language occupied me before I even knew it, like a new set of clothes that I was glad to flaunt, hanging comfortably on me but not quite fitting to my strangeness. It was some time before I realized that I could have or perhaps already had occupied it with my own strange habitat and made the language uncomfortable with itself, with its own sense of familiarity, and turned its seasons of mist and mellow fruitfulness into my months of dust and dirty sweetness. English became my home but, I found strangeness before and after English, an otherness within its homeliness that I desired would somehow break through in a syncopated rhythm. To find home I had to seek its stories and its melodies. A few years later, during my early adolescence (was it 1965?) Bob Dylan Brought It All Back Home to me, a poet prophet of exit from home and a way home with no direction, on a road not taken, a way of turning my Mediterranean Homesick Blues into Subterranean Homesick Blues: "You don't need a weatherman to know which way the wind blows," he sang. But there were other ways out and other ways in. I had to exit English and make a new entry from the other side. About the same time I heard Dylan, I chanced upon and was entranced by Tom Jobim's "Chega de Saudade." Another way home, and another way out, all the more sweet through the melody of another language I was yet to understand: "Enough of blues," the title and rhythm proclaim, as nostalgia lingers in the melody and pulls you back – não sai, não sai, não sai – an emptiness that is brimming and about to overflow. Rhythm and melody work together and against each other, stitching across the hyphen in the errantry of home. Without remembrance of the story, we would forget the way home.

Decades later I recognized this *saudade* in Orhan Pamuk's vision and feeling of *hüzün*, which is not quite an illness, he says, but a poetic state of grace. For the Sufis, it is the spiritual anguish that causes the sufferer to plummet so far down that his soul soars to its divine desire. The possibility of the impossible, a kind of Supraterranean Homesick Blues in the genealogy of angels like Rainer Maria Rilke, Paul Klee, Walter Benjamin, Wim Wenders – out-of-this-world creatures with panoptic views longing to salvage the centre of their beings in the ruinous human world as they hover around sensed and unseen.

Will I be touched by them at some time? Might they briefly lend me their wings? In the days following April 23, 2003 when history fortuitously opened the internal border gates of this island, many went rushing though not knowing what providence had in mind, and if and when the gates might close. I hovered to the settlement that cradled my childhood. If this had been Ithaka, it was gestating its demise without my knowing by the time I had already departed. It would and could not wait for the impossibility of my return. As I landed, the new settlers followed my drift. They found keys and opened doors. I floated up the stairs to a balcony hanging over rooftops and canopies of acacias and eucalyptus trees, drawn by the waft of the old village sibyls and their fading rueful smiles. They wait for me to hear the fleeting sounds of their interrupted prophecies and stories. Only then will they say: "Now homeward, you have had your fill, eve's star is rising."

Afterword

NATAŠA ĎUROVIČOVÁ

Even in the diminishing optic of hindsight the three New Symposia have kept their clear design and their vividness. The sublime setting of Paros is, of course, impossible to forget. But it's also reassuring to see just how well the essays selected in this volume hold up to the basic test of re-reading (their complete line-up, as well as a documentary film capturing the key moments, ideas and protagonists of each meeting, can be found at http://iwp.uiowa.edu/paros/index.html). We'd like to believe that they reflect, first off, the right choice of participants selected for each year and each topic, and, in turn, the fair amount of preparation as well as post-symposium revisions the writers did in each gathering's wake.

To prepare for the 2006 symposium, on "What We Hold in Common," the work of the essay drafting was primed by a stack of readings we placed on a shared electronic bookshelf. These ranged from the 1968 classic "Tragedy of the Commons" by historian Garrett Hardin, which draws on examples from early English history to assert that anything *shared*, that is, any "commons," is ultimately an unsustainable ownership structure, which sooner or later by necessity had to be replaced by an "enclosure," meaning, by private property. His argument was then counterbalanced by several readings that took the obverse view, or offered an alternative model. The major statements on the "pro-public" end of that spectrum drew on the ideas of Lawrence Lessig, the coiner of the term "creative commons" so central for current intellectual property rights debates, and on another classic, namely *The Gift*, written in 1983 (and reissued in 2010) by Lewis Hyde, one of this symposium's participants. For both Lessig and Hyde, it is instead the strictures of ownership, all too ungenerously applied, that block innovation and the efficient use of finite resources—be they intellectual, economical, or ecological. In the four days of intense conversations around the fifteen drafted texts, arguments for non-proprietary creativity were pitted against commons as inevitably communitarian (Hyde, Utami), sustainability of open spaces rethought against the near-eternal impact of a planet threatened by decay and debris (Norminton, Bharucha), a fundamental psycho-logic of a dependent self refracted against the view that the self's proper scale is the ecosystem itself (B. Sanders, R.S. Sanders). A variety of politically and culturally grounded ideas about identity's ties to ownership (Ouwor, Hussein) took fire.

Where the commons talk was sprawling and centrifugal, the working atmosphere during "Justice: One or Many" (held in May of 2007) was fully focused, and at times tense. If for no other reason than that daily headlines everywhere continuously prompted the question, what exactly makes for a "just war"? And what, in turn, are the strengths and the limits of retributive justice, the philosophical wellspring of "just war"—whether its key trope is the raw tribal rule of *lex talionis*, "an eye for an eye," or the more decorous goddess with her scales-and-sword, one of the abiding gifts to us from the Ancient World?

In preparing for this conversation we sent the writers to assorted definitions of these common and loosely used terms but also directed them to readings about some alternative visions of how rule-boundedness might cohabit with fairness, for instance to excerpts about religious law-making. Where some of the writers then seized on particular events through which they parsed the politics of justice and injustice (Alarcón, Eprile), others again (Hirshfield, Habila, Vistonitis) made the case for literature, art in general, as the proper field of experiment where a writer ought to scrutinize and test emotions – of anger, resentment, trauma – before they become "legally actionable" in the world at large. Yet others took the obverse route, broadening instead the time frame in which "justice" should be sought. For rethinking the time and speed of "retaliation," deferring it to some better time or even to an afterlife, is another way of opening up to a more utopian vision of justice – be it a justice of global emancipation (Magani) or one understood as a spiritual and redemptive metamorphosis (Golubovich, Ma Thida). At the emotional center of that year's session arose thus an elusive figure we seldom have the opportunity to encounter in person – the figure of the writer as Witness, she who puts herself into harm's way in order to use her voice, story, pencil, in place of Athena's sharp-edged tool.

And finally, Home/Land: in our initial planning it was the concept of *homeland*, a space defined by national and perhaps ethnic borders – whether celebrated or contested – that ruled the reading list, an assortment of essays exemplifying various forms of "us vs. them." But as the essay drafts arrived, the space that was, instead, sketched out in most of them was that of *nostos*, home as an inner place, a landscape of childhood, dreams, and sometimes – though not always – loss. The stories told were of the grown self, surveying that terrain (Ní Chuilleanáin), stories of her belonging (Trethewey, Papandreou), eviction (St. John, Miller), the right of return (Carson, Stephanides)... in fact, the very essence of novels, poems, plays, of post-romantic literature itself. Only a couple of the writers wanted to put forth the proposition that a home is above all a matter of *real estate*, an estate whose sentimental value lists far far down below its property/cash nexus (Nambisan).

There is no doubt that all these pieces are of their time: even just in the very few years since they were written some of their points of departure or attack are gone, or moot. But, each having been tailored to the size of a special space, that of a face to face conversation, they are animated by the true genius of the personal essay, the unique voice.

CONTRIBUTORS

DANIEL ALARCÓN (novelist, fiction writer; Peru/USA). His short story collection, *War By Candlelight*, was a finalist for the 2006 PEN/Hemingway Foundation Award. His novel, *Lost City Radio*, was named a Best Book of the Year by the *San Francisco Chronicle*, and won the 2009 International Literature Prize given by the House of World Cultures in Berlin. His fiction and non-fiction regularly appear in *The New Yorker*, *Harper's*, *Etiqueta Negra*, and elsewhere. He lives in Oakland, California, and is a Visiting Scholar at Center for Latin American Studies at U.C. Berkeley.

RUSTOM BHARUCHA (writer, director, dramaturg, and cultural critic based in Kolkata, India) is a leading interlocutor in the field of interculturalism. He is the author of several books including *Theatre and the World*, *The Politics of Cultural Practice*, *The Question of Faith*, *In the Name of the Secular*, *Rajasthan: An Oral History*, and *Another Asia: Rabindranath Tagore and Okakura Tenshin*. Bharucha is currently a Research Fellow at the International Research Centre/Interweaving Performance Cultures in Berlin.

JEFFREY CARSON (translator, poet; USA) was born in New York; since 1970 he has lived with his wife, the photographer Elizabeth Carson, on the island of Paros, where he teaches at the Aegean Center for the Fine Arts. He is a translator of Odysseus Elytis and Andreas Kalvos, among many others. Among his books are *Paros* (1977), *49 Scholia on the Poems of Odysseus Elytis* (1983), *The Temple and the Dolphin* (1995), *Collected Poems of Odysseus Elytis* (1997), and *Poems 1974-1996* (1997). His poems also appeared in the anthology *Kindled Terraces: American Poets in Greece* (2004).

TONY EPRILE (fiction writer, novelist; South Africa/USA) is the author of *The Persistence of Memory* (2004), a New York Times Notable Book of the Year. Eprile was recently visiting writer at the University of Iowa Writers' Workshop and at

BarIlan University's Shaindy Rudoff Graduate Center. He teaches fiction and nonfiction at Lesley University's low residency MFA in Creative Writing and lives in Vermont with his family.

KSENIA GOLUBOVICH (fiction writer, essayist, editor, translator; Russia) has published the poetry collection Personae (2001), the travelogue The Serbian Parables (2003), and the novel Wishes Granted (2007), long-listed for the Russian Booker. She is a regular contributor to newspapers and journals including Logos, a philosophical magazine, and the main opposition daily Novaya gazeta, a co-organizer of the international project Dictionary of War, as well as a translator of W.B. Yeats, Bruce Chatwin and V.S. Naipaul. At Moscow University she teaches courses on poets and power and on modernity in poetic language.

HELON HABILA (poet, novelist; Nigeria) has published three novels, including Measuring Time (2007) and, most recently, Oil on Water (2010). His debut novel, Waiting for an Angel, won the 2003 Commonwealth Prize for Best First Book, African Region. Among his other awards is the 2001 Caine Prize for African Writing, which he received for his short story "Love Poems." He has taught at the University of East Anglia in the U.K. and is now on the faculty at George Mason University in the USA.

JANE HIRSHFIELD (poet, essayist; USA) has published seven books of poetry, most recently Come, Thief (2011); a collection of essays, Nine Gates; and three major anthologies collecting the work of historical women poets. Her work has appeared in The New Yorker, The Atlantic, The Times Literary Supplement, The Nation, and six editions of The Best American Poetry. Her books have been finalists for the National Book Critics Circle Award and England's T.S. Eliot Prize; other honors include The Poetry Center Book Award, The California Book Award; fellowships from the National Endowment for the Arts, Guggenheim and Rockefeller

Foundations; and the 70th Academy Fellowship for distinguished poetic achievement from The Academy of American Poets.

AMEENA HUSSEIN (sociologist, editor, publisher, novelist; Sri Lanka) is the author of the short story collections *Fifteen* (1999) and *Zillij* (2004). Her study on violence against Sri Lankan rural women, *Sometimes There is No Blood*, was published by the International Centre of Ethnic Studies in Colombo in 2000. In 2003 she co-founded the Perera Hussein Publishing House, and from 2004–2007, she was editor of the literary journal *Nethra*. Her novel *The Moon in the Water* was long-listed for the 2007 Man Asia Literary Prize, and appeared in print in 2009. She is the editor of *Race: Identity, Caste & Conflict in the South Asian Context* (2004) as well as *Blue: Stories for Adults* (2010).

LEWIS HYDE (non-fiction writer, translator, poet; USA) is the Richard L. Thomas Professor of Creative Writing at Kenyon College. Hyde's interests center on the public life of the imagination. His 1983 book, *The Gift*, is an inquiry into the situation of creative artists in a commercial society. *Trickster Makes This World* (1998) is a portrait of the kind of disruptive imagination needed to keep any culture flexible and alive. Hyde has also published a book of poems, *This Error is the Sign of Love*, and edited a number of volumes, including *The Essays of Henry D. Thoreau*, a book of responses to the poetry of Allen Ginsberg, and selected poems of the Nobel Prize-winning Spaniard Vicente Aleixandre. His most recent book is *Common as Air: Revolution, Art, and Ownership* (2010).

MA THIDA (fiction writer, physician, activist; Burma) was in medical school when Burma's military junta shut down the universities. She then served as a health care provider and editor for the non-violent National League for Democracy. Her many short stories, containing veiled criticism of the Burmese government, led to six years in solitary confinement. In 1999 she was pardoned and released on humanitarian grounds. A recipient of many international awards, she writes and lectures widely about her experience. She also edits and translates poetry from the Japanese. She lives in Yangon, where she is the editor of the youth magazine *Teen* and works as a surgeon at the Muslim Free Hospital.

MOHAMED MAGANI (novelist, essayist, fiction writer; Algeria) is the author of many novels, including *La Faille du ciel*, which won the Grand Prix Littéraire International de la Ville d'Alger, *Esthétique de boucher*, *Un Temps berlinois*, *Le Refuge des ruines*, *Une Guerre se meurt*, *Scène de pêche en Algérie* and *La Fenêtre rouge*, as well as the short story collections *An Icelandic Dream* and *Please Pardon Our Appearance*. Among his essays are *Histoire et sociologie chez Ibn Khaldoun* and *Enseignement primaire, où en sommes-nous?* From 1995–2000 he was a writer-in-exile in Berlin, at the invitation of the International Parliament of Writers and the city of Berlin. He founded the Algerian PEN Club and is a Board member of International PEN. He lives in Algiers.

KEI MILLER (poet, fiction writer; Jamaica) won the Jamaica Observer Literary Prizes for both fiction and poetry in 2002. His first collection of poetry, *Kingdom of Empty Bellies*, came out in 2005; another volume, *There Is an Anger That Moves*, appeared in 2007. His 2006 short story collection, *The Fear of Stones and Other Stories*, was short-listed for the Commonwealth Writers First Book Prize. Miller is also the editor of *New Caribbean Poetry* (2007). He is the recipient of Jamaica's Silver Musgrave medal and the Una Marson Prize for Literature. He teaches creative writing at the University of Glasgow.

KAVERY NAMBISAN (novelist, fiction writer, essayist; India) has worked as a surgeon in rural areas throughout India. She currently runs a medical center for workers in Maharashtra and a learning center for their children. She has authored five novels, most recently *The Hills of Angheri* (2005) and several children's books. She also writes on healthcare issues for Indian media. Among her honors is a UNICEF-CBT Award for her children's novel *Once Upon a Forest*.

EILÉAN NÍ CHUILLEANÁIN (poet; Ireland) is a founding editor of the literary review *Cyphers*. Her collections of poetry are *Acts and Monuments* (1972), *The Second Voyage* (1977, 1986), *The Rose Geranium* (1981) *The Magdalene Sermon* (1989), *The Brazen Serpent* (1994), *The Girl Who Married the Reindeer* (2001), and *The Sun-fish* (2009). Winner of the Griffin International Prize for Poetry, (2010), she also translates poetry from Irish, Italian, and Romanian. She has taught at Trinity College, Dublin, since 1966, serving as Dean of the Faculty of Arts 2001–2005.

GREGORY NORMINTON (novelist and environmentalist; U.K.) studied English Literature at the University of Oxford. He has received two Writer's Awards from the Arts Councils of England and Scotland. He has published four novels: *The Ship of Fools*, *Arts and Wonders*, *Ghost Portrait*, and *Serious Things*, and has written short stories for BBC Radio, *Prospect*, *The London Magazine*, and PEN *International*. He lives in Edinburgh, where he is currently working on a new novel and, as editor, on a collection of short stories responding to climate change, written by major British authors.

YVONNE OWOUR (fiction writer, conservationist, cultural activist; Kenya) is the former executive director of the Zanzibar International Film Festival. She won the Caine Prize for African Writing in 2003 for "Weight of Whispers," a story told from the perspective of a Rwandan refugee fleeing after the 1994 massacres. She has published several short stories including "Dressing the Dirge," "The State of Tides," and "The Knife Grinder's Tale."

NIKOS PAPANDREOU (fiction writer, essayist; Greece) has had his first novel, *A Crowded Heart* (1999), nominated for the Los Angeles Times First Fiction award. His most recent book is Love, Edited (2010), a collection of short stories. His screen-play based on the life of Mikis Theodorakis will be produced in 2012. Recent work of his has appeared in Kenyon Review Online, POETRY, Threepenny Review, Antioch Review, AGNI, Harvard Review, Quarry, The Journal of the Hellenic Diaspora, Indiana Review, and in Greek literary journals such as LEXI and Entefktirion.

BARRY SANDERS (essayist; USA) is Professor Emeritus of the History of Ideas at Pitzer College in Claremont, California, and currently serves as writer-in-residence at Pacific Northwest College of Art, in Portland, Oregon. He has authored and co-authored more than a dozen books on orality and culture, among them ABC: The Alphabetization of the Popular Mind (1986), and with Ivan Illich; A is for Ox: Violence, Electronic Media, and the Silencing of the Written Word (1994), nominated for the Pulitzer Prize; Sudden Glory: Laughter as Subversive History (1995); and The Private Death of Public Discourse (1998). His most recent work is Alienable Rights: The Exclusion of African Americans in a White Man's Land, 1619 – 2000, nominated in 2004 for the Pulitzer Prize.

SCOTT RUSSELL SANDERS (scholar, novelist, essayist; USA) is Distinguished Professor Emeritus of English at Indiana University, in Bloomington. Among his twenty books are novels, collections of stories, and works of nonfiction, including Staying Put, Hunting for Hope, A Private History of Awe, and A Conservationist Manifesto. For his writing, which has been translated into nine languages, he has won the Lannan Literary Award, the Mark Twain Award, and a Guggenheim Fellowship, among other honors. Sanders is active in organizations devoted to conservation, social justice, peacemaking, and protection of the biosphere. He is currently at work on a novel set against the background of America's recent wars, and a book about the meaning of wealth.

DAVID ST. JOHN (poet; USA) is a professor of English at the University of Southern California, Los Angeles. He is the author of six books of poetry, including *Hush* (1976), *No Heaven* (1985), *Study for the World's Body: New and Selected Poems* (1994), and *Prism* (2002). His work has been published in *The New Yorker*, *The Paris Review*, *Poetry*, *American Poetry Review*, *Harper's*, *Antaeus*, and *The New Republic*, among others. His awards include the Discover/ The Nation prize, the James D. Phelan Prize, and a Prix de Rome fellowship. He has also received a Guggenheim Fellowship and several National Endowment for the Arts Fellowships.

STEPHANOS STEPHANIDES (scholar, poet, essayist, translator; Cyprus). His work includes *Translating Kali's Feast: the Goddess in Indo-Caribbean Ritual and Fiction* (2000), *Beyond the Floating Islands* (2002), *Blue Moon in Rajasthan and Other Poems* (2005), *Cultures of Memory/Memories of Culture* (2007), and two documentary films, *Hail Mother Kali* (1988) and *Kali in the Americas* (2003). He is professor of Comparative Literature at the University of Cyprus, and has served as a judge for the Commonwealth Writers Prize in both 2000 and 2010.

NATASHA TRETHEWEY (poet; USA) is a professor of poetry at Emory University. Her poems have appeared in *The Best American Poetry 2003* and *2000*, *AGNI*, *American Poetry Review*, *Callaloo*, *Gettysburg Review*, *Kenyon Review*, *New England Review*, and *The Southern Review*, among others. She has received fellowships from the Guggenheim Foundation, the Rockefeller Foundation, the Bunting Fellowship Program of the Radcliffe Institute for Advanced Study at Harvard, and the National Endowment for the Arts. Her collection *Native Guard* won the 2007 Pulitzer Prize in Poetry.

AYU UTAMI (novelist, editor, journalist; Indonesia) was banned from writing in 1994 upon completion of a black book on corruption in the Suharto regime. Her debut novel *Saman* (1998), which deals frankly with love and sexuality, and addresses the difficult relationship between Muslims, Christians, and the Chinese minority, received the prize for Best Indonesian Novel in 1998, with a companion novel *Larung* coming out in 2001. Since 1998 Utami has been a radio host and co-publisher of the cultural magazine *Kalam*.

ANASTASSIS VISTONITIS (poet, essayist, journalist, translator; Greece) has published eleven books of poetry, three volumes of essays, four travelogues, a book of short stories, and a book of translations of the Chinese poet Li He. He has served as vice president of the Greek Collecting Society of Literary Works (OSDEL) and as a board member of the European Writers' Congress. He was also the general editor of the candidature file of Athens for the Olympic Games of 2004. His creative work has been translated into seventeen languages.

EDITORS

NATAŠA ĎUROVIČOVÁ (USA) is the editor of the International Writing Program and its on-line journal *91st Meridian*. Her publications are principally on film history, in particular on translation and cinema. She is the co-editor, with K. Newman, of *World Cinemas, Transnational Perspectives* (2009) and, with Beaudelaine Pierre, of a recent collection of Haitian writing *How to Write an Earthquake/Comment ecrire un seisme/ Mo pou 12. Janvye* (2011).

CHRISTOPHER MERRILL (USA) works across genres with books that include four collections of poetry; translations of the poetry of the Slovenian Ale Debeljak; several edited volumes; and four books of nonfiction, *Things of the Hidden God: Journey to the Holy Mountain*, *The Grass of Another Country: A Journey Through the World of Soccer*, *The Old Bridge: The Third Balkan War and the Age of the Refugee*, and *Only the Nails Remain: Scenes from the Balkan Wars*. His work has been translated into twenty-five languages. He directs the International Writing Program at the University of Iowa.

The organizers of the 2006–2008 New Symposium
gatherings gratefully acknowledge the support
of their principal funder, the Bureau of
Educational and Cultural Affairs at
the U.S. Department of State.

Five hundred copies of *The New Symposium*
were printed from Rialto types. The edition was
printed and bound by Edwards Brothers
in Ann Arbor, Michigan.